ENVIRONMENTAL LAW

IN A NUTSHELL

FIFTH EDITION

By

ROGER W. FINDLEY
Professor of Law and Fritz B. Burns
Chair of Real Property
Loyola Law School, Los Angeles

DANIEL A. FARBER
McKnight Presidential Professor
of Public Law
University of Minnesota

WEST GROUP

ST. PAUL, MINN.
2000

COPYRIGHT © 1983, 1988, 1992, 1996 WEST PUBLISHING CO.
COPYRIGHT © 2000 By WEST GROUP
        610 Opperman Drive
        P.O. Box 64526
        St. Paul, MN 55164–0526
        1–800–328–9352

All rights reserved
Printed in the United States of America

ISBN 0–314–23866–2

For Suzy, Sheila and Steve
R.W.F.

For Joe
D.A.F.

OUTLINE

TABLE OF CASES

References are to Pages

TABLE OF CASES

TABLE OF CASES

TABLE OF CASES

TABLE OF CASES

ENVIRONMENTAL LAW
IN A NUTSHELL

FIFTH EDITION

CHAPTER 1

JUDICIAL REVIEW OF GOVERNMENT DECISIONS

Environmental litigation often involves disputes with governmental agencies rather than between private parties. Thus, an understanding of administrative agencies and their relationship with the courts is important. In this chapter, we will begin by discussing the general rules governing judicial review of agency decisions. Those rules are mostly derived from the Administrative Procedure Act (APA). We will then consider the special procedures imposed on federal agencies by the National Environmental Policy Act (NEPA).

A. THE JUDICIAL ROLE IN ENVIRONMENTAL LAW

Apart from the political process, the only check on agency action is found in the courts. Because of the importance of government agencies in environmental law, it is crucial to understand the circumstances under which courts will intervene in environmental decisionmaking. We can break this problem down into three issues. First, when will a court hear a case challenging agency action? Second, if the court does hear the case, what standards will it apply in reviewing the agency's action? And third, what remedies will the court provide?

We will begin with the first of these issues, the limits of a court's ability to hear environmental cases. It is quite possible to conceive of a legal system in which any individual could bring suit to halt any government action that violated the law. It is also possible to conceive of a system in which the only redress against illegal government action would be at the ballot box. American law has taken an intermediate position. Courts can hear some, but not all, claims that a government agency has acted illegally. A plaintiff who seeks to bring such a claim must demonstrate that she is a proper individual to challenge the government action, and that she is raising issues that the court is authorized to consider. The requirement that the suit be brought by the proper individual is known as the doctrine of "standing." The requirement that the issues be suitable for judicial resolution is the doctrine of "reviewability." The standing issue has given rise to a great deal of litigation in environmental cases.

1. STANDING

The Supreme Court has had occasion to consider the standing issue in seven major environmental cases. The first of these cases was Sierra Club v. Morton (S.Ct.1972). This case challenged a plan by Walt Disney Enterprises to build a $35 million resort in the Mineral King Valley, which the Court described as "an area of great natural beauty nestled in the Sierra Nevada Mountains." The Sierra Club opposed construction of the huge resort on the ground that approval of the plan by the Forest Service had violated several federal statutes. The Sierra Club did not base its lawsuit on the claim that its members would be directly injured by the construction of the resort. Instead, it invoked its status as a public interest group with a long-standing focus on preservation of the environment.

Although some lower courts had indicated a willingness to confer standing based on similar allegations, the Supreme Court refused to do so. Instead, it relied on earlier cases establishing a general test for standing under the APA. This test, known as the *Data Processing* test, requires that the plaintiff seeking judicial review of agency action show two things: (1) an "injury in fact"; and (2) an interest "arguably within the zone of interests to be protected or regulated" by the statute that the agency is claimed to have violated. (Later decisions make it clear that the plaintiff must be within the zone of interests of the particular provision involved in the case, not of the statute as a whole.) The "injury in fact" requirement has proved to be the more important of these two elements of the *Data Processing* test.

In *Sierra Club* the Court held that a mere allegation of a sincere interest in a problem, even if the interest has been active and long-standing, is not enough to constitute injury in fact. The practical importance of this holding, however, was diminished by the Court's assertion that the Sierra Club could establish injury in fact merely by alleging that some of its members used the area in question for recreational purposes. The esthetic injury suffered by these members, who would no longer be able to hike through an unspoiled wilderness if the project was built, was sufficient to constitute an injury in fact not only as to themselves, but also as to the organization to which they belonged. Obviously, there was little doubt that the Sierra Club could satisfy this requirement, so the ultimate effect of the Court's holding was simply to require an amendment to the pleadings.

The next Supreme Court case suggested that it would be easy to satisfy the *Sierra Club* requirements. United States v. Students Challenging Regulatory Agency Procedures (S.Ct.1973) [*SCRAP I*] involved a challenge to an ICC decision in a railroad rate case. The railroads had sought permission for a rate increase to expand their revenues and to cover expenses. The ICC had not given final approval for the increase, but did allow it to go into effect pending investigation. The plaintiffs, who had formed an association in order to bring the case, alleged that the existing rate schedule unfairly discriminated against recycled goods. As a result of this rate discrimination, they alleged, recycled goods were used in lower amounts than they otherwise would be. The plaintiffs' theory was that the situation would only be made worse by an across-the-board rate increase. They alleged that the result of this increase would be to discriminate against recycled goods, further diminishing the use of recycling, thereby increasing the amount of litter on a nationwide basis, and thus causing an increase in the amount of litter in the parks near the plaintiffs' homes. In short, their standing argument was that the ICC's approval of the railroad rate increase would ultimately have the effect of making their visits to local parks less pleasant because of an increase in litter. They also alleged that the decrease in recycling would cause an increase in mining and logging in the region. Despite the somewhat tenuous chain of causation alleged by the plaintiffs, and the fairly minimal injury which they claimed as a result of this chain of causation, the Supreme Court held that they did have standing to challenge the ICC's action.

The *SCRAP* decision clarified two elements of standing law. First, the Court made it clear that standing "is not to be denied simply because many people suffer the same injury." As the Court pointed out, to deny standing to individuals who are injured simply because many others are also injured, would mean that the "more injurious Government actions could be questioned by nobody." Second, the Court held that the test for standing was qualitative, not quantitative. Thus the magnitude of the injury in fact makes no difference so long as some injury exists. As the Court said, quoting Professor Davis, "the basic idea that comes out in numerous cases is that an identifiable trifle" is enough to establish standing.

The Supreme Court's next decision also took a generous approach to environmental standing. That case, Duke Power Co. v. Carolina Environmental Study Group, Inc. (S.Ct.1978), involved a chain of causation almost as tenuous as that in the *SCRAP* case. The plaintiffs in *Duke Power* challenged the constitutionality of the Price–Anderson Act. That statute limits the liability of the nuclear industry for damages resulting from a single nuclear accident. The plaintiffs claimed that without this limitation on liability, reactors would not be built, and that this in turn would spare them immediate environmental injuries such as injury to fishing. Their claim on the merits, however, did not relate to these immediate environmental injuries. Instead, it related to the possible limitation on damages if and when a reactor in their vicinity became involved in a nuclear accident. They contended that if they were injured and their damages exceeded the amount allowed by the statute, the statute would constitute an unconstitutional taking of property without compensation. But this claim was too speculative to provide them with standing. Instead, their standing claim was that, as a result of a statute which might be unconstitutional if it were ever applied to them in the future, they were suffering immediate environmental injury today. Despite the tenuousness of the chain of causation, the Court held that there was a "substantial likelihood" that the nuclear plants near the plaintiffs' homes would not be completed or operated without the statute. This was held to be a sufficient basis for standing. The defendants had also attacked the plaintiffs' standing because the injury which they were using to establish their standing had no logical relationship to their claims on the merits. The Court held, however, that such a nexus between the plaintiffs' injury and the claim on the merits was unnecessary. (The nonconstitutional status of the zone of interests test was reaffirmed in Bennett v. Spear (S.Ct.1997), in which the Court upheld the power of Congress to grant standing to anyone suffering an injury in fact, without regard to whether they were within the zone of interests of the statute.)

In *Duke Power* and earlier decisions, the Supreme Court took a liberal approach to standing in environmental cases. In 1990, however, the Court signaled a change in direction. The first indication of a changed attitude was in a reference, in an non-environmental opinion, to *SCRAP I* as involving "[p]robably the most attenuated injury" ever to confer standing, with the additional comment that *SCRAP I* "surely went to the very outer limit of the law." Whitmore v. Arkansas

(S.Ct.1990). A second, more serious signal followed later the same year, in Lujan v. National Wildlife Federation (S.Ct.1990).

National Wildlife Federation involved a Bureau of Land Management review of past executive orders protecting many public lands from resource development. (These "withdrawals" are discussed in Chapter 6.) In 1976, Congress directed BLM to review existing withdrawals in eleven western states and decide whether the lands should be reopened for development. The plaintiff alleged that the BLM had violated the required statutory procedures in numerous respects, and that BLM's action would open up the lands involved to mining. The Court held that the plaintiff lacked standing.

Justice Scalia's opinion for the Court held that the plaintiff's claims were invalid in two respects. First, plaintiff had attempted to comply with *Sierra Club* by filing affidavits attesting to use of the affected lands by some of its members. The affidavits were defective, the Court held, because they only alleged that these members used federal lands "in the vicinity" of those affected by the order. Justice Scalia concluded that actual presence, not merely vague proximity, was required. Second, even if those affidavits had been adequate, they would have established the plaintiff's right to litigate only about the specific lands used by those individuals, not to challenge the entire BLM program. Unless a statute specifically permits broad regulations to be directly reviewed, a plaintiff can only challenge some "concrete action applying the regulation to the claimant's situation in a fashion that harms or threatens to harm him." (The opinion then points out that exceptions exist when provided by statutes such as the Clean Air Act or when a rule "as a practical matter requires the plaintiff to adjust his conduct immediately.")

The first of these holdings requires more careful pleading in environmental cases, and probably will increase the amount of time and energy devoted to disputing standing issues. It should not, however, pose an insuperable barrier to environmental standing. The second holding, requiring piecemeal litigation, may have more serious longterm consequences by preventing unified litigation against broad government programs.

Justice Scalia conceded that "[t]he case-by-case approach that this requires is understandably frustrating to an organization such as respondent's, which has as its objective across-the-board protection of our Nation's wildlife and the streams and forests that support it." What Justice Scalia seemingly failed to realize, however, is that in pursuing this role environmental organizations are not merely satisfying the personal values of their members. They are also enforcing the public policies enacted by Congress, which relies on lawsuits as one way of ensuring agency compliance with the law.

Justice Scalia continued his campaign to restrict standing in Lujan v. Defenders of Wildlife (S.Ct.1992). The ultimate issue in *Defenders*, which the Court never reached, was whether the Endangered Species Act applies only to actions within the United States. The plaintiffs alleged that they would be harmed in various ways by federally supported actions taking place in Egypt and Sri Lanka. The Court held that they lacked standing, in the process striking down the ESA's citizen suit provision, which authorized the suit. Without any injury in fact, the plaintiffs could only be suing to vindicate the abstract interest in administrative compliance with the law—but that interest, the Court said, is properly the concern not of the courts but of the President, who is constitutionally obligated to "take care that the laws be faithfully executed."

The plaintiffs had unsuccessfully alleged several forms of injury. Two members alleged that they had visited the relevant areas of Egypt and Sri Lanka in the past and hoped to do so again in the future. "Such 'some day' intentions—without any description of concrete plans, or indeed even any specification of *when* the some day will be," were not enough to support standing. Justice Scalia was no more impressed with what he described as the plaintiffs' more novel standing theories. The first of these theories was called ecosystem nexus, under which "anyone who uses any part of an affected ecosystem has standing even if the activity is located a great distance away." Although the ESA is aimed in part at the protection of ecosystems, Justice Scalia found no basis for concluding that it created a cause of action on behalf of people who use parts of the ecosystem "not perceptibly affected" by the government's action.

Justice Scalia was equally unimpressed by the plaintiffs' other two theories. One, which they called the animal nexus, would have conveyed standing on anyone who studies or observes an endangered species. The other theory, the vocational nexus, would grant standing to anyone with a professional interest in the animal. To say that Justice Scalia was unpersuaded is an understatement. He found it remarkable that anyone would argue for such a broad theory of standing, under which "anyone who goes to see Asian elephants in the Bronx Zoo . . . has standing to sue because the director of AID did not consult with the Secretary [of Interior] regarding the AID-funded project in Sri Lanka." "It goes beyond the limit," he said, "and into pure speculation and fantasy, to say that anyone who observes or works with an endangered species, anywhere in the world, is appreciably harmed by a single project affecting some portion of that species with which he has not had more specific connection."

A concurrence by Justice Kennedy, who was joined by Justice Souter, attempted to stake out a middle ground. The Kennedy concurrence deserves careful attention because he and Souter were the swing voters. Kennedy entered two caveats to the Scalia opinion. First, he agreed that the record in *Defenders* was inadequate to support the plaintiff's nexus theories, but was not willing to foreclose them as a matter of law in some future case. Second, he saw a greater role for Congress in defining the perimeter of injury in fact:

> As government programs and policies become more complex and far-reaching, we must be sensitive to the articulation of new rights of action that do not have clear analogues in our common-law tradition . . . . In my view, Congress has the power to define injuries and articulate chains of causation that will give rise to a case or controversy where none existed before . . . . In exercising this power, however, Congress must at the very least identify the injury it seeks to vindicate and relate the injury to the class of persons entitled to bring suit. The citizen-suit provision of the Endangered Species Act does not meet these minimal requirements . . . .

Defenders and *National Wildlife Foundation* seemed to signal a sharply restrictive attitude toward standing. This trend seemed to be confirmed by Steel Company v. Citizens for a Better Environment (S.Ct.1998). *Steel Company* stressed another prong of standing: the redressability requirement. The plaintiffs sued to recover civil penalties and for other relief against a company that had failed to make toxic emission disclosures required by federal law. The civil penalties, being payable to the government, were held not to redress any injury of the plaintiff. Because the statutory violation had no prospect of recurring, the Court held that the other claimed relief was unavailable. Hence, the plaintiffs had no available redress for their injury and therefore lacked standing. Justice Scalia, the author of the opinion, had seemingly won another battle in his campaign to restrict standing.

But in the Court's first standing decision of the new century, Friends of the Earth v. Laidlaw Environmental Services (TOC), Inc. (S.Ct.2000), yet another change in direction seemed to occur. *Laidlaw* involved a citizen suit under the Clean Water Act against a polluter that had repeatedly violated the mercury limits in its permit. Although the lower court had held that the discharges did not in fact cause environmental harm, the Court nonetheless found standing. The plaintiffs had alleged that they lived in the area but did not use the river for recreational purposes because of concerns about pollution. Quoting *Sierra Club*, the Court said that "environmental plaintiffs adequately allege injury in fact when they aver that they use the affected area and are persons 'for whom the aesthetic and recreational values of the area will be lessened' by the challenged activity." Because the plaintiffs' "reasonable concerns" about the effects of the discharge "directly affected" their recreational and aesthetic interests, they had standing. This holding, as Justice Scalia complained in dissent, seemed to take a more generous attitude toward injury in fact than *Defenders* and similar cases.

Laidlaw also cut back on *Steel Company*'s redressability holding. Read broadly, *Steel Company* would seem to suggest that private parties never have standing to seek civil penalties payable to the government. In *Laidlaw*, however, the violations had continued through the filing of the law suit. Consequently, the Court said, civil penalties would redress potential future injury to the plaintiffs by deterring further violations. Whether *Laidlaw*'s more generous attitude toward standing marks a doctrinal turning point remains to be seen.

In any event, although the Court is obviously divided in how strictly to apply the standing requirements, it does seem united in its understanding of the basic test. To summarize the law of standing, the Supreme Court has required plaintiffs to prove that they have suffered an injury in fact. In environmental cases, the plaintiff must allege the existence of a chain of causation between the allegedly illegal government action and an injury to some portion of the environment used by the plaintiff. The plaintiff need not allege any health injury or any economic damage; aesthetic injury is enough. To obtain standing, the plaintiff need only demonstrate a "substantial likelihood" that judicial relief against the illegal government action would reduce the plaintiff's environmental injury.

2. REVIEWABILITY

The existence of standing does not mean that the plaintiff will necessarily get a hearing on the merits. Standing involves the relationship between the plaintiff and the issues in the case. Although the plaintiff may stand in the proper relationship to an issue, the issue itself may not be suitable for judicial resolution. If *anyone* could litigate the issue, the plaintiff would be the proper person to do so, but some issues simply cannot be litigated by anyone at all. The question of whether an issue is subject to judicial resolution is called "reviewability."

Fortunately, virtually all issues that might arise in an environmental case are subject to judicial review. This was made clear by the Supreme Court in Citizens to Preserve Overton Park, Inc. v. Volpe (S.Ct.1971). *Overton Park* involved a dispute over the use of federal highway funds to finance the construction of an inter-state highway through Overton Park, a 342–acre city park in Memphis. The applicable statute prohibited the Secretary of Transportation from using federal funds to finance the construction of highways through a public park if a "feasible and prudent" alternative route existed. The plaintiffs contended that the Secretary had violated this restriction. The Supreme Court held that the plaintiffs were entitled to judicial review on this issue. The Court found the key to the reviewability problem in section 701 of the Administrative Procedure Act, 5 U.S.C.A. § 701. Section 701 provides that the action of every administrative agency is subject to judicial review except (1) where there is a statutory prohibition on review or (2) where "agency action is committed to agency discretion by law." In order to find the first exception applicable, a court must find "clear and convincing evidence" that Congress intended to restrict access to judicial review. Such evidence is rarely available. The second exception, action "committed to agency discretion," is not easy to understand, inasmuch as even discretionary agency actions can be reviewed by a court to determine if the agency has abused its discretion. In *Overton Park*, the Court concluded that the "committed to agency discretion" exception is very narrow and applies only where statutes are drawn in such broad terms that "there is no law to apply." Thus, this exception really applies only in cases in which a statute gives an agency such broad powers, subject to so few restrictions, that a court could never reasonably conclude in any given case that the agency had exceeded its powers. This seems to be another way of saying that judicial review is pointless because we can conclude without considering the specific facts of the case that the agency could not possibly have acted illegally. Thus, holding that a question is "committed to agency discretion" comes very close to a holding on the merits that whatever the agency has done is necessarily lawful. In the specific case before it, the *Overton Park* Court concluded that the decision was not committed to agency discretion because the statute provided specific criteria which the Secretary of Transportation was supposed to apply.

In a few exceptional cases, the issue of reviewability has proved to be troublesome. Generally, these cases have involved statutes which provide either no limitations on administrative action or limitations which are so broad as to be almost nonexistent. Occasionally, administrative action may be held to be unreviewable because it involves some special area in which courts are hesitant to become involved, such as foreign affairs or military decisions. In the typical environmental law case, however, reviewability is unlikely to be a serious issue.

3. STANDARD OF REVIEW

We have seen that the plaintiff in an environmental law case must establish that she has standing and that the issues involved in the case are reviewable. Making this showing gets the plaintiff through the courtroom door. Of course, getting into the courtroom is not an end in itself; it is merely a means of getting a decision on the merits of the case. Thus, for many plaintiffs, the important question is not whether a court will be willing to hear the case, but rather what kind of hearing the court will provide. In particular, a great deal turns on the degree to which the court is willing to second-guess the administrative agency as opposed to deferring to the agency's expertise. The extent of judicial review generally depends on the kind of issues involved in the case. In particular, it is useful to distinguish between issues relating to pure questions of law, issues relating to the factual basis for the agency's action, and issues relating to the agency's procedures. Courts apply a different level of scrutiny to each of these three kinds of issues.

The first kind of issue involves only questions of law. Several practical reasons exist for giving some degree of deference to the administrative agency's view of the law. In a highly technical area, the agency has more experience than any particular judge in applying the statute. Also, Congress has given the agency, rather than the court, primary responsibility for carrying out the law. Furthermore, it is often important that private individuals or local governments be able to rely immediately on an agency's view of the statute. If the agency's view of the statute were given no credence at all by the courts, it would be unsafe to rely on the agency's position until the issue had been litigated all the way to the Supreme Court. Thus, giving deference to the agency's view serves the purpose of expediting compliance with the law.

The Supreme Court has also emphasized an additional reason for deferring to administrative agencies on statutory interpretation issues. In Chevron U.S.A., Inc. v. NRDC (S.Ct.1984), which is discussed in greater detail in Chapter 3, the Court stressed that policy choices should be made by the political branches of government, rather than the courts. Where Congress has delegated regulatory authority to an administrative agency, that agency should decide upon public policy in the area, not federal judges. Of course, the agency must act within the scope of the authority delegated by Congress. Thus, the Court still plays an important role in assuring that the agency decision is consistent with the statutory mandate. Nevertheless, while *Chevron* does not give agencies unlimited discretion with respect to statutory interpretation, their decisions are entitled to a high level of deference.

The standard of review applied to legal issues is not determined by the form of the administrative action. In order to discuss the level of review for procedural or factual issues, however, it is necessary to understand the basics of administrative procedure. What follows is a brief sketch of the various forms of administrative procedure, which should help the reader understand the judicial review process more fully.

Under the Administrative Procedure Act, there are three important categories of administrative actions. The first category consists of adjudications. This form of procedure normally applies whenever the specific statute governing the agency requires an issue to be "determined on the record after opportunity for an agency hearing." The procedures required are essentially similar to those of a civil trial. The second category of administrative action is rulemaking. With the limited exception of a few situations in which a "formal rulemaking" is required, the procedure is relatively simple. The initial step is the publication of a notice in the Federal Register describing the proposed rule. The agency must then allow interested parties an "opportunity to comment" for at least thirty days. Then, the agency must issue, in conjunction with its promulgation of the rule, a "concise general statement" of the rule's basis and purpose. (There are a limited number of exceptions to these requirements.) The third category of administrative action consists of a vast number of government decisions that neither impose sanctions on individuals, grant licenses to them, nor impose rules governing future conduct. The APA does not specify any procedures for these actions.

With respect to factual issues, the standard of review depends on the type of proceeding. In an adjudicative action, the standard for review of factual issues is the "substantial evidence" test. The agency's action must be upheld by the court unless there is no substantial evidence in the record to support the agency ruling. With respect to other forms of administrative action, the leading authority on review of factual issues is *Overton Park*. In that case, the Court held that the standard of review for non-adjudicative administrative decisions was the "arbitrary and capricious" test. In applying this test, a court must examine the record considered by the administrative agency. On the basis of that record, the court must decide whether the agency considered all of the relevant factors and whether the agency made a clear error of judgment. In practice, this standard of review may involve either a very cursory examination of the administrative action or an intense scrutiny of the reasons given for the administrative decision to determine whether adequate support exists in the record. In environmental cases, some courts apply the "arbitrary and capricious" test in a way that closely resembles the application of the "substantial evidence" test. This has become known as the "hard look" approach. Thus, agencies may face intensive judicial scrutiny of their factual determinations. At the same time, of course, courts have not forgotten that many of these determinations involve highly technical matters with which judges have little familiarity. Hence, some tendency still exists toward deference to the agency, but less than one might expect from the phrase "arbitrary and capricious."

Judges sometimes have felt uncomfortable about attempting to assess an agency's technical judgment on factual issues. Feeling more comfortable in assessing procedural issues, some of these judges, led by Judge Bazelon of the D.C. Circuit, imposed procedural requirements on some administrative agencies beyond those contained in the APA. While this approach had some arguable merit, it was rejected by the Supreme

Court in Vermont Yankee Nuclear Power Corp. v. NRDC (S.Ct.1978), a case involving rulemaking about nuclear waste disposal. The lower court had faulted the NRDC for relying heavily on a conclusory statement by one of its own staff members, which had not been subject to cross-examination. In *Vermont Yankee* the Court held that judges normally lack the authority to impose any additional procedures on agencies beyond those required by statute, the Constitution, or the agency's own rules. The decision leaves open the possibility that in extremely compelling circumstances some additional procedures might be imposed. Fundamentally, the Court's rationale was that the agency itself is in the best position to decide on procedures.

Vermont Yankee was subject to some sharp criticism. Some scholars such as Professor Nathanson, argued persuasively that the Court misconstrued the original intent of the Administrative Procedure Act. Other scholars such as Professor Davis argued that the lower courts were correct in constructing a "common law" of agency procedure. Whatever criticisms may be made of the Court's opinion, it is clear that *Vermont Yankee* represents the current law on the subject.

Lower courts have found, however, that *Vermont Yankee* does leave them some room for maneuver. One exception to the *Vermont Yankee* rule is that courts may reverse agency actions when the agency has violated statutory procedural requirements. Some lower courts responded to *Vermont Yankee* by giving an expansive reading to statutes relating to agency procedures. For example, the APA on its face requires only a brief explanation of the agency's rule and an opportunity to comment by outsiders. Several lower courts have held that the opportunity to comment is not "adequate" unless the agency has fully disclosed in advance the technical data which it is considering. In effect, these courts have required an additional procedure on the part of agencies. Although courts applying this rationale have stopped short of requiring agencies to allow oral presentation of testimony or cross-examination, they have required procedures which have been aptly described as involving a "paper hearing." In addition, it should be remembered that many individual statutes such as the Clean Air Act contain detailed provisions concerning agency procedures in certain kinds of cases. These provisions often go far beyond the minimum requirements of the APA.

4. REMEDIES

Once the court decides that an agency has violated the law, the plaintiff is clearly entitled to some form of relief, if only an order directing the agency to give further consideration to the issue before acting. It has sometimes been argued that a court should withhold any remedy from the plaintiff if granting relief would be "unreasonable." The Supreme Court has clearly rejected that position. In TVA v. Hill (S.Ct.1978), the Court authorized an injunction against the completion of a multi-million dollar dam because the dam would threaten an endangered species of fish known as the snail darter. The Court found that completion of the dam would violate the Endangered Species Act. Having reached this conclusion, the Court held that it had no choice but to issue an injunction against completion of the dam. An enormous amount of money had already been spent on the dam and little work remained to be done, but the Court held that these factors were simply irrelevant. In passing the statute, Congress had weighed the importance of saving an endangered species against other government policies, and had found the policy of saving endangered species to be paramount. The Court held that it was not its function to reassess a Congressional balancing of these policies.

Courts do retain some discretion, however. In a later case, Weinberger v. Romero–Barcelo (S.Ct.1982), the Court held that a statutory violation need not always result in an injunction against the activity. The violation in question was the Navy's failure to get a permit under the Clean Water Act before a training exercise. The permit was technically required because munitions fell in the water, but the lower court found that no harm to the coastal waters would in fact result. Under the circumstances, the Court held that ordering the Navy to apply for a permit was a sufficient remedy.

The latest case on the subject of remedial discretion is Amoco Production Co. v. Village of Gambell, Alaska (S.Ct.1987). *Gambell* involved a grant of oil and gas leases covering tracts offshore of Alaska. The environmental effects on Alaskan lands allegedly required the use of special procedures designed to protect the interests of Alaskan Natives. The Court found *Weinberger* controlling because only a procedural violation rather than an actual environmental injury was present. If an actual environmental injury had been present, however, the result would probably have been different. As the Court said:

> Environmental injury, by its nature, can seldom be adequately remedied by money damages and is often permanent or at least of long duration, i.e.,

irreparable. If such injury is sufficiently likely, therefore, the balance of harms will usually favor the issuance of an injunction to protect the environment.

In the language following this passage, the Court stressed that injury to the environment was unlikely and that the countervailing interest in oil exploration was itself the goal of another federal statute.

The Court has not clearly explained how these three cases fit together. One way of harmonizing the cases is as follows. In issuing relief, a court's primary duty is to effectuate the goals of the statute. In *TVA v. Hill,* the statutory purpose was to protect endangered species at virtually all cost; the only way to effectuate that intent was to enjoin the dam. In *Weinberger,* the goal of the statute was to eliminate water pollution to the extent practicable. That goal was not compromised by the district judge's order, which had directed the Navy to apply for a permit but had allowed the military exercises to continue in the meantime. Similarly, in *Gambell,* a preliminary injunction was not required to accomplish the statutory goal of environmental protection. On the other hand, as the *Gambell* Court pointed out, where a procedural violation results in environmental harm, generally an injunction will be required to effectuate federal policy. Thus, the choice of a remedy is neither mechanical nor left to the district judge's unguided discretion; rather, the judge must act as an agent of Congress in effectuating national policy.

Another important remedial issue relates to attorneys' fees. Much of the most important environmental litigation is brought by public interest groups. Their ability to bring these suits, thereby acting as private attorneys general policing agency compliance with federal statutes, is dependent on their access to funding. One of the most important sources of funding for these groups consists of the awards of attorneys' fees provided by many environmental statutes. The availability of fee awards and their size have been the subject of tremendous litigation, both in the environmental area and elsewhere. Two basic rules are that (1) fees are available only to "prevailing parties," and (2) the fee is usually calculated by multiplying a reasonable hourly rate times the number of hours reasonably invested in the suit. The parameters and qualifications attaching to these rules are, not unexpectedly, quite complex, and will not be discussed here.

Many of the issues we have been discussing are considered in far more depth in an administrative procedure class. The discussion given here, however, should be enough to enable the reader to understand how courts function in environmental law cases.

One restriction on agency action takes the form of judicial review. Each agency is also restricted by the particular statutes governing its activities. In addition, all federal agencies are restricted by a statute known as the National Environmental Policy Act or NEPA. The next section will consider this environmental statute in detail.

B. THE NATIONAL ENVIRONMENTAL POLICY ACT

NEPA imposes environmental responsibilities on all agencies of the federal government. Most of our discussion of NEPA will relate to § 102(2)(c), which concerns the environmental impact statement (EIS). Before turning to the EIS requirement, however, it is worth reviewing some of the other provisions of NEPA.

Section 101 of NEPA makes it the policy of the federal government to use all practicable means to administer federal programs in the most environmentally sound fashion. Section 102(1) requires that the laws and regulations of the United States be "administered in accordance with the policies set forth in this chapter." Prior to NEPA, some agencies contended that they lacked the statutory authority to consider environmental issues even if they wanted to do so. For example, the Atomic Energy Commission (now the NRC) contended that the thermal pollution caused by nuclear power plants was a matter beyond its jurisdiction. One important result of NEPA is to ensure that every agency has the authority to consider the environmental consequences of its actions. Of course, granting agencies the authority to consider the environment does not guarantee that they will actually do so, but it does open the door for those agencies which are willing to take this step.

Section 102(2) contains several provisions that are intended to force agencies to take this step. Subsections (a) and (b) require new agency procedures to ensure that the decisionmaking process takes into account environmental factors. When a proposal involves conflicts between alternative uses of available resources—which is likely to be true of any important government decision—subsection (e) requires the agency to develop alternatives to recommended courses of action. These provisions supplement the EIS requirement and provide a basis for judicial intervention where the EIS requirement does not apply. Another important aspect of NEPA was the establishment of the Council on Environmental Quality (CEQ), which is primarily charged with advising the President about environmental matters.

The most significant provision of NEPA is undoubtedly § 102(2)(c). The primary purpose of this provision is to force agencies to take environmental factors into consideration when making significant decisions. The crucial language of this subsection reads as follows:

> The Congress authorizes and directs that, to the fullest extent possible: . . . (2) all agencies of the federal government shall—
>
> . . .
>
> (c) include in every recommendation or report on proposals for legislation and other major Federal actions significantly affecting the quality of the human environment, a detailed statement by the responsible official on—
>
> (i) the environmental impact of the proposed action,
>
> (ii) any adverse environmental effects which cannot be avoided should the proposal be implemented,
>
> (iii) alternatives to the proposed action,
>
> . . .

The subsection goes on to require the federal agency to consult other agencies with jurisdiction over or special expertise concerning the environmental problem involved. Copies of the EIS are to be circulated among federal, state and local agencies, to the President, to the CEQ, and to the public. The EIS is also supposed to "accompany the proposal through the existing agency review processes."

In essence, the statute requires the agency to prepare a detailed explanation of the environmental consequences of its actions, and to make that report available to higher-level agency officials, other agencies, and the public. The EIS provision in NEPA makes no reference to judicial enforcement. Indeed, the drafter of the provision apparently did not have such enforcement specifically in mind. Nevertheless, soon after the statute was passed, it became clear that courts would become actively involved in enforcing it.

With this background in mind, we turn to a detailed consideration of the EIS requirement. For convenience, we divide our inquiry into two parts. The first issue to be considered is whether an agency needs to prepare any EIS at all. If the answer is affirmative, it is then necessary to consider the scope, timing and content of the EIS.

1. THRESHOLD REQUIREMENTS

We will begin by discussing the threshold question: Is any EIS necessary? A reading of the statute indicates that three requirements must be met before an EIS is necessary. The proposed action must (1) be federal, (2) qualify as "major", and (3) have a significant environmental impact. There has been considerable litigation about these requirements.

We can begin with the first issue. In general, a proposed action is considered "federal" if some federal agency has the power to control the action. Thus, building a nuclear reactor involves a federal major action because a federal license is required. Sometimes the federal control takes the form of licensing, sometimes of funding, and sometimes of direct federal involvement, as in projects constructed by the Army Corps of Engineers. Occasionally, problems arise when an attempt is made to structure a project so as to "defederalize" all or part of it. Nevertheless, in most cases the "federal" requirement poses little difficulty.

The second requirement, that the project be "major," has proved to pose few problems. Any substantial commitment of resources, whether monetary or otherwise, is enough to qualify a project as "major." Indeed, there is considerable dispute as to whether any project having a significant environmental impact could ever be considered "minor." In any event, neither of the first two requirements poses serious conceptual problems, although there are problems of line-drawing.

The final requirement, "significant environmental impact," is analytically more difficult. It poses two questions. First, what counts as an "environmental" impact? Second, when is such an impact "significant"? There is a temptation to assume that "environmental" refers only to the natural environment (wilderness areas, rivers, beaches, etc.). Nevertheless, the statute itself indicates that Congress had broader concerns. Section 101 of NEPA speaks of the need to assure all Americans "safe, healthful, productive, and esthetically and culturally pleasing surroundings." The same section speaks of the need to preserve the important historical and cultural aspects of our national heritage, to enhance the quality of renewable resources, and to achieve a balance between population and resource use. These goals extend beyond undisturbed natural areas.

Judicial decisions confirm that NEPA is not limited to the natural environment. For example, in Hanly v. Mitchell (2d Cir.1972), the Second Circuit held that the construction of a new jail in Manhattan potentially involved significant environmental impact. In addition to air pollution, among the impacts considered were the possibility of increased crime in the area, the esthetic impact of the building, and other socio-economic effects. Given this reading, the scope of NEPA could be virtually unlimited. Almost everything the federal government does has some effect on the quality of life. Yet, the drafters of NEPA presumably did not intend that the government issue an EIS for every decision about foreign policy, medicaid, or tax law, even though these decisions presumably do affect the quality of human life.

The problem of defining the meaning of "environmental impact" reached the Supreme Court in Metropolitan Edison Co. v. People Against Nuclear Energy (S.Ct.1983). The question before the Court was whether the NRC was required to prepare an EIS before allowing Metropolitan Edison to resume operation of one of the reactors at Three Mile Island. The D.C. Circuit held that an EIS was required because the psychological stress caused by reopening the plant would have a significant health effect on residents of the surrounding communities. The Supreme Court apparently agreed with the lower court that "effects on human health can be cognizable under NEPA, and that human health may include psychological health." Generally speaking, however, the Court believed that in NEPA "Congress was talking about the physical environment—the world around us, so to speak."

Under *Metropolitan Edison*, an effect qualifies as environmental only if it has a "reasonably close causal relation" to a change in the physical environment. NEPA requires consideration of the direct effects of present physical actions and of the possible effects should future risks materialize. It does not, however, require consideration of the psychological impact that the mere existence of a risk may have before that risk has materialized. Similarly, as the Court pointed out, in cases involving the construction of a new jail or other public facility, "the psychological health damage to neighboring residents resulting from unrealized risks of crime is too far removed from that event [the operation of the facility] to be covered by NEPA." In short, a psychological effect can only qualify as environmental if it is proximately caused by a physical event.

In addition to the problem of deciding what impacts count as being "environmental", there is also the problem of deciding when an environmental impact is sufficiently serious to be "significant." Courts have taken various approaches to this problem. The Second Circuit in Hanly v. Kleindienst (2d Cir.1972) [*Hanly II*] adopted a two-part test involving the degree of change from current land use and the absolute quantity of the impact. Formulations adopted by other courts include "significant degradation of the environment", and "arguably adverse environmental impact", as well as other attempts to paraphrase the statute. The CEQ regulations, which are made binding by a Presidential

executive order, instruct agencies to consider factors
such as impact on public health, unique features of the
geographic area, the precedential effect of the action,
and whether the action is highly controversial. Even
after considering these factors, a determination must be
made about their magnitude. This is a "judgment call"
about which very little can be said, except to observe
that courts seem to have some tendency to resolve close
cases in favor of requiring an impact statement.

Prior to *Metropolitan Edison*, the Supreme Court
had considered NEPA's threshold requirements on only
two occasions. Both involved rather atypical factual
situations. The first case, Flint Ridge Development Co.
v. Scenic Rivers Association of Oklahoma (S.Ct.1976),
involved a statute requiring certain real estate developers to file a disclosure statement with HUD. The issue
before the Court was whether HUD was required to file
an EIS. The Court held that no EIS was required
because the statutory 30–day deadline was too short to
permit HUD to prepare an EIS. Hence, requiring an
EIS "would create an irreconcilable and fundamental
conflict with the Secretary's duties under the Disclosure
Act." The second case, Andrus v. Sierra Club
(S.Ct.1979), involved the question of whether appropriations requests are covered by NEPA. Although a
federal agency's annual appropriation request might
seem to be a "proposal for legislation," the Court held
that no impact statement was required. The only aspect
of *Andrus* that appears to have broader significance is
the Court's reliance on the CEQ regulations. The
Court held that these regulations were entitled to
substantial judicial deference.

Before 1989, the lower courts were sharply divided regarding the proper scope of review when an agency decides not to prepare an EIS. The Supreme Court resolved the issue in Marsh v. Oregon Natural Resources Council (S.Ct.1989). The plaintiffs in *Marsh* claimed that a dam required a supplemental EIS [SEIS] because of two new documents: a report from the state department of fish and wildlife suggesting that the dam would have more effect on downstream fishing, and a federal soil survey that implied greater downstream turbidity than the original EIS suggested. Although the issue was whether a supplemental EIS was needed, rather than the threshold requirements for an initial EIS, the Court stressed that the two issues are similar. If new information shows that a federal action will affect the environment "in a significant way or to a significant extent not already considered," a supplemental EIS is required. This is obviously very similar to the threshold requirement for an EIS. In both situations, the Court said, NEPA requires an agency to take a "hard look" at the environmental effects of its proposal. The Court held the proper standard for review is the arbitrary and capricious test, because the agency's decision whether to issue an EIS or SEIS involves "a factual dispute the resolution of which implicates substantial agency expertise." After *Marsh*, the same standard should apply to review of an agency's decision to forego an EIS entirely, although some confusion on this point remains in the lower courts.

As noted earlier, the "arbitrary and capricious" test can result in either cursory or searching review of the agency decision, depending on how the court applies the standard. *Marsh* calls for fairly careful review of the agency decision. Lower court judges, the Court said, "should not automatically defer to the [agency] without carefully reviewing the record and satisfying themselves that the agency has made a reasoned decision . . . ." On the other hand, where experts disagree, the agency may "rely on the reasonable opinions of its own qualified experts even if, as an original matter, a court might find contrary views more persuasive." In applying this test, the Court reviewed the record in great detail before upholding the agency decision. Thus, the Court's embrace of the "arbitrary and capricious" test does not free the agency's decision from serious scrutiny on review.

2. SCOPE AND TIMING

This brings us to the most important set of issues relating to NEPA. If an EIS is necessary, *what* must it contain and *when* must it be prepared? As we shall see, although the Supreme Court has not addressed the threshold issues to any significant extent, it has addressed repeatedly the issues relating to the scope and content of the EIS.

Before considering the EIS's *content*, it may be helpful to review briefly the procedure used in preparing an EIS. The CEQ regulations now contain detailed procedural requirements for the entire EIS process. The process begins with an "environmental assessment" (EA), which is a brief analysis of the need for an EIS. The EA must also consider alternatives to the proposed action, as required by § 102(2)(E) of NEPA. If the agency decides not to prepare an EIS, it must make a "finding of no significant impact" (FONSI) available to the public. Under *Marsh*, this finding is subject to judicial review using the arbitrary and capricious standard.

If the agency does decide to prepare an EIS, the first step in the EIS process is called "scoping." Scoping is intended to obtain early participation by other agencies and the public in planning the EIS, to determine the scope of the EIS, and to determine the significant issues to be discussed in the EIS. The actual preparation of the EIS itself involves a draft EIS, a comment period, and a final EIS. Agencies with jurisdiction or special expertise relating to the project are required to comment. Major inter-agency disagreements are to be referred to CEQ for its recommendation. When an agency reaches a final decision on the project, it must prepare a "record of decision" summarizing its actions and explaining why it rejected environmentally preferable alternatives and mitigation measures.

As reflected by the CEQ regulations, one of the most important issues relating to the content of an EIS is its scope. This is the reason why CEQ included a special stage in the procedure focusing on this issue. *Segmentation* of a project is one means of evading NEPA. For example, suppose the Department of Transportation planned to fund construction of a highway through an environmentally sensitive area such as a wildlife preserve. If it did not wish to give full consideration to this environmental impact, it might proceed as follows: first, it could prepare an environmental impact statement on the highway segment terminating on one side of the preserve. Since this segment of the highway would not involve any environmentally sensitive areas, the agency would then conclude that that segment was environmentally sound. It could then do the same for the segment terminating near the other side of the preserve. Finally, when it got to the segment involving the preserve, it would simply note the obvious fact that millions of dollars spent on the other segments would go to waste unless the segments were connected. Thus, by the time it got around to considering the environmental impact of the final segment, the decision would be a foregone conclusion. At no stage in the process would the agency have really given consideration to the overall environmental costs and countervailing benefits of the project. This would defeat the purpose of NEPA. In order to prevent such evasion of NEPA's purpose, courts must be prepared to determine the proper scope of an EIS. In this hypothetical, for example, a court must have some means of determining whether the scope of the EIS can be restricted to these individual segments, considered one by one, or whether a single EIS must be prepared covering the entire project.

The answer to the scope question posed in the previous paragraph is an obvious one. In many cases, however, the issue is not nearly so clear-cut. A good example of the kind of problem faced by courts and agencies is provided by the D.C. Circuit decision in Scientists' Institute for Public Information, Inc. v. AEC (D.C.Cir.1973). That case, commonly referred to as the *SIPI* decision, involved the AEC's breeder reactor program. A breeder reactor is a nuclear reactor which not only consumes nuclear fuel but also produces such fuel. In the early 1970s, the government announced a commitment to complete the successful demonstration of a breeder reactor by 1980 and to proceed toward a full-scale development of the program. The expected cost of the program was well over $2 billion. The AEC predicted that by the year 2000 breeder reactor capacity would equal the total generating capacity of the United States in 1973. The AEC conceded that before building any particular breeder reactor plant, it would have to prepare an EIS on that plant. It argued, however, that it was not required to prepare an EIS covering the breeder reactor program as a whole.

In an opinion by Judge Skelly Wright, the D.C. Circuit held that an EIS covering the whole program was required. In deciding this issue, the court looked to two factors. The first was the extent to which meaningful information was available on the proposed technology and its alternatives. This factor was relevant because without such meaningful information the EIS itself would be pointless. Second, the court asked whether irretrievable commitments were being made, and other options were being precluded, as the program progressed. To the extent that irreversible decisions are being made, it is obviously important to consider their environmental impact now, rather than some years in the future when it is too late to change the decision anyway. Applying these factors to the case before it, the court concluded that the AEC "could have no rational basis for deciding that the time is not yet right for drafting an impact statement." The court noted that by the year 2000, some 600,000 cubic feet of high-level concentrated radioactive wastes would be generated, which would pose an admitted hazard to human health for thousands of years. This and related environmental impacts, according to the court, required "the most searching scrutiny under NEPA." Thus, the D.C.

Circuit's approach was functional, looking to the purposes of the EIS requirement rather than to a formalistic test. Because it found that the purposes of NEPA would be served by early preparation of an impact statement covering the entire program, the court ruled that such an impact statement was necessary.

The Supreme Court has taken quite a different approach to the issue of "programmatic" impact statements. The Court has considered three cases involving the scope and timing issues. The first case involved rather unusual facts and attracted little notice at the time. This case was Aberdeen & Rockfish Railroad Co. v. Students Challenging Regulatory Agency Procedures (S.Ct.1975) [*SCRAP II*], a continuation of the lawsuit which was discussed in connection with the doctrine of standing. After the Supreme Court's standing decision, the case was remanded to the District Court, which held that the ICC had failed to comply with NEPA. On appeal, the Supreme Court reversed. In deciding both the scope and the timing of the EIS, the Court used a relatively mechanical test. According to the Court:

Under ... the statute, the time at which the agency must prepare the final "statement" is the time at which it makes a recommendation or report on a *proposal* for federal action. Where an agency initiates federal action by publishing a proposal and then holding hearings on the proposal, the statute would appear to require an impact statement to be included in the proposal and to be considered at the hearing. Here, however, [until its actual decision], the ICC had made no proposal, recommendation, or report. The only proposal was the proposed new rates filed by the railroads. Thus, the earliest time at which the *statute* required a statement was the time of the ICC's report . . . .

In order to decide what kind of an environmental impact statement need be prepared, it is necessary first to describe accurately the "federal action" being taken.

Having defined the scope of the "federal action" being taken . . . our decision of this case becomes easy.

Thus, in *SCRAP II,* the Court used a fairly mechanistic test. Under *SCRAP,* the key to determining the scope and timing of the EIS is simply to identify carefully the "proposal" in question. The EIS is due at the same time, and not before, the proposal is issued. Moreover, the scope of the EIS is simply determined by the scope of the proposal itself. The scope, impact, and alternatives to *that* proposal must be discussed, not some broader set of issues.

Despite this relatively clear language in *SCRAP,* it failed to receive careful attention from either federal agencies or the lower federal courts. The reason is that much of the other language in the Court's opinion seemed more specifically related to the special characteristics of ICC law.

The Supreme Court's next decision on this issue made it clear that *SCRAP II* was intended to have a broader effect. That decision, Kleppe v. Sierra Club (S.Ct.1976), is the Court's definitive statement on the scope and timing issues. *Kleppe* involved the leasing of coal reserves on public lands to private mining companies. The Sierra Club alleged that individual leasing proposals in an area identified as the "Northern Great Plains region" involved such interrelated environmental effects that a single EIS was necessary for the entire region. Applying a further development of the *SIPI* test, the D.C. Circuit agreed. The Supreme Court made its own disagreement with the lower court's approach unmistakable. The Court faulted the lower court for creating a balancing test to decide the issue rather than focusing on the language of the statute. Looking to the language of the statute, the Supreme Court found it clear that an EIS is required only if there has been a report on a formal proposal for major federal action. On examining the record, the Court concluded that no proposal existed with respect to the Northern Great Plains region; instead, there were only proposals for actions of either local or national scope. The Court noted that an EIS was plainly required both for the local issuance of a lease and for the adoption of a national coal-leasing program. But, according to the Court, there was "no evidence in the record of an action or a proposal for an action of regional scope." Hence, the Court applied the *SCRAP* test and concluded that no regional EIS was necessary.

Having disposed of the argument adopted by the lower court, the Supreme Court then turned to an additional argument made by the Sierra Club. The Sierra Club stressed, not the possibility that some proposal on this region was "contemplated," but rather the inter-related environmental impacts of individual mining operations in this region. The Court rejected this argument also. The Court pointed out that this argument could be viewed in two different ways. First, it could be viewed as an attack on the sufficiency of the

EISs already prepared by the government on those projects already approved. As such, the Court held that the issue was not properly before it since the case was not brought as a challenge to any particular EIS. Second, the argument could also be viewed as an attack on the decision not to prepare one comprehensive impact statement on all proposed projects in the region. The Court conceded that when several proposals are pending before an agency at the same time, and when those proposals have cumulative or synergistic environmental impacts, their environmental consequences must be considered together. This apparent concession was undermined by serious qualifications. The Court indicated in *dicta* that this consideration could be made as part of the issuance of the individual EIS governing each site. That is, a discussion of the general program could be tacked onto the EIS about each specific mine. Also, the Court held that judicial review of the synergism issue would be based on the arbitrary and capricious standard. So long as the agency does not act arbitrarily in deciding on the scope of the impact statement, the Court held that judicial interference was inappropriate. The Sierra Club was unable to meet this standard.

Two important criticisms can be made of the *Kleppe* opinion. To begin with, the opinion indicates little sympathy with the purposes of NEPA. The Court exhibits little concern over whether its test would advance or frustrate the underlying statutory purpose — which is ensuring that agencies seriously consider environmental factors, not simply prepare additional paperwork in the course of making a decision. Under the *Kleppe* Court's view, the statute seems to require

only the preparation of an additional report at the time
a decision is announced, rather than serious consideration by the agency of the environmental factors discussed in the report. This seems to substantially undermine the purposes of NEPA. The Court's position can
best be understood as reflecting a desire to require the
minimum change in agency decisionmaking processes in
order to comply with the statutory language. Thus, the
Court seems to view NEPA as merely a gloss on a
general body of federal administrative law, rather than
as reflecting any congressional desire for a radically new
approach by agencies. In part, the Court seems to have
been motivated also by the desire to have a clear,
predictable test rather than requiring the kind of
case-by-case balancing adopted by the D.C. Circuit.

This brings us to the other major criticism of the
Court's opinion. The Court seems to have believed that
it was adopting a clear, almost mechanical test. In fact,
however, there is no talismanic significance to the word
"proposal." The *SIPI* case is a good illustration. In the
course of the development of the breeder reactor
project, there were probably dozens and perhaps even
hundreds of major memoranda prepared by various
agency officials either sketching possible courses of
action or attempting to evaluate those courses of action.
Some reports are made at higher levels within the
agency than others, and some seem to reflect a more
definitive disposition of the issues than others. Nevertheless, no bright line divides those memoranda which
are merely evaluations of possible courses of action
from those which constitute "recommendations or
reports on proposals for action," to use the statutory
language.

Of course, the breeder reactor program involved in *SIPI* was not a routine government program. But even in more ordinary contexts the existence of a "proposal" is often unclear. For example, in a rate case such as that involved in *SCRAP,* the ICC staff often participates in hearings and files briefs much like a party to the proceedings. These constitute recommendations or reports by the staff concerning a proposal, namely the staff's proposed disposition of the case. The Court gives little guidance as to whether these reports should be considered "reports on a proposal" as that phrase is used in the statute. Moreover, it is hard to see how this issue can be decided simply on the basis of labeling. Instead, a court considering this issue must clearly look, as the D.C. Circuit did in *SIPI,* to the functions of the EIS, to the extent to which a preparation of an EIS under these circumstances would be feasible, and to the extent to which such an EIS would be productive.

The Supreme Court's attempt to replace this functional analysis with a mechanistic test was doomed to frustration because the administrative process is simply too complex to lend itself to such simplistic treatment. This is not to say that the lower court's decision in the *Kleppe* case itself was correct. That opinion went far beyond the earlier decision in *SIPI* and may well have intruded too deeply into the administrative process. But the Supreme Court's cure in this case may have been as bad as the situation it was attempting to remedy.

The *Kleppe* test surfaced again in an unexpected context. In Weinberger v. Catholic Action of Hawaii (S.Ct.1981), the issue before the Court was how to apply the EIS requirement when the government's action involved classified information. Specifically, the government established "nuclear capable" storage facilities, but would neither admit nor deny (for security reasons) that nuclear weapons were actually stored there. The Court held that if nuclear weapons were indeed stored at the facilities, an EIS had to be prepared, but this duty was not judicially enforceable. The plaintiffs were unable to prove the existence of a specific proposal to store nuclear weapons (because any such proposal would be classified) — so under *Kleppe* they were unable to prove that an EIS was required. Consequently, the suit was dismissed for the plaintiffs' failure to prove their cause of action, but with an admonition to the agency that a classified EIS had to be prepared if the military actually was storing nuclear weapons. Thus, both the need for an EIS and the actual contents of the EIS were committed solely to the agency's good faith. Whatever else might be said about it, this case does little to clarify any ambiguities in the *Kleppe* test.

The CEQ has attempted to clarify both the timing and scope issues. The current regulation defines the term "proposal" as follows:

> "Proposal" exists at that stage in the development of an action when an agency subject to the Act has a goal and is actively preparing to make a decision on one or more alternative means of accomplishing that goal and the effects can be meaningfully evaluated.

This definition essentially captures the functional approach used in *SIPI* but restates that test in terms of the Supreme Court's emphasis on the determination of whether a "proposal" exists. Other CEQ regulations make it clear that the EIS should be "prepared early enough so that it can serve practically as an important contribution to the decisionmaking process," not simply "to rationalize or justify decisions already made." The CEQ regulations also require the EIS to consider (a) connected actions which are closely related, (b) actions which may have a cumulative effect with the proposed action under consideration, and (c) similar actions that should be considered together in view of other "reasonably foreseeable or proposed agency action." This seems to reflect an expansion on the *Kleppe* test by requiring agencies to consider other foreseeable actions even if there has been no formal proposal as to those actions.

3. CONTENT OF THE EIS

Determining the scope of the EIS essentially decides what the precise subject-matter of the EIS will be. The next important question, of course, is what must be said about that subject-matter. In particular, what alternatives and environmental impacts must be discussed?

The leading case on the issue of what alternatives must be included in the EIS is NRDC v. Morton (D.C.Cir.1972). This case involved the lease of eighty tracts of submerged land off eastern Louisiana. These tracts included about 10% of the total leased area. The purpose of the suit was to enjoin sale of oil and gas leases pending compliance with NEPA. The sale was a part of President Nixon's energy program. The plaintiffs attacked the EIS for failing to consider a number of alternative approaches to the energy problem, such as relaxing oil quotas. The plaintiffs argued that the need to discuss such alternatives was especially acute in view of the impact of the project. The lease area was adjacent to the greatest estuary and marsh area in the United States. It was agreed that if substantial oil pollution resulted from off-shore operations, serious damage to the biological community in the area could occur.

The D.C. Circuit held that the test in determining which alternatives must be discussed in the EIS is the "rule of reason." The court rejected the argument that the Interior Department was only required to discuss alternatives that were within its own jurisdiction. Instead, the court held that the Interior Department must discuss all reasonable alternatives within the jurisdiction of *any* part of the federal government. The court also held that the EIS must discuss the environmental effects of all the reasonable alternatives. The less likely an alternative is to be implemented, however, the less need there is to discuss it in detail. Alternatives which are extremely implausible need not be discussed at all. The test for deciding these issues is whether a reasonable person would think that an alternative was sufficiently significant to warrant extended discussion.

This test was endorsed by the Supreme Court in the *Vermont Yankee* case. In addition to the rule-making procedure discussed earlier, *Vermont Yankee* also involved a challenge to the issuance of a particular license. In attacking the issuance of the license, the plaintiffs argued that the AEC failed adequately to discuss energy conservation as an alternative to building new nuclear plants. Applying the "rule of reason" approach, the Supreme Court rejected this argument for several reasons. First, energy conservation had not become an important subject of discussion at the time this particular license was issued. It was only shortly thereafter, with the advent of the OPEC oil embargo, that conservation became highlighted. Second, the plaintiffs involved in this aspect of the litigation had failed to participate adequately in the proceedings before the agency. They had filed a list of objections to the grant of the license, but only 17 out of 119 of these objections related to the general topic of energy conservation. This group participated in none of the hearings in the final stage of the proceedings. The Court stressed that the plaintiffs should have structured their participation so that it would alert the agency to their position. This was "especially true when [the plaintiffs] are requesting the agency to embark upon an exploration of uncharted territory, as was the question of energy conservation in the late 60's and early 70's." The Court also stressed that the deceptively simple phrase "energy conservation" involves a vast number of possible actions that might in one way or another ultimately reduce projected demands for electricity. The plaintiffs had done nothing to specify which of these alternatives should be considered. The Court stressed the need for a reasonable approach to the question of inclusion of alternatives:

> Common sense also teaches us that the "detailed statement of alternatives" cannot be found wanting simply because the agency failed to include every alternative device and thought conceivable by the mind of man. Time and resources are simply too limited to hold that an impact statement fails because the agency failed to ferret out every possible alternative, regardless of how uncommon or

unknown that alternative may have been at the time the project was approved.

For this reason, the Court adopted the "rule of reason" test promulgated in NRDC v. Morton, supra.

Under the CEQ regulations, one alternative which must always be discussed is the alternative of doing nothing. The momentum of decisionmaking often creates a desire on the part of the agency to take action about a particular problem. Often, however, the most important alternative to the agency's projected form of action is not some modification in the agency action, but rather a decision to take no action at all. For this reason, the regulations require that the agency explain why it has not chosen the alternative of "no action."

If the EIS is to be more than a checklist of alternative actions, the consequences of each alternative must be discussed in detail. One frequently litigated issue is whether the discussion of the environmental impacts of the alternatives was adequate. In deciding which impacts must be discussed, the test once again is the "rule of reason." Speculative impacts need not be discussed. Unfortunately, courts have not done well in deciding what impacts are too speculative to require discussion. For example, in Carolina Environmental Study Group v. United States (D.C.Cir.1975) the D.C. Circuit held that the possibility of a Class Nine accident to a nuclear reactor was too unlikely to require discussion in an environmental impact statement. The NRC staff later classified the accident at Three Mile Island as a Class Nine accident. Following TMI, but before Chernobyl, the D.C. Circuit held again that NEPA does not require discussion of Class Nine accidents in an EIS, although the NRC had voluntarily decided to require such discussion in future impact statements. The court reasoned that the chance that a Class Nine accident would actually cause any environmental damage was negligible. The Third Circuit, however, rejected that view.

Often, the consequences of an agency action are highly uncertain due to lack of scientific information. Under a CEQ regulation, agencies were required to deal with this problem by including a "worst case scenario" in the EIS. Although the regulation was later rescinded by CEQ, some lower courts held that the "worst case" discussion was still required by the statute. In Robertson v. Methow Valley Citizens Council (S.Ct.1989), however, the Court rejected the "worst case" requirement. The plaintiffs claimed the agency should have considered the "worst case" impact of a planned ski resort on a herd of mule deer. The Court held that CEQ's decision to repeal the worst case regulation was entitled to judicial deference. The Court also upheld CEQ's replacement for the worst case regulation. The amended regulation requires agencies, in the face of "unavailable information concerning a reasonably foreseeable significant environmental consequence," to prepare "a summary of existing credible scientific evidence" and present an "evaluation of such impacts based upon theoretical approaches or research methods generally accepted in the scientific community."

The preceding discussion gives only an overview of the general issues likely to arise in an EIS case. Courts are often forced to engage in extensive factual inquiries concerning the agency's evaluation of the seriousness of the various impacts and its explanations of the counter-vailing benefits of the project. Agencies often engage in slipshod cost-benefit analysis of their proposals, fre-quently biasing their results in favor of their projected course of action. Courts have proved capable on a number of occasions of perceiving the unreliability of the agency's analysis and have not hesitated to require the agency to redo its work. Very little can be said in the way of general rules governing the disposition of these issues, because the issues are generally tied to the specific facts of each individual case.

4. REVIEW ON THE MERITS

Thus far, we have been concerned with the contents of and necessity for an EIS. The reader may well be asking a question which goes beyond the EIS itself: What happens if the EIS is perfect, the project is clearly an environmental disaster, and the agency decides to go ahead anyway? Is NEPA only a procedural require-ment imposing additional paperwork on agencies, or does it also impose substantive limits on agency deci-sions? The courts of appeals were split on this issue. The majority view was apparently that NEPA does impose substantive limits on agencies and that agency action is subject to judicial review if it transgresses these limits. However, except for a single Second Circuit decision, which was reversed by the Supreme Court in Strycker's Bay Neighborhood Council, Inc. v. Karlen (S.Ct.1980), no court of appeals had actually overturned an agency for violating NEPA's substantive limits.

Strycker's Bay involved construction of a housing project in a middle income area. The Second Circuit held that the agency's choice of site was unjustifiable.

According to the Second Circuit, when the agency considers such projects, "environmental factors such as crowding low-income housing into a concentrated area, should be given determinative weight." The Supreme Court summarily reversed the Second Circuit decision. The Court stated:

> [I]n the present case there is no doubt that [the agency] considered the environmental consequences of its decision to redesignate the proposed site for low-income housing. NEPA requires no more.

This statement by the Court implies that NEPA imposes no substantive duties on agencies, or at least that violation of such duties is not subject to judicial review. An accompanying footnote, however, seemed to leave the door open to review under the arbitrary and capricious standard.

That door was firmly shut in *Robertson*. Apart from the need for a "worst case" discussion in the EIS (discussed above), the plaintiffs also argued that the agency had failed to adopt an adequate mitigation plan. In rejecting that argument, the Court made clear its view that NEPA is purely procedural:

> If the adverse environmental effects of the proposed action are adequately identified and evaluated, the agency is not constrained by NEPA from deciding that other values outweigh the environmental costs. In this case, for example, it would not have violated NEPA if the Forest Service, after complying with the Act's procedural prerequisites, had decided that the benefits to be derived from downhill skiing at Sandy Butte justi-

fied the issuance of a special use permit, notwithstanding the loss of 15 percent, 50 percent, or even
100 percent of the mule deer herd. Other statutes
may impose substantive environmental obligations
on federal agencies, but NEPA merely prohibits
uninformed—rather than unwise—agency action.

In concluding that NEPA is purely procedural, the
Court referred to the statement of environmental
policies in § 101 as "precatory." This description seems
to fly in the face of the language of § 102, which "directs
that, to the fullest extent possible: (1) the policies,
regulations, and public laws of the United States shall
be interpreted and administered in accordance with the
policies set forth in this chapter . . . ." Section 102(2)
seems never to have come to the Court's attention.

Given the language of § 102(2), the Supreme
Court's rejection of substantive review under NEPA
seems unjustifiable in principle. Nevertheless, it probably does not make much practical difference. Even if
substantive review were allowed, the arbitrary and
capricious test would require only that the agency
present a "reasoned explanation" for its decision.
Review of the EIS provides an alternative method of
ensuring that the agency has a reasoned explanation for
its decision. (Only in law professors' hypotheticals does
the agency candidly announce that it is planning to
cause a total environmental disaster for no good reason!) So in practice, substantive review and review of
the EIS may amount to much the same thing—an
agency that is making an arbitrary and capricious
decision will be hard pressed to prepare an EIS that a
court will uphold.

5. EVALUATION OF NEPA

We have not yet dealt with one important question about NEPA, the question of whether NEPA has served a useful purpose. There seems to be no objective way of answering this question, and opinions by experts differ. Very few federal projects have actually been halted by permanent injunctions based on NEPA. NEPA litigation does cause substantial delays in a significant number of projects. Not infrequently, projects are halted at some point after initiation of the NEPA litigation, most often because either a local agency or a federal agency decided to withdraw from the project. It is unclear how often such decisions to abandon projects result from the delays caused by the NEPA litigation. It is also impossible to know the extent to which agencies have refrained from taking controversial actions because of the desire to avoid the expense and delay of NEPA litigation. At least some environmentally unjustifiable projects surely have either been abandoned or never begun because of NEPA. In addition, a number of other projects have been modified to reduce their environmental impact. The unanswered question is whether the benefits thus attained are sufficient to justify the expense and delay created in all those instances in which the project ultimately proceeds.

If it turns out that NEPA has not made a major contribution to preserving the environment—a matter which is itself hotly disputed—perhaps some of the blame should go to the Supreme Court. Since NEPA was passed, the Court has decided twelve NEPA cases on the merits. It never once has upheld a NEPA claim. Indeed, it has never taken a case for review in which the lower court rejected a NEPA claim. Only lower courts that upheld NEPA claims have found their decisions subjected to Supreme Court review. A cynical observer might say that the Court's sole interest in NEPA seems to be that of reining in lower court judges who exhibit undue enthusiasm for the statute. Perhaps that is an unfair interpretation, but the fact remains that the Court has given little support to vigorous application of the statute by the lower courts, and has shown little enthusiasm in its own opinions about the statutory scheme. The Supreme Court's attitude toward that statute can hardly have increased NEPA's effectiveness.

It may be useful at this point to summarize briefly the discussion of NEPA. As we have seen, NEPA requires an EIS when an agency has made a report on a proposal for a major federal action with a substantial environmental impact. In deciding whether any EIS is required, the most difficult question to answer has been whether there will be a substantial environmental impact. Once it has been concluded that an EIS is required, the next question is the scope of the EIS. The Supreme Court has made it clear that the answer to this question is to be found by determining the precise scope of the agency "proposal" which is under consideration. The alternatives to that proposal and the environmental impact of the proposal must be discussed in detail. In deciding which alternatives and which environmental impacts must be discussed, the applicable standard is the "rule of reason." This statutory scheme, whatever uncertainties may exist about its effectiveness, has now stood the test of time. Indeed, it has been emulated by many states and by many other countries.

CHAPTER 2

FEDERALISM AND THE ENVIRONMENT

Our nation is divided into fifty states along with the District of Columbia. Environmental problems pay no heed to these geographic lines. Frequently, an environmental problem in one state is caused by conduct in another. Hence, any one state may be effectively unable to protect its own environment. On the other hand, when a state does attempt to engage in environmental regulation, its actions may well have repercussions elsewhere. The regulating state may fail to take into account the costs imposed by its regulations on individuals or firms in other jurisdictions. Moreover, the ability of individual states to regulate may be frustrated by a "race to the bottom," in which states are forced to lower their standards to retain and attract industry. Thus, problems inevitably result from the division of governmental power into units that do not correspond with sharp divisions in either the environment or the economy.

In partial compensation for these problems, however, we obtain the benefits of fuller local government. As a result, individual states in which the public is more strongly motivated to deal with environmental problems may do so without being held back by the less interested citizens of other states. This allows the government to be more responsive to the desires of the population.

Furthermore, states may act as laboratories, in which various forms of environmental regulation may be tried out before being used on a nationwide scale. In short, federalism is both a problem and a useful tool.

To a great extent, the idea of federalism has its impact through the political process. Congress may be reluctant to enact legislation that infringes the traditional prerogatives of the states. The discussion in this chapter, however, will be limited to the constitutional dimensions of federalism. In the first part of the chapter we will consider constitutional limits on environmental regulation by the federal government. In the second part of the chapter, we will consider the extent to which the Constitution limits environmental regulation by the individual states.

A. SCOPE OF FEDERAL POWER

One of the basic assumptions of American constitutional law is that Congress does not have unlimited powers. The federal government does not have the power to take any action it deems in the public interest. Instead, it is a government of limited, delegated powers. Environmental regulation by the federal government must utilize one of a limited group of specific powers. For present purposes, the most important of these specific powers are the power to regulate interstate commerce, the power to tax and spend, the power to enter into treaties, and the power to regulate the use of public lands. Together, these specific powers form an imposing arsenal of regulatory authority.

1. THE COMMERCE POWER

In practice, the most important of these federal powers is the power to regulate interstate commerce.

The broad scope of this power is illustrated in Hodel v. Virginia Surface Mining and Reclamation Association, Inc. (S.Ct.1981). *Hodel* involved the Surface Mining and Reclamation Act, 30 U.S.C.A. § 1201 et seq. The Act imposes a detailed series of regulatory restrictions on strip-mining. The most important of these restrictions require restoration of the land to approximately its original state. A mining association argued that the Act's principal goal was regulating the use of private lands rather than regulating the effects of coal mining on interstate commerce. Thus, the association contended, the ultimate issue was whether land as such was subject to regulation under the commerce clause. The Court rejected the attempt to frame the question in this manner. According to the Court:

> The task of a court that is asked to determine whether a particular exercise of congressional power is valid under the Commerce Clause is relatively narrow. The court must defer to a congressional finding that a regulated activity affects interstate commerce, if there is any rational basis for such a finding. . . .

> Judicial review in this area is influenced above all by the fact that the Commerce Clause is a grant of plenary authority to Congress. This power is "complete in itself, may be exercised to its utmost extent, and acknowledges no limitations other than prescribed in the constitution." Moreover, this Court has made clear that the commerce power not only extends to "the use of channels of interstate or foreign commerce" and to "protection of the instrumentalities of interstate commerce . . . or persons or things in commerce," but also to "activi-

ties affecting commerce." As we explained in Fry v. United States, 421 U.S. 542, 547 (1975), "[e]ven activity that is purely intrastate in character may be regulated by Congress, where the activity, combined with like conduct by others similarly situated, affects commerce among the States or with foreign nations."

Applying this test to the Surface Mining Act, the Court found a rational basis for the congressional determination that surface mining affects interstate commerce. The effect of mining on water pollution was especially significant. The Court also noted that uniform national standards were necessary because of the difficulties encountered by attempts of individual states to regulate the problem.

The Court went on to hold that it was irrelevant whether land use is properly considered a "local" activity. So long as Congress rationally determines that regulation is necessary to protect interstate commerce from adverse effects, characterization of the activity as local is irrelevant. The Court also rejected the argument that the Act was unnecessary because various other federal standards already adequately addressed the federal interests in controlling the environmental effects of surface mining. According to the Court, the "short answer to this argument is that the effectiveness of existing laws in dealing with the problems identified by Congress is ordinarily a matter committed to legislative judgment."

In the companion case of Hodel v. Indiana (S.Ct.1981), the Court rejected another attack on the same statute. The district court in this case had struck down the provisions of the Act which attempted to protect prime farm land. The district court found that only .006% of the total prime farm land in the nation was affected annually by mining. It termed the effect on interstate commerce "infinitesimal." The Supreme Court rejected this quantitative test. According to the Court, the "pertinent inquiry therefore is not how much commerce is involved but whether Congress could rationally conclude that the regulated activity affects interstate commerce." The Court found an ample basis for this conclusion. There was testimony before Congress about the effects of strip mining on agricultural productivity. The Court noted that even given the District Court's finding concerning the amount of land affected, the amount of grain production involved would still be in the neighborhood of $56 million per year, which as the Court observed "surely is not an insignificant amount of commerce."

Until recently, it could be safely said that the commerce power was effectively unlimited. Cases such as *Hodel* gave such a high degree of deference to Congress that almost any imaginable statute seemed likely to be upheld. For this reason, the Court's decision in United States v. Lopez (S.Ct.1995), surprised many observers. A majority of the Court in *Lopez* departed from almost sixty years of past practice by ruling that Congress had exceeded its powers under the Commerce Clause in a regulation of private activity. Specifically, the Court struck down a federal statute prohibiting the possession of firearms in the vicinity of schools. The implications of *Lopez* remain unclear, but the opinion probably does not jeopardize previous cases such as the *Hodel* decisions.

Chief Justice Rehnquist's opinion for the five-person majority in *Lopez* attempts to erect a limit on the commerce power, without overruling any cases or imperiling any well-entrenched federal programs. The opinion begins by invoking the original understanding that federal powers are "few and defined" while state powers are "numerous and indefinite." Rehnquist emphasized that the original function of this division of powers was to assist in preserving liberty. Admittedly, he added, the scope of federal power had greatly increased in the post-New Deal era, partly because of the "great changes" in the economy, and partly because of a desire to eliminate what were considered "artificial" restraints on federal power. Having analyzed the post-New Deal case law, however, Rehnquist concluded that the school gun law did not fall squarely within the previously recognized scope of congressional power, and he declined to further expand that scope. In reaching this conclusion, he noted that the statute related to education, traditionally a core area of state concern, that Congress had made no findings at the time about the effect of the prohibited activity on interstate commerce, and that the statute contained no requirement of proof of any nexus between the defendant's activity and interstate commerce.

Justice Kennedy, joined by Justice O'Connor, agreed that the statute "upsets the federal balance to a degree that renders it an unconstitutional assertion of the commerce power." But Justice Kennedy's concurrence is more tentative than the majority opinion, and repeatedly suggests that the Court's role is to police against disturbance of the *current* balance of regulatory power between the states and the federal government, rather than to begin a roll-back of federal power.

Justice Kennedy concluded that the statute intruded on state sovereignty. In the absence of a stronger link with commercial activities, "that interference contradicts the federal balance the Framers designed and that this Court is obliged to enforce."

Both the majority opinion and the Kennedy concurrence emphasize the non-commercial nature of the defendant's activity, which was simply to be present in the vicinity of a school while in possession of a firearm. A more recent decision struck down a federal law concerning violence against women, also emphasizing the completely noncommercial aspect of the problem. In contrast, environmental statutes are heavily focused on regulating commercial activities such as industry, agriculture, and logging. Moreover, the interstate repercussions of pollution are more obvious than those of gun possession. For these reasons, *Lopez* probably does not pose a threat to the current federal regulatory regime as a whole. It may, however, have some impact on marginal applications of environmental statutes to seemingly local, noncommercial activities. In particular, *Lopez* raises some question about the application of federal wetlands and endangered species regulation in some borderline situations, particularly when the regulated party is not engaged in a commercial enterprise. At this printing, the Supreme Court has agreed to hear a case regarding congressional power to regulate isolated wetlands. This ruling should help clarify the scope of *Lopez*.

Even before *Lopez*, congressional power had already been placed in question in the special context of federal regulation of the activities of state governments. The Tenth Amendment has often served as the basis for efforts to protect state sovereignty. On occasion, the Supreme Court has struck down such a federal statute on federalism grounds, even while conceding that the statute was otherwise within Congress's power under the commerce clause. The Tenth Amendment served as one basis of important federalism rulings before the New Deal, but was widely considered defunct after 1937. For almost forty years, the Tenth Amendment was considered to be nothing more than a truism stating that "all is retained which has not been surrendered." United States v. Darby (S.Ct.1941). In 1976, however, the Court resurrected the Amendment in National League of Cities v. Usery (S.Ct.1976), striking down an extension of the federal minimum wage to cover state employees.

Largely as a result of *League of Cities*, some important federal statutes were challenged on Tenth Amendment grounds. The result was considerable confusion about the limits of Congressional power. For example, the lower courts disagreed about whether Congress could force the states to administer inspection programs for automobiles. Although the Supreme Court never resolved that issue, it did reject Tenth Amendment challenges to other important environmental legislation. In the *Hodel* cases, the Court upheld the Surface Mining Act against a Tenth Amendment challenge. The Court unanimously rejected the claim that land use regulation is an inherently state concern beyond federal power under the Tenth Amendment. Only when Congress directly imposes duties on state officers, the Court held, does the Tenth Amendment come into play. Even then, the statute may be valid. In FERC v. Mississippi (S.Ct.1982), a sharply divided Court upheld portions of a 1978 energy conservation act, even though the statute imposed some affirmative duties on state administrative agencies.

Justice Blackmun had been the swing vote in *League of Cities.* In Garcia v. San Antonio Metropolitan Transit Authority (S.Ct.1985), he changed his mind and became the decisive vote to overrule *League of Cities.* Like the earlier case, *Garcia* involved the federal minimum wage law, this time as applied to public transit workers. Despairing of the effort to distinguish integral state functions from other state activities, the Court held that the political process is the states' primary shield against Congress. At least in the absence of a clear breakdown in the political process, courts should not intervene when Congress regulates state activities.

If *League of Cities* is defunct as a constitutional rule, it may live on as a guide to statutory interpretation. Gregory v. Ashcroft (S.Ct.1991) involved the application of the federal age discrimination act (ADEA) to state judges. Because the case involved a core aspect of state sovereignty, the Court concluded that the statute had to be read narrowly. "Indeed," Justice O'Connor wrote for the Court, "inasmuch as this Court in *Garcia* has left primarily to the political process the protection of the States against intrusive exercises of Congress' Commerce Clause powers, we must be absolutely certain that Congress intended such an exercise." After reviewing the statute, she concluded that it was "at least ambiguous whether Congress intended" the ADEA to cover appointed judges. "In the face of such ambiguity, we will not attribute to Congress an intent to intrude on state governmental functions. . . ." The parameters of the *Gregory* test are still quite unclear, but the test may require that federal environmental statutes that attempt to control state governmental functions be written with unusual clarity.

It is one thing for Congress to restrict the state's activities; it is another to impose affirmative duties on state officials. In New York v. United States (S.Ct.1992) the issue was whether Congress could force states to establish programs for disposing of low-level radioactive waste, at penalty of "taking title" to the waste if they failed to enact such a program on schedule. The statute is obviously designed to deal with the NIMBY syndrome (Not in My Back Yard): every state wanted to generate low-level waste in local medical facilities, but every state wanted some other state to take the responsibility of providing a site for disposal. While it did not quarrel with the purpose of the statute, the Court found the "take title" provision to be an unprecedented effort to mandate affirmative legislative activity by the states. Reinforcing her discussion of the values of federalism in *Gregory*, Justice O'Connor ruled that the immunity of states from such federal coercion is so fundamental that it can never be allowed — even if state officials initiate the federal legislation (as they had in *New York*) and regardless of the strength of the government's regulatory interest. The latter holding, notably, elevates state sovereignty above such less substantial interests as racial equality and freedom of speech, both of which can be impaired on the basis of a sufficiently compelling government interest. It should be noted, however, that the statute also provided a number of other incentives for states to legislate, which the Court upheld.

In analyzing congressional power under the commerce clause, it is wise to begin with a strong presumption in favor of the government. Beginning in 1937, the Supreme Court has been careful to give Congress broad leeway in regulating, particularly with respect to commercial activities. Currently, however, congressional power is suspect in two areas. First, with respect to regulations of private individuals, *Lopez* suggests that congressional power is doubtful if the activity is noncommercial, takes places in an area of traditional state concern, and has no apparent interstate connection. Second, regulations that impinge directly on state government have been under a cloud since 1976, when *League of Cities* was decided. Although *League of Cities* has currently been replaced by *Garcia*, the current trend seems to be back toward the protection of state rights. This trend has surfaced in *Gregory*, which resurrects the *League of Cities* approach in a nonconstitutional setting, and in *New York*, which bans a specific form of particularly objectionable federal regulation. Perhaps the only safe prediction that can be made about the future is that federalism will remain a dynamic and uncertain area of the law, in sharp contrast to most of the past half century when federal power was at its apex. These developments seem unlikely, however, to threaten the core of federal environmental law.

2. OTHER FEDERAL POWERS

Perhaps the most important of these other federal powers arises from the property clause of the Constitution. This clause provides that "Congress shall have Power to dispose of and make all needful Rules and Regulations respecting the Territory or other Property belonging to the United States." This clause is of great significance because of the vast amount of land owned by the federal government, which comprises an area nearly the size of India. About one half of this land was located in Alaska; most of the remainder was in the western United States. Almost 180 million acres have been reserved for national forests and parks. These enormous tracts of land contain much of the nation's remaining wilderness. It is the property clause that gives Congress the power to protect these lands.

Historically, the federal government's main goal was to divest itself as quickly as possible of its lands. Indeed, at one time, it was argued to the Supreme Court that this was the only permissible purpose for which Congress can manage the public lands. It is now clear, however, that Congress is entitled to retain ownership of public lands and to use those lands for whatever purpose Congress believes is in the public interest. When it chooses to do so, its legislative power over the retained lands is extremely broad.

The leading case on congressional power under the property clause is Kleppe v. New Mexico (S.Ct.1976). *Kleppe* involved the Wild Free–Roaming Horses and Burros Act. The Act protects all unbranded horses and burros on public lands from capture. If the animals stray onto private land, the landowner may require the government to retrieve them. In *Kleppe,* state game wardens entered public land to remove wild horses. The state argued that the statute could not be supported by the property clause. According to the state, the clause grants Congress only the powers to dispose of federal land and to protect federal land. The first power was allegedly not broad enough to support legislation protecting wild animals that live on federal land, while the second power was not implicated because the Act allegedly was designed to protect only the animals, which are not themselves federal property. The Court rejected the narrow reading of the property clause implicit in these arguments. According to the Court, the clause is not limited to rules regarding disposal, use, and protection of federal lands. Rather, Congress possesses the powers of both a proprietor and a legislature over the public domain. With respect to public lands, Congress has the full regulatory power which the state has with respect to its own lands. Thus, Congress may regulate for any public purpose concerning activities on public lands.

It is less clear how much regulatory power the property clause gives Congress over private lands which adjoin public lands. In one early case, the Supreme Court held that Congress had the power to order the removal of a fence built on private land which limited access to public land. Camfield v. United States (S.Ct.1897). The Court held that the fence constituted a nuisance and that Congress had the power to abate this nuisance. The Court remarked more generally that Congress has the power to protect the public lands without being required to seek the aid of state legislatures. Following the logic of these remarks, some lower court opinions have read the property clause quite broadly to allow Congress to prevent any activity on private lands that would interfere with Congress's goals respecting the public lands. See Minnesota v. Block (8th Cir.1981); United States v. Brown (8th Cir.1977). Thus, if Congress sets aside public lands for quiet, peaceful enjoyment, it may prevent activities on adjoining private lands that would produce excessive noise. This reading of the property clause seems to be correct. If the Constitution gives Congress the power to dedicate public lands to a particular purpose, it must surely give

Congress the power to effectuate that decision by preventing interference from private parties.

Some lower courts construed *Kleppe* to mean that federal power over public lands was not only broad but exclusive, so that any state laws dealing with public lands would be preempted. In California Coastal Commission v. Granite Rock Co. (S.Ct.1987), the Court made it clear that the Congressional power over public lands is not necessarily exclusive. Applying the standard preemption analysis discussed in Part C of this chapter, the Court upheld a state law requiring a permit for mining on public lands. (Note that the mining was being done by private parties; state power to regulate the activities of the federal government itself is sharply limited by the notion of federal sovereign immunity.)

Two other sources of federal power deserve at least brief mention. One is the treaty power. Congress has broad powers to make treaties with foreign nations on matters of international concern. Thus, the Court in Missouri v. Holland (S.Ct.1920) upheld a treaty restricting the hunting of migratory birds. Today, legislation on this subject would be upheld under the commerce clause. The Court in *Missouri v. Holland* held, however, that even if Congress' power under the commerce clause did not extend to the subject of migratory birds, a treaty on the subject was still a proper basis for implementing congressional legislation.

A final source of congressional power is the spending clause. The Constitution authorizes Congress to spend money in pursuit of the public interest. The Supreme Court has generally held that Congress has free rein in determining where that public interest lies. This clause rarely gives rise to litigation but has vast importance to the economy. It has been used, for example, to authorize the spending of vast amounts of money to enable local governments to build municipal treatment works.

As we have seen, congressional power in the environmental area is extremely broad. The commerce clause reaches virtually any private activity that has significant environmental consequences. That power, broad as it is, is augmented by the other broad powers to protect public property, to deal with matters of international concern, and to spend money in the public interest.

The Constitution not only grants powers to the federal government but also limits the activities of state governments. In the next section we will consider those limitations as they are relevant in the environmental area.

B. COMMERCE CLAUSE RESTRICTIONS ON STATE POWER

In a unified national economy, the existence of a multitude of differing state environmental laws can impede the flow of commerce. Yet, the states have often been in the lead in the environmental area because of pressing local problems. The conflict between the local interest in regulation and the economic interest of other states cannot be resolved effectively by the courts of any of the states involved. Obviously, both the state which is engaging in regulation and the states which are affected by the regulation have interests which disable them from providing a completely neutral forum. For this reason, the federal courts have emerged as the tribunals in which these conflicting interests can be assessed.

Balancing the need for environmental regulations against their economic impact on outsiders is not a uniquely American problem. The European Court of Justice has also attempted to strike such a balance within the European Union. In the broader international arena, WTO rules regarding free trade can also call local environmental regulations into question. Under Article III of the GATT agreement, regulations that discriminate against imports are prima facie illegal. They can be defended, however, on the basis of Article XX, which authorizes protectionist regulations when necessary for certain crucial governmental interests. One particularly controversial area has been the extent to which a government can exclude imports in order to prevent harm to the environment relating to the production of those goods. For example, can the United States exclude tuna caught in a way that poses an undue threat to dolphins? WTO issues can also arise with respect to more mundane environmental regulations when they have the effect of favoring domestic products over imports. WTO tribunals are only now beginning to analyze the knotty issues that U.S. courts have struggled with since the days of John Marshall.

The basis for federal court involvement in these issues is the commerce clause of the Constitution. The commerce clause, on its face, is a grant of power to Congress, not a grant of power to the federal courts or a restriction on state legislation. Yet, since the early 19th century, the Supreme Court has always construed the commerce clause as preventing certain kinds of state legislation even when Congress has not spoken. Various doctrinal explanations have been utilized in an effort to support judicial intervention. Moreover, the restrictions have been subject to changing formulations. For present purposes, however, we can ignore the rather tangled history of commerce clause theory and concentrate on the theory as it exists today.

At present, there are three strands to commerce clause theory. One test governs state legislation that discriminates against interstate commerce. Such legislation is virtually *per se* unconstitutional. A second test applies to the State's proprietary activities. Such activities are virtually immune from restriction under the dormant commerce clause. The third test applies to the remaining forms of state legislation. These forms of legislation are dealt with by a balancing test.

1. DISCRIMINATORY LEGISLATION

The first test is illustrated by City of Philadelphia v. New Jersey (S.Ct.1978). This case involved a New Jersey statute prohibiting the import of most waste originating outside the state. The Supreme Court struck down this restriction. The parties in the case disputed whether the purpose of the restriction was economic favoritism toward local industry or environmental protection of the state's resources from overuse. The Court found it unnecessary to resolve this dispute. According to the Court, "the evil of protectionism can reside in legislative means as well as legislative ends." Thus, "whatever New Jersey's ultimate purpose, it may not be accomplished by discriminating against articles of commerce coming from outside the State unless there is some reason, apart from their origin, to treat them differently." Having found that the statute was discriminatory, the Court found it easy to resolve the case:

The New Jersey law at issue in this case falls squarely within the area that the Commerce Clause puts off-limits to state regulation. On its face, it imposes on out-of-state commercial interests the full burden of conserving the State's remaining landfill space. It is true in our previous cases the scarce natural resource was itself the article of commerce, whereas here the scarce resource and the article in the commerce are distinct. But that difference is without consequence. In both instances, the State has overtly moved to slow or freeze the flow of commerce for protectionist reasons. It does not matter that the State has shut the article of commerce inside the State in one case and outside the State in the other. What is crucial is the attempt by one State to isolate itself from a problem common to many by erecting a barrier against the movement of interstate trade.

The Court conceded that certain quarantine laws have not been considered forbidden by the commerce clause even though they were directed against out-of-state commerce. The Court distinguished those quarantine laws, however, on the ground that in those cases the "very movement" of the articles risked contagion and other evils. According to the Court, "[t]hose laws thus did not discriminate against interstate commerce as such, but simply prevented traffic of noxious articles, whatever their origin." Subject to this very narrow exception, legislation which on its face distinguishes out-of-state items from domestic items seems likely to be held unconstitutional, in the absence of compelling justification.

As it turned out, Philadelphia v. New Jersey was simply the first in a series of cases in which the Court has thwarted efforts by states to control the flow of garbage. In two 1992 cases, the Court struck down two variations on the New Jersey statute. One variation was to impose a tax on garbage imports rather than banning them. In Chemical Waste Management v. Hunt (S.Ct.1992), the Court struck down a special tax imposed on waste generated outside the state. A second variation was to delegate import controls to the local level. In Fort Gratiot Sanitary Landfill, Inc. v. Michigan Department of Natural Resources (S.Ct.1992), the Court struck down a state law forbidding landfills from accepting garbage generated elsewhere unless the county's landfill plan authorized them to do so.

The most recent decision in this series involves the converse of Philadelphia v. New Jersey: rather than attempting to exclude garbage *imports*, the government was trying to ban garbage *exports*. Many municipalities adopted flow control ordinances that require all waste generated in the locality to be sent to a designated facility. The main reason for the requirement was to assure a sufficient flow of waste in order to finance expensive new, state-of-the-art waste disposal facilities. A five-Justice majority in C & A Carbone, Inc. v. Town of Clarkstown (S.Ct.1994) found that flow control was facially discriminatory and struck it down under the Philadelphia v. New Jersey test. The majority pointed to several alternatives to flow control, including the use of property taxes to subsidize the local disposal facility. Justice O'Connor concurred in the result. She considered the ordinance to be nondiscriminatory but struck it down as an undue burden on commerce under the balancing test discussed below. Applying the same balancing test, Justice Souter and two other dissenters would have upheld the local ordinance. He argued that none of the alternatives to flow control were as desirable, and that the locality should be free to impose on its own residents the increased costs caused by flow control. As *Carbone* illustrates, what constitutes "discrimination" is sometimes in the eye of the beholder: what five Justices considered to be patent discrimination, the other four did not find to be discriminatory at all.

2. PROPRIETARY ACTIVITIES

The second class of state regulations involved proprietary or quasi-proprietary activities by the State. Here, the leading case is Hughes v. Alexandria Scrap Corp. (S.Ct.1976). This case involved a Maryland bounty system for old, abandoned cars ("hulks"). Prior to 1974, no title certificate was needed by the scrap processor in order to claim the bounty. After 1974, Maryland processors needed only to submit an indemnity agreement in which their suppliers certified their own rights to the hulks. In contrast, out-of-state processors were required to submit title certificates or police certificates. The legislation was challenged by a Virginia processor. The Court held that this statute was valid because the State was not exercising a regulatory function but rather had itself entered the market in order to bid up prices. As Justice Stevens noted in his concurrence, the interstate commerce at issue would never have existed except for the state's bounty system. Because the state's failure to create such commerce would have been unobjectionable under the commerce clause, Justice Stevens believed that out-of-state processors had no grounds for complaint if they were excluded from this commerce. Justice Brennan filed a strong dissent. Because *Hughes* came down on the same day as *National League of Cities,* Justice Brennan apparently feared that the Court was creating tremendous loopholes in the commerce clause in the name of state sovereignty.

In a later decision, the Court extended this rationale by holding that South Dakota could refuse to sell cement from a state-owned plant to out-of-state buyers during a shortage. Reeves, Inc. v. Stake (S.Ct.1980). This decision seems to be a recognition that quasi-proprietary state activities are not subject to normal commerce clause restrictions. As the Court held in Hughes v. Oklahoma (S.Ct.1979), however, the state's theoretical title in wild animals does not justify discrimination against out-of-state businesses.

3. BALANCING TEST

Most state legislation is neither proprietary nor discriminatory, and thus falls into the third class. State legislation of this kind is not as suspect as legislation which is discriminatory on its face. Nevertheless, there is a real risk that the state may pass legislation without adequately considering its impact elsewhere in the country. In addition, the risk also exists that a state will use what appears to be nondiscriminatory legislation as covert means of burdening out-of-state businesses. In order to guard against these risks, the Court subjects nondiscriminatory state legislation to a balancing test. Under this test, the impact of a statute on interstate commerce is balanced against the state's justifications for the statute. The Seventh Circuit decision in Procter & Gamble Co. v. Chicago (7th Cir.1975) is a good illustration of the balancing test. The case involved a

Chicago ordinance banning the use of detergents containing phosphates. The Seventh Circuit found that the ordinance did place a burden on interstate commerce. Due to the warehousing methods used in the industry, the Chicago ordinance would restrict sales of phosphate detergents in a wide area including parts of Wisconsin, Indiana, and Michigan. Nevertheless, the court found that the possible contribution of the ordinance to controlling the growth of algae in the Illinois River and in Lake Michigan was sufficiently great to justify the burden placed on commerce.

Balancing tests are not always predictable in their application. This one is no exception. On the whole, however, environmental laws have fared well in commerce clause litigation. For example, the Supreme Court found that the burden on commerce created by a Minnesota container law was not "clearly excessive," even though the Minnesota Supreme Court had found the supposed benefits of the statute to be illusory. Minnesota v. Clover Leaf Creamery Co. (S.Ct.1981).

The use of this balancing test has been attacked by Justice Scalia, some lower court judges, and several scholars. These critics have assembled several arguments against the use of a balancing test to assess nondiscriminatory legislation. If a state law does not discriminate against interstate commerce, they argue, the federal courts should not second-guess the state legislature about the balance between a statute's costs and benefits. Moreover, ill-advised but nondiscriminatory statutes are subject to a built-in political check, because the adversely affected local industry will lobby for repeal. Thus, these laws can be handled by the political process without judicial intervention. Finally, these critics argue, the judicial balancing in these cases is unhappily reminiscent of the era in which courts routinely overturned statutes they considered unwise—an approach that has long since been repudiated in other contexts. Although these arguments against the balancing test have some force, so far they have failed to make much headway on the Court. On the other hand, perhaps in response to these concerns, most judges have applied the balancing test cautiously, tending to defer strongly to state environmental policies. Some lower courts apply the balancing test only to laws that have a disparate impact on out-of-state firms.

C. FEDERAL PREEMPTION

The preceding section dealt with the validity of state regulation in the absence of federal regulation. In this section we will be concerned with the validity of state regulations in areas where Congress has acted. It is clear, of course, that in cases of direct conflict, the state statute must give way. The Supremacy Clause of the Constitution provides:

> This Constitution, and the Laws of the United States which shall be made in Pursuance thereof; and all Treaties made, or which shall be made, under the authority of the United States, shall be the Supreme Law of the Land; and the Judges in every State shall be bound thereby, any Thing in the Constitution or Laws of any State to the Contrary not withstanding.

The presence of a conflict between federal and state law, however, is often less than obvious.

The Supreme Court has set forth various factors which are to be considered in preemption cases. First, the federal regulatory scheme may be so pervasive and detailed as to suggest that Congress left no room for the state to supplement it. Or the statute enacted by Congress may involve a field in which the federal interest is so dominant that enforcement of state laws is precluded. Other aspects of the regulatory scheme imposed by Congress may also support the inference that Congress has completely foreclosed state legislation in a particular area. (This is often called "field" pre-emption.) Even where Congress has not completely foreclosed state regulation, a state statute is void to the extent that it actually conflicts with a valid federal statute. Such a conflict can be found where compliance with both the federal and state regulations is impossible, or more often, where the state law interferes with the accomplishment of the full objectives of Congress.

These factors are obviously rather vague and difficult to apply. The Supreme Court has done little to create any more rigorous framework for analysis. Therefore, the only way to get some degree of under-standing of the field is to examine particular cases in order to see what kinds of situations have been found appropriate for application of the preemption doctrine.

One controversial preemption issue involves nuclear energy. In a 1971 case, Northern States Power Co. v. Minnesota (8th Cir.1971), the court held that the state lacked the authority to impose conditions on nuclear waste releases stricter than those imposed by the AEC. The court relied heavily on a provision of the Atomic Energy Act which allows the federal govern-ment to delegate regulatory authority to the states over certain categories of nuclear materials. Radioactive releases from nuclear power plants did not fall within any of these categories, which the court considered the exclusive areas in which states may regulate with respect to radiation hazards. The court concluded that state regulation would interfere with the Congressional objectives expressed in the 1954 Act:

> Thus, through direction of the licensing scheme for nuclear reactors, Congress vested the AEC with the authority to resolve the proper balance between desired industrial progress and adequate health and safety standards. Only through the application and enforcements of uniform standards promulgated by a national agency will these dual objectives be assured. Were the states allowed to impose stricter standards on the level of radioactive waste releases discharged from nuclear power plants, they might conceivably be so overprotective in the area of health and safety as to unnecessarily stultify the industrial development and use of atomic energy for the production of electric power.

In contrast, the Supreme Court upheld a California nuclear moratorium in a later decision, Pacific Gas & Electric Co. v. State Energy Resources Conservation & Development Commission (S.Ct.1983). In an opinion by Justice White, the Court upheld a California statute prohibiting nuclear plant operation until the federal government approved a permanent method of waste disposal. The Court found that the state statutes were not aimed at radiation hazards, but instead at economic problems posed by the failure of the federal government to approve a permanent method of waste disposal. The Court concluded that Congress had not intended to promote nuclear power at all costs. Rather, Congress had decided to leave the choice as to the necessity or economic benefits of a nuclear plant to the state through its utility regulatory powers. Thus, it appears that if the state casts its legislation in the form of utility regulation, it may indirectly accomplish what federal law would not allow it to do directly—that is, impose its own views as to the safety of nuclear reactors under various circumstances. So long as it can reasonably be argued that a possible safety risk would have repercussions on the economic desirability of nuclear energy, the Supreme Court would apparently allow the state to regulate.

A year after the *PG & E* case, the Court again displayed a permissive attitude toward state laws dealing with the nuclear industry. In Silkwood v. Kerr–McGee Corp. (S.Ct.1984), the Court upheld an award of punitive damages against a utility for an employee's radiation injuries. As the dissent pointed out, the jury was told it could impose punitive damages even if the defendant had complied with all federal regulations. Thus, the state was allowed to hold the defendant to higher standards of conduct in the handling of radioactive materials than those imposed by the federal government. Together with *PG & E, Silkwood* makes it clear that the Court's enthusiasm for preemption in the nuclear area had waned considerably since it affirmed *Northern States Power* in 1972.

Every preemption case in a sense is unique. Apart from some vague and usually unhelpful maxims, little can be said about this area of law that is of much help in deciding individual cases. The question before the court in each case is whether Congress in passing a particular statute would have been willing to allow the state to impose certain kinds of regulations in the same area.

This is essentially an issue of statutory construction. It can only be resolved by close attention to the language of the federal statute, to its legislative history, and to its purposes. Thus, the best advice in analyzing preemption problems is to probe the legislative materials and the extent to which the state statute would have a practical effect on the implementation of the federal statute.

Even when a federal statute itself does not preempt state law, the federal administrative agency implementing the statute may issue a regulation that preempts state law. The Court is reluctant to infer preemption merely from the presence of comprehensive federal regulations. The state law will stand unless it directly conflicts with the federal regulation. This reluctance to infer preemption makes sense, because the agency can readily adopt an express preemption regulation. Congress, on the other hand, must overcome considerably more inertia to respond to a state law that interferes with a federal statute. Hence, there is less reason for courts to apply preemption doctrines expansively when agency regulations are involved.

In this chapter, we have seen that the federal regulatory power in the environmental area is broad indeed. Questions about the scope of this power arise only when Congress directly attempts to regulate the activities of state government, or when it attempts to reach noncommercial activities that are traditionally state concerns and have no apparent interstate implications. The vast majority of federal regulations fall outside of these gray zones and are clearly constitutional. When the federal government has acted, any state legislation which interferes with the accomplishment of the congressional purpose or the operation of the regulatory scheme is unconstitutional under the supremacy clause. Even when Congress has not acted, a state statute may run afoul of the dominant federal interest in the free flow of interstate commerce. Thus, while federalism imposes only relatively minor restraints today on the national government, it continues to circumscribe the actions of state governments.

CHAPTER 3

POLLUTION CONTROL

Consider the problem of a common pasture open to all, posed by Garrett Hardin in his classic article, "The Tragedy of the Commons." Even as the number of cattle begins to exceed the pasture's carrying capacity, each herder benefits from increasing his own herd. The marginal utility of adding one more animal always seems positive, since he receives all the benefits from the animal, while most of the resulting costs of overgrazing are borne by other herders. Since the herders all act in the same way, freedom in the commons brings ruin to all. Land can be protected from overexploitation by allocating ownership among individuals as private property. But protection of a commons from waste discharges cannot be managed so handily: unlike land, the air and waters cannot readily be fenced.

Thus, the market may not strike a proper balance between economic output and environmental quality because the costs of pollution are borne by someone besides the polluter. As a result, these "externalized" costs will not be taken into account by polluters. Without the incentive to reduce the amount of pollution, insufficient resources are devoted to this objective. Insofar as pollution costs are not borne by polluters or their customers, some of the total welfare resulting from economic activity is redistributed away from the victims of pollution to other groups in the society. In a sense, the polluter is subsidized by others who bear the environmental costs of his activities. Because of this subsidy, the polluter's conduct is not economically efficient: total social wealth (without regard for its distribution) is not maximized.

An economic activity may also confer external *benefits*. For example, renovation of a deteriorated building improves aesthetic and property values for nearby landowners. External benefits, like external costs, usually are not reflected in the producer's balance sheet. Closely related to the concept of external benefits is that of collective or public goods, commodities that cannot efficiently be supplied to one person without enabling others to enjoy them. Examples are national defense and clean air. Consumption of such goods is collective, because enjoyment by any one person does not significantly diminish the enjoyment available to others. The nonexcludability that characterizes collective goods causes underproduction by the market, even though their total value may substantially exceed the production costs.

Theoretically, as Professor Coase demonstrated, even these problems could be surmounted by the free market. Without barriers to transactions, such as imperfect knowledge, limited rationality, or negotiation expenses, individuals could enter into enforceable bargains to produce public goods or to refrain from producing externalities such as pollution. Indeed, Coase argued, absent impediments to bargaining, individuals would bargain their way to the same levels of public goods or externalities regardless of the legal rule. This analysis has become known as the Coase Theorem and has had a powerful impact on scholarship in "Law and Economics." Although Coase used pollution as an example, he acknowledged that the large number of victims of pollution would make a contractual solution impossible. The idea of using market transactions to control pollution, however, has proved useful. Later in this chapter, we will examine innovative ways for the government to utilize market forces to help control pollution. The Coase Theorem also may be relevant to analyzing situations involving relatively small numbers of individuals, such as some nuisance cases. It does not, however, eliminate the need for government intervention in the pollution area.

Because the free market provides inadequate incentives, government must intervene to limit external costs and facilitate production of external benefits and collective goods. The following basic approaches are available:

Property Rights. The common law doctrine of nuisance offers injured landowners the remedies of damages and injunctions against pollution. Litigation, however, is ill-suited to dealing with widespread environmental problems involving highly technical issues or difficult tradeoffs between conflicting interests. Usually government resorts to the other approaches described below or provides collective goods itself, using tax revenues.

Direct Regulation. The principal method to control pollution has been to prohibit emissions beyond prescribed limits. When the method of enforcement is imposition of financial penalties, rather than injunctions or jail sentences, the boundary between direct regulation and effluent charges (the last method below) becomes blurred.

Subsidies. Another approach, frequently used in combination with direct regulation, is for government to subsidize private activities that avoid external costs or produce collective goods. Examples are special tax deductions and credits for installation of pollution control equipment, and federal grants to municipalities for construction of waste treatment facilities.

Charges. Besides the foregoing approaches, government can require payment of penalties or fees for private activities that generate external costs or fail to provide collective goods. Relating the amount of the charge to the estimated cost (to the producer) or benefit (to the public) can create a market incentive for the producer to alter his activities. Rather than setting the level of charges itself, the government can use market mechanisms to price pollution. For example, it can auction off pollution rights.

The following sections discuss methods of controlling pollution through application of nuisance law, by regulation under the federal Clean Air and Clean Water Acts, and through creation of economic incentives. Special emphasis is given to the consideration of economic and technological feasibility in a regulatory system.

A. COMMON LAW REMEDIES

Boomer v. Atlantic Cement Co. (N.Y.1970) involved a classic nuisance. Defendant operated a large cement plant, and neighbors incurred damages from dirt, smoke and vibration emanating from the plant. The neighbors sought an injunction and compensatory damages for past injuries. The court found that the total damages to plaintiffs' properties were relatively small compared with the value of defendant's plant, and that enjoining further pollution would force closure of the plant. The plant was the core of the local economy and already employed the best available pollution control.

In such situations, most courts "balance the equities" and deny injunctions, on the ground that the hardships on defendants and the community would be greater than the hardships suffered by plaintiffs left to their damage remedies. In New York, however, a line of cases held that once a nuisance was found and substantial damage was shown by the plaintiff, an injunction would be granted notwithstanding any disparity in economic consequences between the effect of the injunction and the effect of the nuisance.

In *Boomer* that rule finally was disavowed. The court considered granting the injunction but postponing its effect to a specified future date, to allow the defendant to develop the technology to eliminate the nuisance. But the court was uncertain of defendant's ability to achieve such advances, which it believed were the responsibility of the entire cement industry rather than one company. Furthermore, the court believed that the state's extensive regulatory scheme covering air pollution provided a better mechanism for addressing this problem than a nuisance action.

The New York court deviated from the usual path of awarding compensatory damages only for past injuries (leaving plaintiffs free to sue again for future injuries). Instead, the court ordered that the injunction issue unless defendant paid permanent damages to plaintiffs, which would include compensation for the total economic loss to their properties, present and future, caused by defendant's operations. A dissenting judge said that the decision was in effect "licensing a continuing wrong [by] saying to the cement company, you may continue to do harm to your neighbors so long as you pay a fee for it." The dissenter likened the result to conferring the power of eminent domain—the power to condemn an easement—upon a private corporation, to be used for private gain rather than for public use.

The courts' tendency to balance hardships and deny injunctions is not the only factor that has made nuisance law inadequate to control widespread pollution. Another is lack of standing to sue. The common law distinguished public and private nuisances. A public nuisance was one that damaged a large number of persons. Only the attorney general or local prosecutor could sue to abate a public nuisance, unless a private individual could show "special" damage, distinct from that of the public generally. Elected officials frequently were hesitant to seek injunctions that might shut down major industries. Only if a private plaintiff could prove special damage, or show that damages were limited to him or a small group (thus making the nuisance private rather than public), was he recognized by the courts as having standing to seek injunctive relief. While today some states do allow private suits to abate public nuisances, lack of standing remains a problem elsewhere. Still another difficulty can be the plaintiff's burden of proving material harm attributable to unreasonable conduct of defendants. Frequently effluents derive from many sources, none of which alone would produce the alleged damage. It may be impossible to prove any particular polluter responsible for the poor air or water quality. Also, attempts to join multiple defendants and allocate damages among them can pose difficult procedural problems. Finally, nuisance law fails to provide a systematic mechanism for supervising pollutant discharges. Just as the common law has had to be supplemented in most communities by land use planning and zoning, so it also has had to be supplemented by legislative intervention in the area of pollution control.

Nevertheless, nuisance law sometimes remains a useful tool. An interesting example is Spur Industries, Inc. v. Del E. Webb Development Co. (Ariz.1972). In 1957, Del Webb began construction of a retirement community called Sun City, west of Phoenix. By 1967, the development had moved close to Spur's feedlot, which had been in operation for several years before Webb came into the area. Webb complained that Spur's feeding operation was a nuisance because the flies and the odor spilled over into parts of Sun City. Some residents were unable to enjoy the outdoor living which Webb had advertised, and Webb was faced with sales resistance from prospective purchasers. The court found that Spur's feedlot was both a public and a private nuisance as to citizens of Sun City. Webb, having shown a special injury in the loss of sales, was found to have standing to bring suit to enjoin the nuisance.

If only Webb had been injured, the court said, the doctrine of "coming to the nuisance" would have barred relief. In Arizona and some other states, courts have denied relief to homeowners knowingly entering areas with industrial or agricultural uses. In *Spur*, the court found that Webb was entitled to injunctive relief because of the harm to people who had purchased homes in Sun City. However, the court also concluded that Webb should not be free of liability to Spur, because Webb was the cause of damage sustained by Spur. Having brought people to the nuisance, to the foreseeable detriment of Spur, Webb was required to indemnify Spur for a reasonable amount of the cost of moving or shutting down, as a condition to obtaining the injunction.

Interstate air and water pollution formerly were governed by a federal common law of nuisance. Thus, in Georgia v. Tennessee Copper Co. (S.Ct.1907), the State of Georgia obtained an injunction against a Tennessee company whose sulfur oxide emissions were causing wholesale destruction of forests, orchards and crops in Georgia. However, in Milwaukee v. Illinois (S.Ct.1981) [*Milwaukee II*], a case involving discharges of untreated sewage into Lake Michigan, the Supreme Court held that the comprehensive regulatory system established by the federal Clean Water Act had completely preempted federal common law. The Clean Air Act probably has also displaced the federal common law pertaining to interstate air pollution.

The decision in *Milwaukee II* is open to serious criticism. The Clean Water Act expressly provides that it does not preempt more stringent state laws. Indeed, the Supreme Court has more recently held that federal courts *can* hear nuisance suits arising under state law, so long as they apply the nuisance law of the state where the discharger is located. International Paper Co. v. Ouellette (S.Ct.1987). The result of *Milwaukee II*, then, is to leave dischargers subject to common law liability in federal court, but to make the remedies available to downstream victims depend on the law of the upstream state. This result is difficult to discern in the language of the Clean Water Act, and seems to present no practical advantages over the application of federal common law. Moreover, the Court's desire to give sole regulatory authority to the discharging state has been undermined by later regulatory developments. EPA now requires permits to ensure compliance with the water quality standards set by downstream states. This requirement was upheld in Arkansas v. Oklahoma (S.Ct.1992). Thus, the original rationale for *Milwaukee II* now seem to have evaporated.

B. REGULATION UNDER THE CLEAN AIR ACT

Five main classes of air pollutants are emitted by a variety of sources. *Carbon monoxide* (CO) is a colorless, odorless, poisonous gas, slightly lighter than air, that is produced by the incomplete burning of carbon. The main sources are internal combustion engines, mostly in motor vehicles. *Particulates* are solids or liquids in a wide range of sizes, produced primarily by stationary fuel combustion and industrial processes. Control techniques include filtering, washing, centrifugal separation, and electrostatic precipitation. These work well for most of the particles, but complete removal, especially of the very finest particles, is difficult. *Sulfur oxides* (SO_x) are corrosive, poisonous gases produced when fuel containing sulfur is burned. Electric utilities and industrial plants are the principal producers. *Nitrogen oxides* (NO_x) are produced when fuel is burned at very high temperatures. The main sources are vehicles and combustion plants. Sulfur dioxide and nitric oxides, after being emitted into the atmosphere, can be chemically converted into sulfates and nitrates, which may return to earth as components of rain or snow, known as acid precipitation. *Hydrocarbons* (HC), like carbon monoxide, represent unburned and wasted fuel. Unlike carbon monoxide, gaseous hydrocarbons at concentrations normally found in the atmosphere are not toxic. They are a major pollutant, however, because they combine with NO_x under the influence of sunlight to form photochemical oxidants (or smog), a complex mixture of secondary pollutants including ozone (an unstable, toxic form of oxygen) as well as nitrogen dioxide. They can cause eye and lung irritation, damage to vegetation, offensive odor, and thick haze.

The most important effect of air pollution is its threat to human health. Occasional acute episodes have been marked by dramatic increases in death and illness rates, especially among the elderly and those with preexisting respiratory or cardiac conditions. Of much greater significance for the general population are the subtle, long-range effects of exposure to low level, long-lasting pollution. Such pollution contributes to chronic diseases like emphysema, bronchitis and other respiratory ailments. Air pollution is also linked to higher mortality from other causes such as cancer and arteriosclerosis. Smokers in polluted cities have a much higher rate of lung cancer than smokers in rural areas.

Overall health effects of air pollution are not known to possess meaningful thresholds or safe levels. For example, scientists cannot demonstrate that exposure to one hundred parts per million of a pollutant for twenty-four hours is "safe" while exposures above that level are "dangerous." It is not even possible to establish that effects of exposure become rapidly more serious around some particular exposure level.

1. OVERVIEW OF THE CLEAN AIR ACT

In 1955, Congress began to respond to the problem of air pollution by offering technical and financial assistance to states. Amendments in the 1960s authorized federal agencies to expand their research, to intervene directly to abate *interstate* pollution in limited circumstances, to control emissions from new motor vehicles, and to exercise certain powers of supervision and enforcement of state controls. By the end of the decade states had made little progress, and Congress responded with the Clean Air Amendments of 1970. The Environmental Protection Agency [EPA] also was created in 1970, by an executive order of President Nixon combining preexisting units from various federal departments.

The 1970 amendments sharply increased federal authority. For example, § 111 mandated uniform national standards of performance for new sources of air pollution. ("New" sources included preexisting sources subsequently modified by any physical change or change in the method of operation which increased emissions of any pollutant.) Similarly, § 112 provided for uniform national emission standards for hazardous air pollutants likely to cause an increase in mortality or in serious illness. Nevertheless, § 107(a) still provided that each state "shall have the primary responsibility for assuring air quality within the entire geographic area comprising such state." But states no longer were given a choice as to whether they would attain air quality of specified standards.

Section 109 directed the EPA Administrator to establish national ambient air quality standards (NAAQSs) for pollutants that endanger public health or welfare. Each pollutant is subject to two types of standards: *primary* standards which, "allowing an adequate margin of safety, are requisite to protect the public health"; and *secondary* standards "to protect the public welfare from any known or anticipated adverse effect." Within nine months of promulgation of an NAAQS, each state was required to submit to EPA a plan to implement that standard within its boundaries. § 110(a)(1). EPA, in turn, was required to approve a state implementation plan (SIP) if it had been adopted after public hearings and satisfied the conditions specified in § 110(a)(2). The most important condition was that the SIP provide for attainment of primary NAAQSs "as expeditiously as practicable" but no more than three years later. Secondary standards were to be achieved within "a reasonable time." A SIP had to include "emission limitations, schedules, and timetables for compliance with such limitations," as well as assurances of appropriate resources to enforce the plan.

As with many other deadlines set in environmental statutes, the goals set in 1970 were never attained in many areas. Special provisions were added to the statute in 1977 and further strengthened in 1990 to deal with these "nonattainment areas." In nonattainment areas where pollutant concentrations exceed NAAQSs, § 172 requires at a minimum that SIPs impose "reasonably available control technology" (RACT) on existing sources. If EPA determines that state standards are not sufficient to attain primary NAAQSs on schedule or to attain secondary NAAQSs within a "reasonable time," under § 110 it must issue a federal implementation plan within two years which will assure timely attainment. The fact that compliance may be difficult or even impossible for some sources does not excuse promulgation of the required implementation plans.

Once EPA approves a state plan, it is enforceable not only as state law but also as federal law under § 113. If EPA finds a proposed SIP to be inadequate to attain any NAAQS in any region of a state, and if the state fails to make adequate amendments, § 110(c)(1) directs the agency to issue amendments which are binding on the state.

EPA has established NAAQSs for carbon monoxide, particulates, sulfur dioxide, nitrogen dioxide, hydrocarbons, ozone, and lead. Initially, the NAAQSs were the driving force behind EPA's control strategy, since all emissions contributing to violation of the standards were to be eliminated by 1975–1977. This did not happen, however, and the Act has been amended to extend the deadlines, thereby reducing the "absolute" nature of the standards. In 1982 EPA rescinded the hydrocarbon standard as unnecessary, but the remaining NAAQSs continue to play an important role in air pollution policy. EPA has sometimes approved or promulgated SIP provisions which for economic or political reasons were unlikely to be enforced, such as an EPA mandate to reduce automobile traffic in Los Angeles by 70–80% in 1975. In 1990, Congress enacted major amendments intended to accelerate attainment of the standards, as well as dealing with other major problems such as acid rain and toxic pollutants.

As the foregoing indicates, the basic approach of the 1970 Clean Air Act with respect to existing stationary sources and motor vehicles was that EPA would establish uniform NAAQSs and the states would adopt the emission standards necessary to meet the statutory deadlines. However, with respect to new vehicles, new stationary sources, and hazardous air pollutants, EPA was required to establish nationally uniform emission standards.

For new motor vehicles, the aim was to reduce 1970 emission levels by 90% by 1975. The Act was later amended, however, extending the deadline to 1983–model vehicles and to 1985 models for NO emissions.

The 1990 Amendments Act further tightened vehicle emission standards. By 1998, hydrocarbon emissions had to be cut 30% below the prior standard, while nitrogen oxides had to be cut 60%. The standards were phased in during 1994–98. Unless EPA determines that tougher standards are unnecessary or infeasible, a second tier of reductions would be required by 2003, cutting emissions by about another 50%. States have the option of adopting the even tougher California emission standards.

In addition to these new emission standards, the 1990 amendments create an ambitious new program to change the composition of gasoline in heavily polluted cities. There are two reasons for this program. First, the changed tailpipe standards will have only a gradual impact on pollution levels since they affect only new cars. Second, leaks from the system may defeat even the best exhaust treatment. The reformulated gasoline must contain fewer volatile organic compounds and more oxygen in the form of alcohol or an ether compound. These changes in fuel composition were designed to reduce ozone and carbon monoxide levels in the most smog-ridden cities.

The 1970 Act also addressed new stationary sources. New source performance standards (NSPSs) for stationary sources reflect best available control technology, taking into account the costs of compliance. The NSPSs normally specify how many pounds of a pollutant may be emitted per unit of plant input or output, leaving each source to decide what combination of technological measures and fuel changes to use.

A 1977 amendment to § 111 directed EPA to take a different approach to setting NSPSs for three pollutants from combustion of fossil fuels—sulfur dioxide, nitrogen dioxide, and particulates. Emissions were to be reduced by a specified *percentage* below what they would be without technological control measures—changes in fuel to reduce emissions were not sufficient. The political intent of these amendments was not only to reduce total pollutant emissions but also to reduce the economic incentive for eastern industries to use low sulfur western coal instead of high sulfur eastern coal. EPA implemented this provision with a "sliding scale" regulation, under which the degree of emission control varied with the sulfur content of the fuel. This regulation was upheld in Sierra Club v. Costle (D.C.Cir.1981), despite the statutory command to use "the best technological system of continuous emissions control."

The 1990 Amendments took a new approach to this issue. In place of the "percentage reduction" provision, the amendments rely on a complex system of sulfur dioxide "allowances" to control emissions. These allowances are discussed in the materials on acid rain in the final section of this chapter. Plants using scrubbers were able to postpone compliance with the new acid rain requirements until 1997, and the statute also grants additional emission allowances to those plants. To cushion the impact of the new requirements, the amendments authorized $250 million in "transition assistance" for workers fired or laid off because of compliance with the Clean Air Act.

With respect to hazardous air pollutants, § 112 initially required that EPA establish emission standards with "an ample margin of safety to protect public health." The 1990 Amendments added complex new regulatory requirements to § 112, which are discussed in Chapter 5.

For geographic areas with superior air quality, where pollutant levels are substantially below an NAAQS, the 1977 amendments asserted a congressional commitment to the principle of prevention of significant deterioration (PSD). A region that complies with the NAAQS is put into one of three classes. Large national parks and wilderness areas are Class I areas, where very little deterioration of air quality is allowed. All other areas are Class II, where moderate increases in ambient concentrations are allowed (but not to exceed NAAQS). A governor may reclassify a Class II area in his state as Class I, or as Class III, where larger increments are allowed, usually to permit new industry. To establish a major new source in any PSD area, the owner must apply for a permit. (The 1990 Amendments expanded the permit requirement to include all major sources and all new plants.) The permit requires that the new emissions remain within the allowed increments, and that the source use "best available control technology" for *all* pollutants, quite apart from the allowable increments.

The following section focuses on probably the most important issue, economically and politically, in implementing the Clean Air Act: the extent to which the difficulty of compliance is considered in establishing and enforcing limits on pollutant emissions by individual sources. Different categories of sources and pollutants recognized by the Act are discussed in separate subsections.

2. CONSIDERATION OF ECONOMIC AND TECHNOLOGICAL FEASIBILITY

In establishing national ambient air quality standards, EPA cannot consider the feasibility of attaining them. Under § 109 of the Act, NAAQSs must be fixed at levels necessary to protect the public health (with an "adequate margin of safety"), as well as public welfare. If EPA has evidence that primary standards are necessary to protect the health of substantial numbers of people (including the most sensitive segments of the population, such as the elderly and persons with respiratory diseases), the standards will not be overturned judicially. Lead Industries Association, Inc. v. EPA (D.C.Cir.1980).

Air pollutants do not generally exhibit thresholds. That is, there is no cutoff level, above which there is a known risk of harm and below which there is some assurance of harmlessness. Instead, at any given level, there is at least some possibility of risk. Cost-benefit analysis, or simply consideration of the feasibility of compliance, could help draw the line, but the statute precludes these considerations. Hence, EPA is faced with a considerable difficulty in setting NAAQS. Its ability to revise existing NAAQSs was thrown into question by American Trucking Associations v. EPA

(D.C.Cir.1999). In *American Trucking*, the court held that EPA's failure to set forth an "intelligible standard" governing the selection of risk levels rendered § 109 an unconstitutional delegation of power. The court therefore vacated important new NAAQSs governing ozone and fine particulates, pending EPA's development and application of a new risk methodology. Observers considered this a rather startling application of the nondelegation doctrine, and whether the D.C. Circuit's current approach will hold up remains to be seen. The Supreme Court will review the case during its October 2000 term.

Despite EPA's inability to consider feasibility when setting an NAAQS, it would be a mistake to view the CAA as a whole as being oblivious to cost. In fixing emission standards and timetables applicable to various pollution sources and pollutants, EPA is sometimes required to consider economic and technological difficulties of compliance.

a. New Motor Vehicles

Section 202(b) provided that, beginning with the 1975 model year, exhaust emissions of hydrocarbons and carbon monoxide from "light duty vehicles" must be reduced at least 90% from the permissible emission levels in 1970. As noted by Judge Leventhal in International Harvester Co. v. Ruckelshaus (D.C.Cir.1973), Congress was aware that these standards were "drastic medicine," designed to "force the state of the art." Because of doubts whether manufacturers would be able to comply, Congress provided a "realistic escape hatch": the automakers could petition EPA for a one year suspension of the 1975 requirements. EPA could grant the suspension only if the applicant proved that "effective control technology, processes, operating methods, or other alternatives are not available or have not been available for a sufficient period of time" to achieve timely compliance. In 1972, International Harvester, Ford, Chrysler, General Motors and Volvo applied for suspensions. EPA denied the applications because it could not make the required finding that technology was unavailable. Although in actual tests no car had conformed to the standard, EPA adjusted the auto companies' test data by use of several assumptions and predicted that the necessary technology would be available by the 1975 model year.

The court in *International Harvester* agreed with EPA that the proper question was whether technology would be available in time for 1975 models, not whether it was already available when the manufacturers applied for suspensions in 1972. But the court reversed EPA's determination that technology would permit compliance without the one year suspension. The court cited EPA's "unexplained assumptions," the "absence of an indication of the statistical reliability" of the prediction that technology would be available by the 1975 model year, and the "economic and ecological risks inherent in a 'wrong decision'." Realistically, if the prediction of availability proved wrong, the court did not expect an enforced shutdown of one or more auto companies. Instead, the likely response would be a last-minute congressional or administrative forgiveness of noncompliance, imposing a competitive disadvantage on companies able to comply (because their vehicles would cost more and be less fuel efficient). On the other hand, the court believed that the environmental risks of suspension were small, especially given EPA's authority to prescribe special interim emission standards for 1975 model vehicles. The court concluded that EPA had failed to produce a reasoned basis supporting the reliability of its methodology for predicting the avail- ability of technology. In so holding, the court seems to have ignored the statutory provision placing the burden of proof regarding technological availability on the industry rather than on EPA. Under the terms of the statute, if the availability of the technology was unclear, EPA should have prevailed; the burden was on industry to furnish a reliable prediction of unavailability. Pre- sumably, Congress felt the risk of an erroneous denial of suspension to be less severe, or the urgency of pollution control to be greater, than did Judge Levanthal.

Following the court's decision, the Administrator granted the extension and imposed interim standards more lenient than the 90% reduction. As noted earlier, the industry later received additional extensions of time from Congress.

b. Existing Stationary Sources

The Act does not preclude a state from adopting an implementation plan exceeding national ambient standards, i.e., producing ambient air even cleaner than that mandated by NAAQSs. In Union Electric Co. v. EPA (S.Ct.1976), an electric utility company petitioned EPA to disapprove Missouri's SIP, on the ground that compliance by its coal-fired generating plants in St. Louis was economically and technologically infeasible. Union Electric argued that an infeasibly strict state plan should be rejected under § 110 as not "practicable" or "reasonable." A single state cannot, the company argued, engage in technology-forcing on its own. However, the Court upheld EPA's position, holding claims of economic and technological infeasibility irrelevant to EPA consideration of a SIP.

Union Electric does not mean that claims of infeasibility are never relevant. As the Court pointed out, the most important forum for consideration of feasibility is the state agency which initially formulates the SIP. So long as NAAQSs and PSD requirements will be met, the state generally may select any mix of controls that it desires for existing stationary sources (subject since 1977 to the RACT requirement in nonattainment areas). Industries with particular economic or technological problems may seek special treatment in the plan. Moreover, once a SIP is in place, individual plants within the industry may be able to obtain a revision of the provisions applying to those plants, providing the revised plan still complies with § 110.

If denied variances, sources may also assert claims of infeasibility in the state courts. In Illinois, for example, the courts invalidated both statewide emission limitations and individual enforcement orders when the state agency failed to sufficiently consider the "technical feasibility and economic reasonableness" of compliance, as required by Illinois law. Commonwealth Edison Co. v. Pollution Control Board (Ill.1976); Wells Manufacturing Co. v. Pollution Control Board (Ill.1978).

State courts can not, however, provide polluters with a complete screen from liability. Even though a state court has enjoined or invalidated a SIP, it is still enforceable as a matter of federal law. Thus, EPA may still be able to obtain a federal court order enforcing the plan even though the state courts have held the plan invalid as a matter of state law. See United States v.

Ford Motor Co. (6th Cir.1987). EPA does not, however, frequently exercise this power.

A state does not have complete freedom to select any mix of controls which will result in attainment of NAAQSs. For example, one requirement is that the SIP mandate "continuous" emission limitations where possible, rather than "intermittent" and "dispersion" techniques. Prior to 1990, § 110(a)(2)(B) required each SIP to include "emission limitations, schedules, and timetables for compliance with such limitations, and such other measures as may be necessary to insure attainment and maintenance" of NAAQSs. In Kennecott Copper Corp. v. Train (9th Cir.1975), the court struck down portions of Nevada's SIP. The SIP required that Kennecott's smelter reduce SO_2 emissions by 60% through installation of a plant to convert SO_2 to sulfuric acid, i.e., by continuous controls. Further emission reductions, required when weather conditions threatened maintenance of the ambient standard, were to be achieved by reducing temporarily the production level at the smelter, i.e., by intermittent controls. EPA rejected the Nevada plan on the ground that noncontinuous controls (including also use of a tall stack, a dispersion technique) were acceptable only after Kennecott employed continuous controls to the limit of economic and technological feasibility. Kennecott contended that the agency was not authorized to require continuous emission reduction techniques in preference to intermittent controls or dispersion methods, and that EPA must approve a SIP that provided for attainment of the NAAQS by any combination of controls. Citing congressional actions in 1974 indicating approval of the EPA position and also the CAA's general policy of nondegradation, the court held that the phrase "as may be necessary" in § 110(a)(2)(B) modified only "such other measures," and not "emission limitations." Thus, noncontinuous emission limitations were appropriate only when continuous controls were infeasible. The court said that the reliability and enforceability of intermittent control systems was questionable, since they may not be implemented when needed; and that dispersion techniques do not reduce emissions but only spread out the pollution, threatening other clean air areas.

In 1990, § 110(a)(2)(B) was rephrased in a way that undercuts the court's reading of that section. In the meantime, however, *Kennecott* had been codified elsewhere in the Act. Section 123, the "tall stacks" provision added after *Kennecott* in 1977, provides that the "degree of emission limitation required for control of any air pollutant" under a SIP "shall not be affected in any manner" by (1) stack height in excess of "good engineering practice," or (2) any other dispersion technique. Good engineering practice means the height necessary to ensure that emissions from the stack do not result in "excessive concentrations" of any pollutant in the "immediate vicinity" of the source. Ordinarily, such height may not exceed 2 1/2 times the height of the source. Section 123(b) treats intermittent controls as a form of dispersion technique.

Variances from SIP-prescribed emission standards are granted by state agencies subject to approval by EPA. Such variances are treated as "revisions" of the SIP. Under § 110(a)(3)(A), EPA was required to approve any revision if it did not jeopardize timely attainment and subsequent maintenance of NAAQSs, if it required continuous emission controls to the maximum extent feasible, and if it satisfied the other requirements of § 110(a)(2). Train v. NRDC (S.Ct.1975). This provision was repealed in 1990, but § 110(k) now requires EPA to approve revisions if they are properly documented and meet the requirements of the Act.

In 1977 the Clean Air Act was amended by the addition of several relief provisions for stationary sources unable to meet the statutory deadlines. The most important was § 113(d). Section 113(d) authorized "delayed compliance orders" for any stationary source which was "unable to comply" with a SIP. Among other things, the order had to provide for final compliance "as expeditiously as practicable" but no later than three years after the date for final compliance in the SIP. Such a state order became part of the SIP and was a defense to any federal or private effort to compel earlier compliance. This provision was repealed in 1990.

Having exhausted the statutory and administrative possibilities for an extension of time, a firm may then be faced with an EPA enforcement proceeding or a citizen suit under § 304. At that point, the firm may seek to invoke the equitable discretion of the federal court to obtain a further delay. As we saw in the previous chapter, the extent of equitable discretion to delay compliance with federal statutes is somewhat unclear. When Congress has so carefully structured the statutory mechanisms for considering feasibility, however, a free-wheeling exercise of discretion by the courts is surely out of place. Thus, as the Third Circuit has said, any remaining judicial discretion to delay compliance must be narrow indeed. United States v. Wheeling-Pittsburgh Steel Corp. (3d Cir.1987).

The foregoing paragraphs have focused on the feasibility of individual sources complying with emission limitations. But what if an entire air quality control region is unable to achieve timely attainment of an NAAQS? Section 172, as amended in 1977, authorized postponement of the date for compliance with primary standards until 1982, or 1987 for oxidants and carbon monoxide, if that was "as expeditiously as practicable." Under §§ 110(a)(2)(I), 172 and 173, the main sanction for nonattainment of primary NAAQSs by the statutory deadlines was a moratorium on construction and operation of new or modified major stationary sources. Section 176 also contemplated denial of federal grants for highway construction and various other purposes. Early in 1983 EPA designated more than 100 counties nationwide as probable noncompliance areas and announced procedures for making final determinations, prior to imposing sanctions. EPA was able to avoid imposing stringent sanctions by approving unrealistic SIP amendments for some states and granting "conditional approval" of others, subject to a requirement that states revise them later to assure attainment.

The arrival of the 1987 deadline placed EPA in an even more uncomfortable position. Over 70 cities missed the deadline for the ozone and carbon monoxide standards. One response was a series of attempts by states to carve attainment areas out of larger nonattainment areas. This tactic, however, at best reduced but did not eliminate state's noncompliance problem. In Abramowitz v. United States EPA (9th Cir.1987), the court rejected the California SIP because it would not result in attainment of the standards by the statutory deadline. EPA had attempted to temporize by allowing California to take "reasonable extra efforts" to comply.

In Delaney v. EPA (9th Cir.1990), the court again rebuffed EPA's efforts to give states more time to comply.

Nonattainment was one of the central concerns of the 1990 amendments. The amendments limited the ability of states to carve up nonattainment areas. A nonattainment area now must include the entire metropolitan area, unless the state can show that some sub-area does not contribute significantly to the nonattainment problem. The relatively simple noncompliance provisions of the 1977 amendments are replaced by a far more elaborate scheme.

The amendments require another round of SIP amendments to achieve compliance. In this connection, it is worth noting some changes in the procedures governing plan revisions. EPA must issue minimum standards that a plan revision must meet in order to be considered a "complete" submission. Within sixty days of a plan submission, EPA must consider whether the submission is complete. If not, EPA may treat it in whole or in part as a nullity; if the submission is complete, EPA must approve or disapprove the plan within twelve months. (EPA's failure to meet this deadline arguably may affect its ability to collect penalties from some non-complying sources. The Supreme Court had ducked this issue under the pre–1990 version of the Act.) See General Motors Corp. v. United States (S.Ct.1990). EPA may issue a conditional approval if the state commits itself to adopt specific enforceable measures within a year.

If a SIP for a nonattainment area is inadequate, EPA must issue a federal implementation plan within two years. The amendments provide several other sanctions, including a cutoff of federal highway funds. Another important sanction is an upward adjustment of the "offset" requirements, which are discussed later in this chapter. The effect of the adjustment is to limit economic growth in the offending region. Areas that fall behind schedule may be "bumped up" to higher categories, resulting in more stringent requirements. Finally, depending on the severity of the non-attainment problem, the term "major source" is redefined to include smaller sources, which will have to implement tough technology-based standards such as LAER and RACT.

Apart from these general provisions, the amendments also contain a series of complex provisions relating specifically to ozone, NO_x, CO, and particulates. The ozone provisions are illustrative. The statute divides ozone non-attainment areas into five classes, depending on the severity of the pollution. Only Los Angeles is in the worst class (extreme nonattainment). Compliance requirements are keyed to this classification scheme. For example, marginal areas must achieve attainment within three years, while serious areas have nine years, and Los Angeles is given 20 years. Except for marginal areas, all ozone non-attainment areas must reduce emissions of volatile organic compounds by 15% by 1996, and further reductions of 3% must be achieved annually. Major sources are also defined differently for the different categories: 100 tons per year in the marginal and moderate areas, but only 50, 25, and 10 tons per year in the serious, severe and extreme areas. Offset requirements also vary among these areas. The statute requires various specific control measures in different categories. For example, in areas ranked serious or worse, gas stations are required to install special hose-and-nozzle controls on gas pumps to capture fuel vapors. These areas are also required to have more stringent vehicle inspection and maintenance programs.

The ozone reduction measures have an estimated cost of $9–12 billion annually after they are fully implemented in 2004. Benefits from reduced acute health effects and increased agricultural output were conservatively estimated at $5 billion. Other possible benefits include a possible (but conjectural) decrease in chronic respiratory disease, reductions in damage to forests, improved visibility, and incidental reductions in carcinogenic emissions.

The nonattainment provisions for other pollutants are generally similar, but give EPA somewhat more discretion. One particularly interesting feature of the CO provisions is that they require the use of oxygenated fuels (such as gasoline containing ethanol) in certain areas. As discussed earlier, the fuel additives increase the amount of oxygen available for combustion and thereby decrease emissions of carbon monoxide.

Congress has obviously learned a lot about the noncompliance problem in the two decades following the original enactment of the Clean Air Act. It remains to be seen whether this increased regulatory sophistication will be reflected in improved air quality, but the 1990 amendments do seem to promise significant further progress.

c. New Stationary Sources

Section 111 directs the Administrator to promulgate "standards of performance" governing emissions of air pollutants by "new" stationary sources, i.e., sources constructed or modified after the effective date of pertinent regulations. The term "modification" means any physical change or change in the method of operation which increases the amount of any air pollutant. The emission standard must reflect "the degree of emission reduction achievable through the application of the best system of continuous emission reduction which (taking into consideration the cost of achieving such emission reduction, and any nonair quality health and environmental impact and energy requirements) the Administrator determines has been adequately demonstrated." (If such a standard is not feasible, under § 111(h) the EPA may issue operating or work practice standards instead.) In Portland Cement Association v. Ruckelshaus (D.C.Cir.1973), industry sought judicial review of EPA's standards of performance for cement plants. The companies contended that EPA had violated the mandate to "take into consideration the cost" of achieving the prescribed emission reductions, because it had not prepared a quantified cost-benefit analysis. What EPA had done was to estimate that the cost of pollution control was affordable by the industry and could be passed on to customers, without substantially affecting competition with substitutes such as steel, asphalt and aluminum. Noting that the kind of cost-benefit analysis urged by petitioners would conflict with the Act's specific time constraints, and that quantifying the benefit to ambient air conditions would be difficult if not impossible, the court held that EPA had given sufficient consideration to economic costs to satisfy the requirement of § 111.

In 1977, the Clean Air Act was amended by addition of § 317. It provides that before publishing notice of a proposal to adopt or revise any standard of performance under § 111, EPA shall prepare an "economic impact assessment respecting such standard or regulation." This assessment, which shall be available to the public, must analyze costs of compliance, potential inflationary or recessionary effects, and effects on competition, consumer costs, and energy use. However, § 317 expressly did not "alter the basis on which a standard or regulation is promulgated" or "authorize or require any judicial review of any such standard or regulation."

Beginning with the Reagan Administration in 1981, more extensive use of cost-benefit analysis has been required by executive order. Executive Order 12,291 required that "major" regulations must satisfy a cost-benefit analysis, unless such an analysis is precluded by statute. Later Presidents have modified the order but continued its basic mandate. The cost-benefit requirement is enforced by the Office of Management and Budget. OMB's increasingly active role in agency rulemaking has been a source of political controversy, and has given rise to disputes about whether OMB has violated the statutory procedures governing rulemaking. Congress has repeatedly considered whether to strengthen the role of cost-benefit analysis, but has failed to do so.

Under § 172 of the Act, a SIP applicable to any nonattainment area must "require permits for the construction and operation of new or modified major stationary sources." To qualify for a permit, a major source must comply with the "lowest achievable emission rate" (LAER) and satisfy certain pollution "offset" requirements (discussed in section 3 below). Section 171 defines LAER as "the most stringent emission limitation ... contained in the implementation plan of any state" (unless shown to be unachievable), or "the most stringent emission limitation achieved in practice, ... whichever is more stringent." Since LAER may not be less stringent than standards of performance for new sources under § 111, LAER must be at least "the best system of continuous emission reduction ... adequately demonstrated," considering cost.

As amended in 1977 by addition of §§ 160–169, the Clean Air Act requires that SIPs include measures to "prevent the significant deterioration" of air quality. This requirement applies to areas designated by the states under § 107 as having ambient air quality better than any applicable NAAQS, or for which there is insufficient data to determine air quality. Since classification of areas is pollutant-specific, the same geographic area may be a PSD area for one pollutant but a nonattainment area for another.

Areas subject to PSD are divided into three classes. Separate ceilings on increases in ambient concentrations of air pollutants are defined for each class. Class I areas, for which very small increments apply, include international parks and large national parks and wilderness areas. All other areas were initially designated Class II, for which increments were set permitting moderate economic growth. However, some Class II areas can be redesignated Class III, for which increases in pollutants are allowed up to the national ambient standards. No major stationary source may be constructed or modified in a PSD area without a permit, and no permit shall be issued unless (1) the applicant demonstrates that emissions will not contribute to air pollution in excess of the allowable increment or concentration for any pollutant in the PSD area, and (2) the facility's emission limitations reflect "best available control technology" (BACT) for each pollutant subject to PSD regulation. Demonstrations that emissions will not violate applicable increments are to be based on monitoring and diffusion modeling.

The actual operation of the PSD requirements has diverged somewhat from what one might infer from reading the statute. Reclassification has been minimal: virtually no area has been reclassified as either Class I or Class III. Except for national parks, essentially the entire nation has been set at Class II. SIP revisions have been problematic because of modeling difficulties. About one hundred projects, mostly modifications, pass through the permit process every year. Because PSD has had little effect on plant siting, the technology standards have become the focus of PSD policy. This technology requirement (BACT) has resulted in significant decreases in emissions below the § 111 new source standards. For example, there has been more than a 20% reduction in particulates and sulfur dioxide below new source standards. EPA has implemented a "top down" review process, under which a source must use the most stringent control technology available unless it can demonstrate that use of this technology is infeasible based on "substantial and unique local factors."

A related requirement is intended to protect visibility in national parks because of complaints that haze was seriously impairing their scenic beauty. Section 169A declares as a national goal the prevention of visibility impairment in mandatory Class I federal areas (primarily national parks). Some limited amount of "retrofitting"—that is, upgrading equipment in existing plants—is mandated to help achieve this goal.

3. OFFSETS AND BUBBLES

As mentioned earlier, § 173 requires permits for the construction and operation of "new or modified major stationary sources" in nonattainment areas. Permits are issued only if "total allowable emissions" from existing sources and new non-major sources are "sufficiently less than total emissions from existing sources allowed under the applicable implementation plan" when the permit is sought, "so as to represent . . . reasonable progress." Thus total emissions of each pollutant must be *reduced* even though a new source is added. Under the 1990 amendments, the amount of the reduction varies with the severity of the area's non-attainment problem. New or modified major sources receive credit only for reducing emissions which are allowed under the SIP, not for reductions already overdue.

Section 173 does not require that the source reducing its emissions be owned or operated by the person proposing a new major source. Section 173 refers to "total allowable emissions from existing sources in the region," and EPA guidelines allow offsets based on reductions at sources owned by others. As long as net emissions are reduced, it is immaterial who reduces them. Thus, someone wishing to create a new source could pay another firm to close down a marginal plant, to control it beyond SIP requirements, or to move to another air quality control region. The result is that § 173 creates a private market in emission rights.

Since 1979 the EPA has allowed "banking" of unused emission reduction credits, for offset against

future new sources. For example, localities may bank
reductions that result from firms going out of business.
These clean air credits could later be transferred to new
firms locating in the community. But who owns offsets
that are not used immediately, and how should they be
allocated among potential new sources? According to
EPA, "the State is free to govern ownership, use, sale,
and commercial transactions in banked emission offsets
as it sees fit." The offsets might be considered the
exclusive property of the parent source which produced
them; they might be treated as public property, even
though created by private investments; or the offsets
might be viewed as privately owned rights which can be
made available either to the parent source or to other
investors. If a state or local government becomes the
"banker" of emission rights, how should it allocate the
rights among potential users? The offsets could be
allocated on a first-come-first-served basis, but that
would give little control to state or local officials in
planning the economic development of the region.
Allocation by auction, to the highest bidder, a more
traditional free market approach, would also undermine
state control. Another alternative might be for the
government to condition permit approval upon the
satisfaction of specified social, employment or tax-base
criteria.

The preceding paragraphs were concerned with
inter-source offsets. The following paragraphs deal with
intra-source offsets and the so-called "bubble" concept.
The basic idea behind the bubble is to treat the various
components of an industrial complex as a single source
for regulatory purposes. Thus, emissions from all stacks
are considered only in the aggregate. (If only stacks at
a single plant are involved, this concept is called "net-

ting." "Bubbles" involve multi-plant facilities under common ownership. In practice, netting is much more common than the use of bubbles.)

The bubble policy was the source of conflicting rulings in the D.C. Circuit. That court considered bubbles in a series of three cases. In two cases dealing with § 111 new source standards and nonattainment standards, bubbles were declared invalid. In a case dealing with PSD rules, however, use of bubbles was upheld.

The issue reached the Supreme Court in Chevron, U.S.A., Inc. v. NRDC (S.Ct.1984). *Chevron* involved the use of bubbles in state nonattainment regulations. The effect of using a bubble was effectively to allow the firm to offset one source of pollution with a reduction in another source, without complying with the other requirements of the offset provisions. Nevertheless, the Supreme Court upheld the use of the bubble. Finding nothing in the language of the statute or its legislative history directly on point, the Court concluded that the issue was really one of how to best implement the general policies of the Act. This policy decision, the Court concluded, was best made by the EPA rather than by the judiciary:

> In this case, the Administrator's interpretation represents a reasonable accommodation of manifestly competing interests and is entitled to deference: the regulatory scheme is technical and complex, the agency considered the matter in a detailed and reasoned fashion, and the decision involves reconciling conflicting policies. Congress intended to accommodate both interests, but did not do so itself on the level of specificity presented by this

case. Perhaps that body consciously desired the Administrator to strike the balance at this level, thinking that those with great expertise and charged with responsibility for administering the provision would be in a better position to do so; perhaps it simply did not consider the question at this level; and perhaps Congress was unable to forge a coalition on either side of the question, and those on each side decided to take their chances with the scheme devised by the agency. For judicial purposes, it matters not which of those things occurred.

Judges are not experts in the field, and are not part of either political branch of government. Courts must, in some cases, reconcile competing political interests, but not on the basis of the judges' personal policy preferences. In contrast, an agency to which Congress has delegated policymaking responsibilities may, within the limits of that delegation, properly rely upon the incumbent administration's views of wise policy to inform its judgments.

As this passage makes clear, a subsequent administration would be free to prohibit states from utilizing bubbles in their nonattainment regulations, based on a reappraisal of the competing policies.

C. REGULATION UNDER THE CLEAN WATER ACT

The major sources of water pollution are industrial, municipal and agricultural. The types of pollutants entering streams, lakes and oceans include organic wastes, other nutrients, toxic chemicals and other hazardous substances, heated water, and sediments.

Organic wastes decompose by bacterial action. They are commonly measured in units of biochemical oxygen demand (BOD), or the amount of oxygen needed to decompose them. Because fish and other aquatic animals need oxygen, the amount of dissolved oxygen in a water body is one of the best measures of its ecological health. If too much oxygen is consumed in decomposition of organic waste, certain desirable types of fish no longer can live there and are replaced by pollution-resistant fish such as carp. If all the dissolved oxygen is gone, an anaerobic (airless) decomposition process occurs. Rather than releasing carbon dioxide, anaerobic decomposition releases methane or hydrogen sulfide, and the stream or lake turns dark and malodorous.

Discharges of heated water into lakes and rivers ("thermal pollution") also can harm aquatic life. Higher temperatures accelerate biological and chemical processes, reducing the water's ability to retain dissolved oxygen and other gases. The growth of aquatic plants like algae is hastened, and fish reproduction may be disrupted.

Eutrophication, or the "dying of lakes," is a natural process resulting from the addition of nutrients and sediments. Over time, lakes become shallower and biologically more productive, eventually evolving into swamps and finally into dry land. Normally this takes thousands of years, but humans greatly accelerate the process when they add nutrients such as detergents, fertilizers, and human and animal wastes, and allow soil runoff from agricultural and other lands.

Discharges of toxic chemicals, heavy metals, and other hazardous substances can impair aquatic life and render both the water (even after treatment) and fish and shellfish unsafe for human consumption.

Most industrial wastes can be controlled by treatment and production process changes. Some types of wastes, like those from food processing, can be treated efficiently—after pretreatment in some cases—in municipal treatment systems. Such systems receive about half of their wastes from industrial sources and about half from homes, stores, and offices.

Three levels of treatment are employed in municipal treatment plants. Primary treatment is a simple gravity process which separates and settles solids. It provides BOD removal levels of 25 to 30%. Secondary treatment is a biological process that speeds up what occurs in natural water bodies. Good secondary treatment plants remove 90% of BOD. Advanced waste treatment involves a wide variety of processes tailored for specific treatment needs. They may remove up to 99% of measured BOD, as well as other pollutants. Even after treatment, however, municipal wastes contribute large amounts of phosphate and nitrate nutrients to water bodies. Secondary treatment plants remove an average of 30% of the phosphorous and up to 20% of the nitrogenous materials, although with modifications higher levels of removal are possible.

Another municipal waste problem is street runoff into storm sewers. Where storm sewers are separated from sanitary sewers, runoff enters receiving waters untreated and can carry a variety of wastes, including organic and toxic wastes. Where storm and sanitary sewers are combined, both runoff and raw sewage pass directly into receiving waters when treatment systems become overloaded during storms or thaws.

1. OVERVIEW OF THE CLEAN WATER ACT

Until 1972, the Federal Water Pollution Control Act prescribed a regulatory system consisting mainly of state-developed ambient water quality standards applicable to interstate or navigable waters. The standards for any particular segment of a water body depended upon the uses (e.g., agricultural, industrial, recreational) which the state wanted to facilitate. Enforcement was possible only to prevent an imminent health hazard or when a discharge reduced the quality of the receiving water below the specified ambient level. This system failed for lack of enforcement. Multiple polluters discharging into the same stream or lake presented problems of proof similar to those encountered under nuisance law. As with air pollution, many states were either unmotivated or incapable of taking effective regulatory action.

In 1972 Congress adopted a totally different approach. The 1972 amendments established a system of standards, permits and enforcement aimed at "goals" of "fishable and swimmable" waters by 1983 and total elimination of pollutant discharges into navigable waters by 1985. Ambient water quality standards were to be supplemented by effluent limitations applicable to all "point sources" ("any discernible, confined and discrete conveyance . . . from which pollutants are or may be discharged"). Under § 301, effluent limitations for all point sources except publicly owned treatment works were required to reflect "best practicable control technology currently available" (BPT) by 1977, and "best available technology economically achievable" (BAT) by 1983. Publicly owned treatment works (POTWs) were required to adopt secondary treatment by 1977, and "best practicable waste treatment over the life of the works" by 1983. In addition, all point sources were required to comply with any more stringent limitations established pursuant to § 302 to achieve ambient water quality standards, or pursuant to any other federal or state law.

Special requirements were imposed on some types of sources. Section 306 required that "new" sources in specified categories meet effluent limitations akin to the 1983 BAT standards. Section 307 required that EPA maintain a list of toxic substances and establish separate limitations for them. These limitations were to be based mainly on protection of public health and water quality, rather than on technological feasibility, and were to provide an "ample margin of safety." Section 307 is discussed in more detail in Chapter 5.

Section 402 created a permit system, the National Pollutant Discharge Elimination System (NPDES), under which discharge permits can be issued by EPA or by states with EPA-approved programs. Discharges by point sources, except in compliance with the limitations imposed in permits, were declared unlawful. Permits must incorporate applicable effluent limitations established under §§ 301, 302, 306 and 307, including enforceable schedules of compliance to meet the 1977 and 1983 deadlines. A 1987 amendment prohibits backsliding; with limited exceptions, new permits cannot be less stringent than existing permits for the same facility.

The 1972 amendments contemplated that states would be primarily responsible for enforcement. However, the federal government was not constrained, as it had been under the previous FWPCA, from acting to enforce state or federal standards. Provisions allowing for inspection, entry and monitoring, EPA enforcement suits, and citizen suits were all designed to facilitate enforcement of the new standards. Under § 505, citizens could sue to enforce effluent limitations in state or EPA permits. (As government enforcement action has been hindered by budgetary constraints, citizen suits have become increasingly important.) Citizens also could sue EPA for failure to perform nondiscretionary regulatory duties. Another provision, discussed in Chapter 6, addressed the problem of wetlands protection.

Like the Clean Air Act, the FWPCA was amended in 1977. It was denominated the Clean Water Act. EPA was authorized to grant case-by-case extensions of the 1977 BPT deadline to industrial dischargers which had attempted in good faith to comply; however, full compliance was required by 1979. If delays in compliance were caused by lack of federal construction grant funds, the agency also could extend the 1977 deadline until 1983. Another provision, § 301(h), authorized EPA to waive the secondary treatment requirement permanently for POTW discharges into "marine waters" (oceans and tidal rivers) if the sewage will not interfere with public water supplies, aquatic life, and recreational activities.

With respect to the previously established 1983 deadline for industry compliance with BAT effluent limitations, the 1977 modifications were more complex. Different requirements were adopted for three categories of pollutants: (1) "toxic" pollutants, including initially a list of 129 specific chemicals; (2) "conventional" pollutants designated by EPA, including BOD, fecal coliform, suspended solids, and pH; and (3) "nonconventional" pollutants, those not classified by EPA as either toxic or conventional. For toxic pollutants, BAT was to be employed by July 1, 1984 (or for pollutants not on the original list, within three years after EPA adoption of applicable effluent limitations); no exceptions were allowed. Under a surviving portion of the pre–1977 law, EPA may establish even stricter toxic standards, including zero discharge, where necessary either to protect public health with an ample margin of safety or to attain applicable ambient water quality standards. Under the 1987 amendments, stricter standards are also required to control toxic "hotspots," where BAT, new source, and pretreatment standards are insufficient to attain water quality standards.

Previous BAT requirements were also modified. For conventional pollutants, a new standard, "best conventional pollutant control technology" (BCT), was to be achieved by July 1, 1984. In establishing effluent limitations for conventional pollutants, EPA was to consider "the reasonableness of the relationship between the costs of attaining a reduction in effluents and the effluent reduction benefits derived." This "reasonable relationship" factor was not included among those to be considered in formulating BAT limitations for toxic and nonconventional pollutants. Effluent limitations based on the BAT standard were to be achieved for nonconventional pollutants, with a deadline that was ultimately extended to 1989.

The deadline for secondary treatment could be extended to 1988 where reductions in federal financial assistance or other changed conditions made it impossible to complete construction by 1983. Further, under § 304(d)(4), the definition of what constitutes acceptable secondary treatment was relaxed in 1981: "such biological treatment facilities as oxidation ponds, lagoons, and ditches," in which sunlight and algae cause decomposition of the wastes, "shall be deemed the equivalent of secondary treatment" so long as receiving water quality will not be "adversely affected." Clearly, this redefinition, together with the provisions of § 301(h) concerning discharges into marine waters, amounts to a partial retreat—with respect to publicly owned treatment works—from technology-based effluent standards, back toward the pre–1972 focus on attainment of ambient water quality standards.

Water quality considerations have continued to play a lesser role in regulating industrial sources. Sections 302 and 303 require stricter effluent limitations when necessary to achieve water quality standards, and provide procedures for classifying waters in terms of desired use and needed purity. States have much leeway in determining the type of use, but less in deciding what water quality is necessary for those uses. Section 302 was amended in 1987 to allow modifications of its requirements when there is "no reasonable relationship" between costs and benefits. The most ambitious water quality provision of the 1987 Amendments relates to non-point source pollution, that is, run-off from agricultural and urban areas. This has proved to be a major yet intractable part of the water pollution problem. Pre–1987 law made an ineffectual effort to grapple with the problem in § 208. The 1987 Act added a new § 319 to address the problem. States were required to identify water bodies in which water quality standards cannot be met without control of non-point source pollutants, and to establish management programs for these water bodies, including "best management practices" for categories of sources.

Although still less significant than technology standards, water quality standards may well attain increasing importance under the Clean Water Act. For example, the Supreme Court recently upheld the use of state water flow requirements, designed to maintain water quality, in the permit for a hydroelectric project. PUD No. 1 of Jefferson County v. Washington Dept. of Ecology (S.Ct.1994). A vociferous dissent by Justice Thomas argued that the Court had allowed the parochial local interest in clean water to overrule the national interest in power generation. The majority not only rejected this argument, but adopted a broad view of the appropriate mechanisms that states could use in defining water quality standards, going well beyond quantitative restrictions on pollutant concentrations.

To date, technology-based effluent limitations are still the key restrictions on industrial point sources. Section 301(b), as noted above, requires that effluent limitations reflecting different levels of technology—BPT, BCT and BAT, depending upon the type of pollutant and the deadline for attainment—"shall be achieved" by dischargers. However, the statute does not state explicitly who is to set the limitations, or how. In E.I. du Pont de Nemours & Co. v. Train (S.Ct.1977), the issue was whether § 301(b) authorized EPA to establish effluent-limitations applicable to *classes* of plants, the class in question being organic chemical plants. The company argued that § 301(b) merely indicated the level of technology to be specially fashioned for each *individual* plant in NPDES permits granted under § 402. Generally, these permits are issued by the states, not by EPA. The critical question was whether the EPA could set effluent limitations by regulation, i.e., by quasi-legislative rulemaking, or whether such limitations had to be established in individualized proceedings by the state officials or regional EPA officials responsible for issuing NPDES permits. The fact that the statute left such a basic question open speaks poorly for the skills of the drafters.

The Supreme Court sided with EPA. After considering the legislative history of § 301, the "impossible burden" of individually considering the unique circumstances of the 42,000 permit applicants, and the judicial deference due EPA's reasonable statutory interpretation, the Court concluded that § 301 authorized both BPT and BAT limitations to be set by regulation. The Court held, however, that some allowance must be made for variations in individual plants, as EPA had done by including a variance clause in the challenged BPT limitations.

2. CONSIDERATION OF ECONOMIC AND TECHNOLOGICAL FEASIBILITY

The § 301 and § 304 definitions of BPT, BCT and BAT leave EPA considerable discretion in establishing effluent limitations for different categories of dischargers. We shall consider the factors to be considered in implementing BPT, BCT and BAT standards, in that order. We also shall review relevant provisions of § 306, concerning national standards of performance for *new* sources of water pollution.

a. BPT

American Meat Institute v. EPA (7th Cir.1975) is illustrative of industry challenges to EPA limitations. The BPT regulations there covered slaughterhouses and meat packing. Under §§ 301(b)(1)(A) and 304(b)(1)(B), BPT is based on consideration of total cost in relation to effluent reduction benefits, age of equipment, production process, engineering aspects of control techniques, and non-water quality environmental impacts. In construing this mandate, EPA relied on legislative history indicating that BPT should reflect "the average of the best existing performance by plants of various sizes, ages, and unit processes within each industrial category," except where existing practices are uniformly inadequate. The court approved this interpretation and sustained the effluent limitations because they had actually been achieved at some time by one or more existing processing plants.

The courts have upheld EPA's refusal to consider water quality in setting BPT limitations. In Weyerhaeuser Co. v. Costle (D.C.Cir.1978), pulp and paper makers challenged the validity of the BPT regulations for their industry. Some of their mills discharged effluents into the Pacific Ocean. They urged that because the amounts of pollutants were small in comparison to the volume of receiving water, they should not have to spend heavily on treatment equipment, or increase their energy requirements and sludge levels, in order to treat wastes that the ocean could dilute or absorb. EPA argued that, based on long experience, Congress in 1972 deliberately ruled out arguments based on the assimilative capacity of receiving waters. The court agreed with EPA. According to the court,

Congress was not only concerned about the lack of enforceability of pre–1972 water quality standards, but also wanted nationwide uniformity to free states from the temptation of relaxing local limitations in order to woo or keep industrial facilities. Water quality was to be considered only in setting *more* stringent standards than those reflected in technology-based effluent limitations.

Although the statute was silent on the question of variances from BPT standards, the Supreme Court held in *du Pont v. Train*, supra, that EPA's practice of allowing such variances was not only permissible but required. EPA allowed adjustment of the category-wide standards for plants that could demonstrate the existence of "fundamentally different factors" compared with the industry norm. In subsequent cases, the Court clarified the nature of these "FDF" variances. First, in EPA v. National Crushed Stone Association (S.Ct.1980), the Court upheld EPA's view that a firm's individual economic inability to comply is not a basis for an FDF variance. Although the relationship between costs and effluent reduction benefits is relevant to setting BPT limits, the extent of an individual firm's financial resources is not a factor in variances. Second, in Chemical Manufacturers Association v. NRDC (S.Ct.1985), the Court held that FDF variances are available for toxic pollutants, despite § 301(*l*) of the Act, which prohibited any modification of effluent standards for toxics. The Court explained that an FDF variance is not a "modification" of the effluent standard, but rather a tailoring of the standard to the individual situation of a particular plant. The 1987 amendments added a new subsection, 301(n), providing for FDF variances from BAT, but was silent about BPT variances.

b. BCT

As amended in 1977, § 304(b)(4)(B) spells out the criteria to be used in establishing BCT effluent limitations. Concerning cost considerations, the statute provides that BCT shall include: (1) "consideration of the reasonableness of the relationship between the costs of attaining a reduction in effluents and the effluent reduction benefits derived"; and (2) "the comparison of the cost and level of reduction of such pollutants from the discharge from publicly owned treatment works to the cost and level of reduction of such pollutants from a class or category of industrial sources." In 1979 EPA promulgated a BCT methodology which reduced this cost-reasonableness analysis to a single test: a comparison of the marginal cost of going from BPT to BCT with the marginal cost of going from "secondary treatment" to "advanced secondary treatment" at publicly owned treatment works (the POTW comparison test). EPA analyzed POTW costs and established a figure of $1.15 per pound as the appropriate marginal cost of advanced secondary treatment at a POTW. It then screened existing BAT rules for 41 industry subcategories to determine which rules passed the POTW comparison test.

Industry groups challenged the new BCT standards in American Paper Institute v. EPA (4th Cir.1981). They argued that § 304(b) called for a two-part cost-reasonableness test: a cost-effectiveness test, and a POTW comparison test. EPA, on the other hand, argued that Congress did not require it to evaluate cost-effectiveness, but only mandated a POTW cost-comparison standard. EPA read the seemingly dual statutory requirements as one, commanding only a consideration of reasonableness. The court rejected EPA's position and invalidated all the BCT regulations. EPA's interpretation of the statute was found to be contrary to its plain meaning, ignoring the mandatory language ("shall") and disregarding the conjunctive ("and"). On the other hand, the court concluded that EPA had not acted arbitrarily or capriciously in choosing advanced secondary treatment as the increment beyond secondary treatment for the POTW comparison test. In 1986, EPA adopted new BCT regulations, adding to the POTW test an industry cost-effectiveness test capping the incremental cost of BCT at 129% of BPT.

A later decision gives additional guidance concerning the role of cost in setting BPT and BCT. In Chemical Mfrs. Ass'n v. EPA (5th Cir.1989), the industry argued that BPT should be governed by a "knee-of-the-curve" test to determine the point at which the marginal cost of removal rises steeply. Increasing the removal of conventional pollutants for this industry from 96% to 99% would allegedly cost almost twice as much per pound of pollutant as current treatment methods. CMA argued that this shift went well beyond the knee of the curve, and was therefore impermissible. EPA countered that the knee-of-the-curve test could be applied only to assess increases in limitations beyond BPT (that is, for BCT). The Fifth Circuit agreed with the agency:

> The BCT provisions were intended to establish an intermediate level between BPT and the stricter BAT limitations for conventional pollutants by adding a cost-effectiveness test for incremental technology requirements that exceed BPT technology. Under BCT, additional limitations on conven-

tional pollutants that are more stringent than BPT
can be imposed only "to the extent that the increased cost of treatment [would] be reasonable in
terms of the degree of environmental benefits."

The court concluded that cost played a different role in
BPT than in BCT. Regarding BPT, the only question is
"whether the costs are 'wholly disproportionate' to the
benefits." In contrast, cost weighs more heavily in
setting BCT. Note that FDF variances are available for
BCT under § 301(n), added by the 1987 amendments.

c. BAT

Section 301(b)(2) prescribes BAT effluent limitations for "nonconventional" and toxic pollutants.
Section 304(b)(2)(B) directs that BAT "shall take into
account" the age of equipment and facilities, the process
employed, engineering aspects of control techniques,
process changes, "the cost of achieving such effluent
reduction," and non-water quality environmental
impacts (including energy requirements). There is no
requirement of a balancing between the costs and
benefits of effluent reduction. Because § 301 mandates
compliance with BAT limitations by 1984 for toxic
pollutants, but fixes no deadline for nonconventional
pollutants, EPA's BAT program now is focused on
toxics. Effluent limitations and other controls on toxic
pollutants under the Clean Water Act are discussed in
Chapter 5. Here, we will consider only the availability
of variances.

Section 301(c) authorizes the Administrator to
grant a variance from BAT upon a showing that modified requirements: "(1) will represent the maximum use
of technology within the economic capacity of the

owner or operator; and (2) will result in reasonable further progress toward the elimination of the discharge of pollutants." Thus, consideration of individual economic impact, as well as environmental impact, is required. However, § 301(*l*) prohibits variances with respect to pollutants on the toxic pollutant list established under § 307. Thus, § 301(c) variances are available only for nonconventional pollutants.

The 1987 amendments added a new subsection, 301(n), expressly sanctioning FDF variances for BAT and BCT. Congress ratified the Supreme Court's views about FDF variances by limiting consideration to the factors involved in establishing the effluent limitations "other than cost," and by amending subsection (*l*) to make FDF variances available for toxics. The amendment also seems to ratify lower court decisions rejecting water quality as a factor in granting variances from BPT. Water quality is not a factor in establishing effluent limitations, and the amendments make it clear that the same factors are relevant at the variance stage as at the regulation stage.

Another source of BAT variances (but only for nontoxics) is § 301(g). This subsection allows variances based on water quality considerations. The applicant must show that the modification will not interfere with public water supplies, prevent a balanced population of wildlife and fish, or allow the discharge of toxics posing an unacceptable risk. The 1987 amendments limit 301(g) variances to a few well-studied nonconventional pollutants.

BCT = best conventional poll. cntrl Technology

d. Standards of Performance for New Sources

Section 306 directs the Administrator to establish federal standards of performance for new sources. The term "new source" includes any source, the "construction" (but not "modification") of which is commenced after EPA *proposal* of a § 306 standard which will apply to such source. "Standards of performance" must reflect the "greatest degree of effluent reduction which the Administrator determines to be achievable through application of the best available demonstrated control technology, processes, operating methods, or other alternatives, including, where practicable, a standard permitting no discharge of pollutants." In establishing such standards, the Administrator "shall take into consideration the cost of achieving such effluent reduction, and any non-water quality environmental impact and energy requirements."

The ability of owners and operators of individual new sources to comply with industry-wide standards may not be considered. In E.I. du Pont de Nemours & Co. v. Train (S.Ct. 1977), the Supreme Court noted that there was no statutory provision for variances, and concluded that variances would be inappropriate for a standard intended to ensure national uniformity and "maximum feasible control" of new sources.

D. ECONOMIC INCENTIVES FOR ENVIRONMENTAL PROTECTION

Preceding portions of this chapter dealt with abatement costs and lack of technology as constraints upon environmental protection. This section examines ways in which government can use economic incentives to promote environmental protection, primarily by increasing the cost of nonabatement to those causing environmental degradation.

Economists view a competitive market as the preferred means of allocating scarce resources in an "efficient" manner, that is, so as to maximize the total value of production. The market mechanism functions correctly, however, only if prices fully reflect the costs and benefits of production to the entire society. As discussed earlier, two factors which tend to distort the market system are the related problems of "externalities" and "collective goods." Pollution is a common form of external cost, a spillover effect of production which uses up other resources by degrading them. Collective goods are commodities which can not readily be supplied to specific persons without enabling large numbers of other persons to enjoy them as well. One example is the clean air produced by installation of emission control equipment.

Because of the free market's failure to provide adequate incentives, government must intervene to limit external costs and to facilitate production of collective goods. As discussed at the beginning of this chapter, the basic approaches are (1) recognition of *property rights,* with damage and injunctive remedies being available to injured owners; (2) *direct regulation,* e.g., emission limitations under the Clean Air Act; (3) *subsidies,* i.e., government payment of some of the expenses of avoiding external costs or producing collective goods; and (4) *charges* for activities generating external costs or failing to provide collective goods.

As we have seen, control of pollution via nuisance actions and direct regulation is not without problems.

Nuisance law proved inadequate to control widespread pollution from multiple sources. Even if plaintiffs can satisfy standing requirements and sustain the burden of proving material harm attributable to defendants' unreasonable conduct, courts may refuse injunctive relief after "balancing the equities." In addition, nuisance law fails to provide a systematic mechanism for supervising emissions. Direct regulation, by contrast, is systematic. However, it can involve enormous administrative costs because of the need to conduct economic analyses of entire industries, as well as mastering the technologies of production and pollution control. As we have seen, the resulting regulatory limits often are challenged in court on the ground that they do not represent "best practicable control technology" or some other statutory standard. Moreover, the economic benefits of delay may be so great in comparison that regulatory agencies may face widespread noncompliance.

One alternative to the regulatory approach is the use of subsidies. Typical subsidies employed for environmental management have included tax breaks (accelerated depreciation and credits), low interest loans, and grants for installation of treatment equipment. However, such financial incentives provide only part of the cost of the equipment. They reduce losses, but they do not make installation of abatement equipment profitable. Such subsidies may "sweeten" a regulatory program but cannot replace it. Furthermore, subsidies provide incentives only for investments in equipment. Often the most efficient ways to reduce discharges are to alter production processes, recover materials, produce marketable goods from by-products, or change the nature or quality of raw materials. Subsidies are better suited to encourage pollution control than pollution reduction.

Because of shortcomings in the first three types of public intervention enumerated above, economists and others have shown increasing interest in effluent charges and marketable discharge permits.

1. EFFLUENT CHARGES AND NON COMPLIANCE PENALTIES

An effluent charge system requires payment of a fee or tax on each unit of pollution released into the air or water. Reducing pollution by, say, 90% may be relatively inexpensive for some plants but very costly for others. Rather than a regulatory system with uniform effluent limitations, it may be preferable to have a variable standard that would focus pollution abatement where it costs the least. Each firm would reduce pollution to the point where the cost of removing an additional unit was the same as that for every other firm. With a fixed charge per unit of pollution, each discharger, if acting rationally, would remove pollution until the cost of removing an additional unit was greater than the effluent charge. The larger the charge, the greater the percentage of pollutants any firm would be motivated to remove, though firms with low costs of control would remove larger percentages than would firms with high abatement costs.

Fixing the levels of effluent charges poses some severe problems. Ideally, the legislature or administrative agency should impose on an environmentally damaging activity all of the external or social costs which it produces. A polluter then would pay for all the resources which it consumes. But computing total social damages involves enormous difficulties and probably is not practical. Other formulas for setting the charges therefore must be considered. One approach is based on the average costs of controlling pollution in various industries. Another is simply to set a charge which in practice provides sufficient incentive to cause polluters to reduce total discharges to socially acceptable levels.

Skepticism concerning the workability of effluent charges stems from concern that fully measuring the effluents actually produced by every source would be too difficult or expensive. While other methods of pollution control, such as direct regulation, do also require some monitoring of discharges, those systems usually do not require *continuous* monitoring for *all* polluters. The necessary technology has only recently become available in certain settings. Obviously the design of charge systems would have to be influenced to some extent by what it is technically and economically feasible to measure, and this may move such systems a considerable distance from the ideal mentioned above.

Despite avowed allegiance to the free market system, private businesses are among the strongest opponents of effluent charges. Many believe they are better off under the present regulatory system than under an effective charge system. Any realistic comparison between the two systems must take into consideration the probabilities of having to comply. Under a charge system, if the problem of monitoring discharges accurately can be solved, a firm is almost certain to have to pay the charge or to spend money to abate its pollution so as to reduce the charge. Under direct regulation, however, some firms decide that, because enforcement is cumbersome and ineffective, they either will never have to pay for expensive controls or can gain the financial advantages of years of delay beyond official deadlines.

Noncompliance penalties under the Clean Air Act are aimed precisely at denying polluters such financial advantages from delay. Section 120, added in 1977, provides that EPA or the state "shall" assess and collect a noncompliance penalty against "every" person who owns or operates (i) a "major" stationary source (other than certain smelters) which violates any applicable implementation plan, (ii) a stationary source which violates an emission limitation, emission standard, standard of performance, or other requirement established under § 111 or 112, or (iii) a stationary source for which an extension, order, suspension, or consent decree is in effect, and which violates any applicable interim control requirement or schedule of compliance. (The owner or operator was formerly exempted from the penalty if it demonstrated that its failure to comply was "due solely" to "an inability to comply . . ., for which inability the source has received [a delayed compliance] order under Section 113(d) . . . [and] which inability results from reasons entirely beyond [its] control." Since EPA and states no longer have authority to issue DCOs, this provision is no longer in effect.) The amount of the penalty assessed under § 120 shall be equal to "no less than the economic value which a delay in compliance beyond July 1, 1979 may have for the owner of such source," including both capital and operating costs, minus any expenditures actually made for the purpose of bringing the source into and maintaining compliance. Fines under § 120 are in addition to other civil or criminal sanctions which may be imposed under the Act or state or local law.

The Clean Water Act, as a result of the 1987 amendments, now provides for administrative penalties of up to $250,000. The amount is to be determined based on a variety of factors, one of which is the degree of "economic benefit or savings (if any) resulting from the violation." These administrative penalties may approximate the noncompliance penalties under the Clean Air Act.

It should be noted that, under a pure effluent charge system, there would be no requirement that a polluter limit its discharges at all. So long as it was willing to pay the charges, then it would be in compliance with the law. This is not true with a system involving charges only for discharges in excess of publicly established effluent limitations. Thus, noncompliance penalties render the regulatory system more effective but do not make the standards more economically efficient, unlike a pure charge system. Another attractive aspect of the pure charge system is that a polluter *always* has some financial incentive to reduce his pollution further, down to zero. No such continuing incentive exists under either a pure regulatory system, or under a system imposing effluent charges only on discharges in excess of regulatory limits.

2. MARKETABLE DISCHARGE PERMITS

Another system of economic incentives that increasingly has attracted attention would allocate discharge rights by means of publicly issued permits, which could be sold to other present or prospective dischargers, or to nondischargers entering the market for speculative or environmentalist purposes. Most proposals would limit the duration of permits to some specified time, such as five or ten years. The initial permittees could be chosen in several ways. Permits could be allocated among existing polluters (free or for a price), or among broader groups of applicants by auction or lottery.

Once the permits have been allocated initially, they become transferable, and sale prices function as free-market equivalents of officially established effluent charges. Like an effluent charge system, a system of marketable permits provides some continuous incentive for individual sources to improve pollution control methods, since funds could be freed by sale of unneeded permits for the going price. However, the permit system would involve two distinct advantages over a charge system. First, the permit system would avoid the problems of setting effluent charges at the proper level. The government would set the price of a permit, if at all, only at the time of its initial issuance. If the price were wrongly fixed in relation to market forces, there would be automatic adjustments as permits were resold. The second advantage would be that, even if prices were "wrongly" fixed by the government or the market, there nevertheless would be a fixed limit on total permissible discharges. Excessive discharges and damage to the environment would not be legal, as they would be under an effluent charge system (assuming willingness to pay the effluent charges), but could occur only through outright violation of the permit.

It should be noted that transfers of permits from one geographic area to another—e.g., from one stretch of a stream to another, or from one portion of an air quality control region to another—might have to be regulated by exchange rates, set by the issuing authority so that trading could not cause water or air quality to fall below the prescribed ambient standard at any site. (Otherwise, the permit system would need to be backed-up by regulatory standards). For example, if discharges of BOD into stream zone B would be twice as harmful to a critical reach as identical discharges into zone A further upstream, a permit might allow a polluter to discharge either one pound per day into zone B or two pounds per day into zone A. Very fine distinctions between zones and the amounts of discharges authorized would better protect water or air quality, but also would complicate transfers and perhaps impair the marketability of permits.

The most ambitious effort to implement a federal marketable permit system is now found in the acid rain provisions of the Clean Air Act. Prior to 1990, the Act had proved completely ineffective in dealing with acid rain. Two provisions of the Act, §§ 110(a)(2)(E) and 126, give EPA limited authority to take action against interstate pollution. EPA declined, however, to implement that authority, and its position was consistently upheld by the courts. (For the first time, EPA has recently broken with this tradition of ignoring interstate spillovers, by invoking these provisions in connection with the problem of interstate transport of ozone.) During the 1980s, acid rain received increasing attention from environmentalists and the general public. Under the Reagan Administration, however, Congress and the executive were at loggerheads over the issue. The deadlock between Congress and the White House was finally broken with the passage of the 1990 amendments. Title IV of the amendments is devoted to acid rain. It imposes a completely new approach to the problem, which was originally devised by the Bush Administration.

The system is based on a system of allowances that can be banked or sold by emitters. Each allowance is equivalent to one ton of emissions. A utility can emit SO_2 only to the extent permitted by its allowances. The allowances are allocated largely on the basis of past emissions and fuel consumption, but there are extra allowances for a variety of purposes. For example, from 1995 to 1999, an extra 200,000 allowances are allocated to power plants in Illinois, Indiana, and Ohio.

A complex set of initial allowances was established to cut SO_2 emissions to 8.9 million tons by 2000. The program is divided into two phases. In Phase I, over a hundred plants (individually listed in the statute) must meet a standard of 2.5 pounds of SO_2 per million Btus. The 111 utility power plants in question are those that in 1990 emitted more than 2.5 pounds of SO_2 per million Btus. (For example, generator # 1 at the Colbert plant in Alabama is given a Phase I allowance of 13,570 tons.) The deadline for this standard was 1995, except that plants using scrubbers to meet the standards were given until 1997. These provisions are intended to encourage the use of scrubbers and thereby continue at least part of the market for eastern high-sulfur coal. The Phase I allowances are expected to reduce SO_2 emissions by about ten million tons per year.

Phase II requires utilities to reduce emissions by an additional 50%. Large, poorly controlled plants must reduce emissions to 1.2 million lbs./mBtu. A complex formula applies to smaller plants. The deadline for compliance is 2000. Total emissions cannot exceed 8.9 million tons annually, but for the first ten years, EPA will have a half million extra allowances in reserve. A further forty thousand allowances can be given to high-growth states. A four-year extension is available for units that use new clean coal technologies.

In part, the system of allocations embodies the efficiency concerns of economists. The system of allowances seems to have been manipulated, however, in the interests of regional equity, so that utilities that are required to engage in heavy investments will be able to recoup part of their expenses. The initial allocations are large enough that some of these utilities will find it feasible to control emissions more than required to stay within their initial allowances, thereby allowing them to sell excess allowances. At least some of these allowances will have to be purchased by new utility plants in order to operate, helping to defray the cost of controlling emissions from the older plants.

Sulfur dioxide allowances became truly marketable when the Chicago Board of Trade voted to create a private market for them. Implementation of the program is now underway. The results of initial auctions of allowances were disappointing. However, private trades between firms now seem more common, and transfers of allowances between a single firm's plants are not infrequent. An ambitious system of marketable air pollution permits has also been established by state regulators for the Los Angeles area. Both programs are being carefully studied. The federal program seems to have succeeded in reducing the cost of controlling acid rain, aided by some fortuitous economic shifts. The

success or failure of these two programs may determine
the future of the concept of marketable permits.

CHAPTER 4

RISK MANAGEMENT AND SCIENTIFIC UNCERTAINTY

This chapter explores some special problems associated with regulation of hazardous and toxic substances. Primary among these is pervasive scientific uncertainty about long-term human effects of exposure to small amounts of such substances. In the face of uncertainty which no party to a regulatory or judicial proceeding may be able to resolve, rules concerning risk assessment, causation, presumptions, burden of proof, sharing of liability, and scope of judicial review become critically important.

A. INTRODUCTION TO RISK ASSESSMENT AND RISK MANAGEMENT

Risk *assessment* is the use of scientific data to define the probability of some harm coming to an individual or a population because of exposure to a substance or situation. Risk *management* is the process of deciding how to deal with a risk that has been determined to exist. Risk management includes taking into account the technical feasibility of reducing risk, in light of social, economic and political factors.

There are three types of risk assessment. They can address short-term health risks (e.g., food poisoning), long-term health risks (e.g., cancer, a focus of this chapter), and ecological risks (e.g., global warming). These assessments employ a variety of methodologies ranging from testing rats to doing fieldwork on a mountain stream. The results can be expressed as a safe-unsafe dichotomy or as a quantitative estimate to six decimal places.

EPA uses risk assessment to predict the probability of developing cancer as a result of exposure to a particular agent. Risk assessment of a carcinogen involves four steps: (1) hazard identification, (2) dose-response evaluation, (3) exposure assessment, and (4) risk characterization. Hazard identification is the process of determining whether an "agent" (for example, an industrial chemical) increases a person's risk of developing cancer. Dose-response evaluation reveals how the likelihood of cancer changes with the level of exposure. A risk assessor might estimate, for example, how the probability of lung cancer changes with the number of cigarettes smoked. The third step, exposure assessment, quantifies the amount, or dose, of the carcinogen to which people may be exposed. This may be the amount of a chemical in the air near a factory or the amounts of various foods which an individual consumes each day. After these quantitative inputs to a risk assessment have been determined, the numbers are combined to yield an, overall estimate of risk. This risk characterization usually is expressed numerically as the incremental lifetime risk of cancer due to a particular agent at a particular level of exposure. Good risk characterizations should contain not only a final risk number but also a discussion of the uncertainties in and assumptions behind the assessment; unfortunately, such discussion rarely is included.

Separating the assessment of risk from its management is often difficult in practice. One reason is that human or social values, which are supposed to be considered in risk management, also may influence risk assessment. For example, suppose that a chemical is tested on laboratory animals to determine whether it can cause cancer, and that a proportion of the animals exposed does develop tumors. In order to assess the risk of humans contracting cancer from exposure to the chemical—that is, to develop a "dose-response curve"—a number of steps are required, each of which usually entails a substantial degree of uncertainty. Thus, the doses given to the laboratory animals are extremely high, while environmental exposures of humans typically are much lower. To determine the human dose-response curve, one must extrapolate down from the high-dose laboratory data. There are various statistical models for doing this, all of which fit the data, are open to debate, and yield very different predictions. Beyond that problem, it is necessary to extrapolate cancer data from animals to humans, and to deal with uncertainty about the levels of human exposure. All of these uncertainties inherent in risk assessment combine to produce a very wide range of risk estimates in most cases. Thus, a National Academy of Sciences report on saccharin concluded that over a period of 70 years the expected number of cases of human bladder cancer resulting from daily exposure to 120 milligrams of saccharin might range from 0.22 to 1,144,000. Because such a range is of limited use to policymakers, a risk assessor may try to narrow it. However, any such narrowing process is influenced by the scientist's personal and professional experience and values.

Scientists now believe that approximately 85% of all cancers are caused by broad environmental factors, including life-style patterns. The rest presumably have a hereditary basis or arise from spontaneous metabolic events. Identifying the environmental factors in cancer has not been easy. Tobacco is thought to be responsible for roughly 30% of all cancers, while a study done for the Congressional Office of Technology Assessment estimated that 35% of all cancer deaths in the United States were caused by dietary factors *other* than chemical additives and pollutants, such as natural carcinogens, excess fats that increase production of carcinogens in the body, and lack of fibers to flush potential carcinogens out of the bowels. The study concluded that less than 8% of cancer deaths resulted from carcinogens in the work place, environmental pollution, food additives, and industrial products.

If indeed almost two-thirds of all cancer deaths are caused by smoking and by dietary factors other than chemical additives and pollutants, while less than one-tenth are caused by carcinogens in the workplace, environmental pollution, food additives, and industrial products, what should be the government's strategy for reducing cancer mortality? As materials in this chapter and Chapter 5 indicate, our regulatory efforts (other than requiring labels warning smokers of health risks) have in fact been directed mostly at the latter four causes.

To date, statistical models that predict chemicals will not cause cancer until humans have been exposed to certain "threshold" levels have failed to gain general acceptance within the scientific community; in regulating suspected carcinogens, agencies therefore assume that risk is linear at lower dose levels, i.e., that there is at least some risk associated with any exposure.

A basic fact about risk management is that there is a difference between a "safe" world and "zero-risk" world. We all encounter risks of many kinds in our lives. Some, like earthquakes and disease, may be attributable to nature while others, such as automobile accidents and mishaps at nuclear power plants, usually are attributable to human actions. Hence, in many situations "safety" can not be absolute but must entail an "acceptable" level of risk, however and by whomever that level may be defined. In some cases the decision may be made by an "expert" risk manager, while in other cases it may be a function of the political process.

Selective aversion to certain risks may entail acceptance of other greater risks. For example, the use of new vaccines entails some risk, but a decision not to use them may be even riskier for the society as a whole. Therefore, the objective of public risk management should be minimization, not elimination, of risk-related costs.

"Public risks" is a recent term for distinctively high-tech hazards. Peter Huber has defined public risks as man-made "threats to human health or safety that are centrally or mass-produced, broadly distributed, and largely outside the individual risk bearer's direct understanding and control." "Private risks," on the other hand, are of natural origin or, if man-made, produced in relatively discrete units, with local impacts more or less subject to personal control. Hence, disease is a natural private risk, automobile accidents are man-made private risks, and effects of new technologies like recombinant DNA are public risks. Many public risks are latent, so that adverse effects do not appear until long after exposure. Such risks also are often diffuse in their impact, spread over many victims, so that the costs to any one victim may be small even though the aggregate costs to all victims may be very large. Two common characteristics of public risks are a potential for catastrophic costs, and a low "subjective" probability (lacking a solid actuarial basis) of the catastrophic outcome. Together, these characteristics can produce a "zero-infinity dilemma" for risk managers dealing with problems such as the threat of a Chernobyl-type nuclear accident.

Technical experts tend to rank the risks of various technologies according to their estimates of annual fatalities. William Lowrance has shown that lay persons, on the other hand, tend to consider a greater number of factors in judging the seriousness of risks: involuntary exposure, delayed effects, "dreaded" versus common hazards, irreversible consequences, and others. The general public is more concerned than the experts about risks that have catastrophic potential, that are unfamiliar, uncontrollable or involuntary, that threaten future generations, that would concentrate fatalities in time or space, that are distinctively threatening as opposed to widespread and shared by the general population, and that have human as opposed to natural origins.

Clayton Gillette and James Krier have analyzed possible reasons for these popular views. With respect to voluntariness, for example, they see underlying concerns about autonomy, equality and power among individuals in the society. The special dislike for latency and irreversibility is explained by the fact that latency frustrates knowledge and irreversibility frustrates control; both impair free choice. As for the bias against man-made rather than natural hazards, people are responsible only for artificial risks, not for natural ones; and the government's job is to regulate what people do. Finally, lay persons' "dread" of catastrophic events is related to notions of inequitable distributions of risk within the society or between generations.

B. JUDICIAL VIEWS CONCERNING MANAGEMENT OF UNCERTAIN RISKS

1. EARLY LOWER COURT DECISIONS

A leading case on the problem of scientific uncertainty was Reserve Mining Co. v. EPA (8th Cir.1975). Reserve Mining disposed of great quantities of mining byproducts by discharging them into Lake Superior. These materials contained asbestos, a known cause of cancer when inhaled. The district court ordered an immediate halt to all further discharges, which would have required closing the facility. On appeal, the Eighth Circuit considered three issues: (1) whether the ingestion of fibers, as opposed to inhalation, posed any health hazard, (2) whether that hazard was sufficiently great to justify judicial intervention, and (3) what form the remedy should take.

In considering the question of risk the court was handicapped by a lack of scientific evidence. The district court had directed a study of the tissues of long-time Duluth residents to determine whether asbestos fibers were present. The plaintiffs' principal medical witness had testified that the study should disclose the presence of asbestos if indeed asbestos is absorbed by the body. Nevertheless, the study failed to indicate that Duluth residents had any greater amounts of asbestos in their tissues than did residents of Houston, where the water was free of asbestos fibers. Moreover, animal tests intended to determine whether ingested fibers penetrate into the body were inconclusive and produced conflicting results. On the other hand, strong evidence did exist that workers exposed to asbestos dust suffered from a moderately increased rate of gastrointestinal cancer. One possible explanation, according to expert witnesses, was that asbestos workers first inhaled the asbestos dust and then coughed up and swallowed the asbestos particles. Taking all of this evidence together, the most the court could conclude was that public exposure to asbestos fibers "creates some health risk." The court was unable to conclude, however, that "the probability of harm is more likely than not."

The next issue to confront the court was whether this showing of harm was sufficient to satisfy the requirements of the Clean Water Act. The Act authorized suit by the federal government to abate discharges in interstate waters where the discharges "endanger ... the health or welfare of persons." (Compare § 504 of the current CWA.) After careful consideration of the statute, the court concluded that the requirement of a danger to public health was satisfied by the evidence before it.

The final question was the form of the relief. The district court had ordered an immediate halt to discharges. Because of the weakness of the evidence of harm, the cost to both industry and the public of closing the plant, and the company's willingness to spend $243 million to dispose of the materials more safely, the court held that closing the plant was unnecessary. Balancing the equities, the court ordered that Reserve be given a reasonable time to stop discharging its wastes into Lake Superior.

The *Reserve Mining* decision received strong support from the D.C. Circuit's opinion in Ethyl Corp. v. EPA (D.C.Cir.1976)(en banc). That case involved § 211(c)(1)(A) of the Clean Air Act, which authorized EPA to regulate gasoline additives whose emission products "will endanger the public health or welfare." EPA determined that lead additives in gasoline presented "a significant risk of harm" to the public health and issued orders limiting the use of such additives. As in *Reserve Mining,* the court was faced with a high degree of scientific uncertainty. The uncertainty was not as to the harmfulness of lead emissions, which were well known to be toxic. Because human beings were exposed to multiple sources of lead, it was difficult to determine whether the incremental increase in the amount of lead in the environment due to gasoline additives had serious health effects. In upholding EPA, the court stressed that assessment of risks involves policy judgments rather than simply factual determinations. Thus, the court accorded substantial deference to EPA's conclusion. As the court explained:

> Questions involving the environment are particularly prone to uncertainty. Technological man has altered his world in ways never before experienced or anticipated. The health effects of

such alterations are often unknown, sometimes unknowable. While a concerned Congress has passed legislation providing for protection of the public health against gross environmental modifications, the regulators entrusted with the enforcement of such laws have not thereby been endowed with a prescience that removes all doubt from their decision making. Rather, speculation, conflicts, and theoretical extrapolation typify their every action. How else can they act, given a mandate to protect the public health but only a slight or non-existent data base upon which to draw? ...

Undoubtedly, certainty is a scientific ideal—to the extent that even science can be certain of its truth. But certainty in the complexities of environmental medicine may be achievable only after the fact, when scientists have the opportunity for leisurely and isolated scrutiny of an entire mechanism. Awaiting certainty will often allow for only reactive, not preventive regulation. Petitioners suggest that anything less than certainty, that any speculation, is irresponsible. But when statutes seek to avoid environmental catastrophe, can preventive, albeit uncertain, decisions legitimately be so labeled?

Thus, the court concluded that a rigorous, step-by-step proof of cause and effect should not be demanded where a statute is precautionary in nature, the evidence is on the frontiers of scientific knowledge, and regulations are designed to protect the public health. Hence, EPA may apply its expertise to draw conclusions from "suspected, but not completely substantiated" relationships between facts, from trends among facts, from theoretical projections, and so forth.

This approach was followed in numerous other lower court opinions. For example, in Lead Industries Association, Inc. v. EPA (D.C.Cir.1980), the D.C. Circuit upheld a primary air quality standard for lead which incorporated an "adequate margin of safety." In setting the margin of safety, EPA had given no consideration to feasibility or cost. Moreover, the evidence of harm was unclear. Nevertheless, the court held that feasibility and cost were irrelevant and that EPA had acted properly in setting the margin of safety. As the court explained, use of a margin of safety is an important method of protecting against effects which have not yet been uncovered by research and effects whose medical significance is a matter of disagreement. As the court also explained, "Congress has recently acknowledged that more often than not the 'margins of safety' that are incorporated into air quality standards turn out to be very modest or non-existent, as new information reveals adverse health effects at pollution levels once thought to be harmless." The court also reiterated the need for deference to EPA's expert judgments on these issues. Finally, the court held that the margin of safety requirement could be fulfilled by making conservative decisions at various points in the regulatory process, rather than by determining a safe level and adding a percentage to that as the "margin of safety."

In general, these lower court decisions demonstrated a high degree of deference to EPA's expert judgment. They gave little weight to questions of cost and feasibility when dealing with toxic chemicals. Finally, these courts recognized that administrative action was justified without a showing that harmful effects were more likely than not. Instead, the courts concluded that regulatory intervention was justified whenever a substantial possibility of danger could be found.

2. SUPREME COURT DECISIONS

The Supreme Court did not have occasion to consider the problem of toxic chemicals until 1980. It has now decided two cases in the area. Before considering these cases, it should be noted that they arose in a somewhat different context from most environmental issues. Both cases involved protection of workers by the Occupational Safety and Health Administration (OSHA). The cases thus involved a rather special kind of environmental problem, since the environments in question were not used by the general public.

The policy issues presented in OSHA cases are rather different from those in normal environmental cases. First, exposure to the risk is somewhat more voluntary than is exposure to, say, ambient air pollution. Second, negotiations between the source of the hazard and the possible victims are feasible to a much greater extent than in the normal pollution case. This is especially true when the victims of the hazard, the employees, are represented by a union. Thus, the transaction costs of private settlements are sometimes much smaller here. Third, the possible victims of the hazard have a much greater stake in the economic health of the enterprise creating the hazard than is the case generally in environmental disputes. The option of closing the plant down in order to end the hazard is generally not acceptable to the workers, nor are actions which would seriously jeopardize the prospects for continued employment. For all of these reasons, the balance between protection from risks versus economic cost may be different than in the normal environmental case.

Moreover, the statutory scheme is primarily concerned with quite different problems of worker protection. The only provision dealing expressly with toxic chemicals is § 6(b)(5) of the Act, 29 U.S.C.A. § 655(d)(5). This provision requires the agency to set a standard for any toxic material "which most adequately assures, to the extent feasible, that no employee will suffer material impairment of health or functional capacity. . . ." Another section of the Act, § 3(8), 29 U.S.C.A. § 652(8), was thought to be relevant by at least some members of the Court. This section simply defines an occupational safety and health standard as a regulation setting any one of a variety of requirements "reasonably necessary or appropriate to provide safe or healthful places of employment." These provisions provide less guidance than most of the analogous provisions of the Clean Air Act or Clean Water Act. In short, both the statutory context and the policy choices presented in this area are atypical.

The Supreme Court's first encounter with the problem of toxic chemicals was Industrial Union Department, AFL–CIO v. American Petroleum Institute (S.Ct.1980). (This decision is generally known as the "benzene case.") The case involved an OSHA regulation governing benzene. Benzene was acknowledged to be a carcinogen, and no safe level of exposure was known. On this basis, the Secretary of Labor had set the permissible exposure level for workers at 1 ppm (part per million), which he considered the lowest

feasible level. OSHA estimated the total cost of compliance as including $266 million in capital investments,
$200 million in first-year start-up costs, and $34 million
in annual costs. About 35,000 employees would benefit
from the regulation. The Fifth Circuit had struck down
the regulation on the theory that the statute implicitly
required a cost-benefit analysis by the agency. On
review, only one member of the Supreme Court reached
this issue; another member of the Court went off on a
constitutional ground; and the Court divided 4–4 on
another statutory issue.

The primary opinion was written by Justice Stevens
but was joined in its entirety by only two other Justices,
Burger and Stewart, who are no longer on the Court.
Justice Powell, also now retired, joined parts of the
opinion. This plurality opinion resolved the case on the
basis of an interpretation of § 3(8) as a limitation on §
6(b). According to the plurality opinion, § 3(8) requires
that OSHA make a threshold finding of a "significant
risk of harm" before issuing any regulation. On close
examination of the record, the plurality observed that
the industry had argued that the regulation would save
at most two lives every six years. According to the
plurality, a risk of one in a billion is clearly insignificant,
but a risk of one in a thousand "might well" be considered significant. The Court declined to determine
whether the risk level alleged by industry would be
considered significant, since the agency itself had made
no finding on this issue, which the plurality thought to
be a critical requirement of the Act.

The plurality opinion went to some lengths to rebut
the dissent's charge that the plurality's approach would
prevent effective regulation until deaths had actually

occurred. First, the plurality stated that what constitutes a "significant" risk was a judgment for the agency to make and plainly involved policy considerations. Second, the plurality noted that the agency's findings need not be supported by "anything approaching scientific certainty." The agency must be given "some leeway" when its findings are made on the frontiers of scientific knowledge. Thus, the plurality concluded:

> [S]o long as they are supported by a body of reputable scientific thought, the Agency is free to use conservative assumptions in interpreting the data with respect to carcinogens, risking error on the side of over-protection rather than under-protection.

In a concurring opinion Chief Justice Burger was careful to stress the limitations of the plurality opinion:

> A holding that the Secretary must retrace his steps with greater care and consideration is not to be taken in derogation of the scope of legitimate Agency discretion. When the facts and arguments have been presented and duly considered, the Secretary must make a policy judgment as to whether a specific risk of health impairment is significant in terms of the policy objectives of the statute. When he acts in this capacity, pursuant to the legislative authority delegated by Congress, he exercises the prerogatives of the legislature—to focus on only one aspect of a larger problem, or to promulgate regulations that, to some, may appear as imprudent policy or inefficient allocation of resources. The judicial function does not extend to substantive revision of regulatory policy.

The Chief Justice noted however, that "[p]erfect safety is a chimera; regulation must not strangle human activity in the search for the impossible."

Justice Powell was the only member of the Court to reach the cost-benefit issue. He agreed with the plurality opinion's reading of the statute. He also concluded, however, that the Agency was required to give fuller consideration to cost than it had done.

Thus, four Justices, three of whom are no longer on the Court, based their votes on statutory grounds. The decisive fifth vote was cast by Justice Rehnquist, who reached his decision on constitutional grounds. He concluded that Congress had in fact provided no standard at all concerning the threshold requirements for regulation. He believed that Congress was simply unwilling to decide the relative weights to be given to protection of human life versus economic cost. Because Congress had failed to make this basic policy decision, Justice Rehnquist argued that the statute was an unconstitutional delegation of legislative authority to the agency. This view was somewhat out of line with the Supreme Court's decisions over the preceding half century. Not since the Court's unsuccessful attempt to block the New Deal has the Court struck down a statute on this basis, though at least three Justices today probably would be willing to revive the so-called nondelegation doctrine.

Justice Marshall wrote a stinging dissent, joined by Justices Brennan, White and Blackmun. All have since left the Court. Justice Marshall found it incredible that the plurality could read any substantive meaning into the statutory definition of a health standard as one "reasonably necessary" to provide safe employment. In his view, the relevant section of the statute was plainly § 6, and the meaning of that section was clear: in dealing with any toxic chemical, the Secretary was to set a standard which would *ensure* that no risk would be presented to any employee. Furthermore, Justice Marshall argued that the "plurality's discussion of the record in this case is both extraordinarily arrogant and extraordinarily unfair." In his view, the Court was usurping the agency's power to make factual findings and was mischaracterizing virtually every aspect of the agency's decision. He concluded by accusing the plurality of "an extreme reaction to a regulatory scheme that, as the members of the plurality perceived it, imposed an unduly harsh burden on regulated industries."

This decision clearly left the law in a state of confusion. Four Justices, only one of whom is still on the Court, believed that a "significant risk" finding was required by the statute. Four other Justices, all of whom have now left the Court, disagreed, while the final member believed that the statute was completely silent on the problem. Moreover, to the extent that the plurality approach represented the law, its meaning was quite unclear. In particular, the test for a "significant risk" was not stated with clarity. Finally, the standard used by the plurality seemed to be set too high. The plurality said a one-in-a-thousand risk "might well" be considered significant. As applied to the general population, such a risk level would mean approximately 240,000 deaths. How many additional deaths would be required before the plurality would find a risk *clearly* significant?

The Supreme Court's second OSHA decision did little to clarify this issue. That case, American Textile Manufacturers Institute, Inc. v. Donovan (S.Ct.1981), was decided one year after the benzene case. *Textile Manufacturers* involved a standard regulating cotton dust. Cotton dust is the cause of a disease called byssinosis, more commonly known as "brown lung" disease. The primary issue before the Supreme Court was whether the agency was required to engage in a cost-benefit analysis when issuing its regulation. In an opinion by Justice Brennan, the Court held that no cost-benefit analysis was necessary. According to the Court, all that is necessary is a feasibility analysis, that is, an analysis showing that performance is possible but not an analysis comparing the cost of compliance with the benefits of the regulation.

The benzene case was discussed only in a footnote in *Textile Manufacturers.* The Court's discussion was not very helpful because the risk issue in *Textile Manufacturers* was easy to resolve. OSHA had expressly found that "exposure to cotton dust presents a significant health hazard to employees." Data relied on by the agency showed that 25% of all industry employees suffered at least low-grade byssinosis, and that even at the level required by the new standard, about half this many employees would suffer from the disease. Thus, the prevalence of the disease "should be significantly reduced" by the new regulation. As the Court said, "It is difficult to imagine what else the Agency could do to comply with this Court's decision in [the benzene case]."

The implications of these OSHA decisions for toxics regulation in general were unclear. The four

dissenters in the benzene case clearly endorsed the
approach previously taken by lower courts in cases like
Reserve Mining. The members of the plurality in the
benzene case took a more cautious view, but did not
squarely reject the then prevailing approach in the
lower courts. One member of the Court, Justice
Rehnquist, never spoke to the merits of any of these
issues. Most members of the present (1996) Court were
not present for the decision of either of these cases.

3. LATER LOWER COURT DECISIONS

Two court of appeals decisions since the Supreme
Court's OSHA cases raise questions concerning the
continuing authority of *Reserve Mining* and its progeny,
pages 151-156 supra. Most importantly, to what extent
may the plurality's "significant risk" regulatory threshold in *Industrial Union* now be applied in non-OSHA
toxics cases? Also, in light of *Textile Manufacturers'*
rejection of the claimed need to employ cost-benefit
analysis under OSHA, when may lower courts require
agencies to engage in such analysis under other environmental laws?

In NRDC v. EPA (D.C.Cir.1987)(en banc), EPA
had refused to set a zero-emission limitation for vinyl
chloride, though acknowledging that such a standard
seemed to be the only one which would offer complete
safety from ambient exposure to this apparently non-
threshold carcinogen. Section 112 of the Clean Air Act
then required the Administrator to regulate hazardous
air pollutants "at a level which in his judgment provides
an ample margin of safety to protect public health."
EPA interpreted this language to authorize regulatory
standards requiring reduction of emissions to the

"lowest level achievable by the use of best available technology in cases involving apparent non-threshold pollutants, where complete emission prohibition would result in widespread industry closure and EPA has determined that the cost of such closure would be grossly disproportionate to the benefits of removing the risk that would remain after imposition of the best available control technology." The court rejected this interpretation, saying that the Administrator had simply substituted technological feasibility for health as the primary consideration under § 112.

However, the court did not order a zero-emission standard. Instead, the court held that the Administrator was required to make an initial determination of what was "safe," based exclusively upon his determination of the risk to health at a particular emission level. Citing the plurality opinion in *Industrial Union,* the court of appeals said specifically that "safe" need not mean "risk-free." Rather, the Administrator's decision should be based upon "expert judgment" regarding the level of emissions that would result in an "acceptable" risk to health. Only after this degree of "safety" was assured could the Administrator consider what was an "ample margin," taking into account the inherent limitations of risk assessment and the limited scientific knowledge of the effects of exposure to carcinogens at various levels. At that point he could "diminish" the statistically determined "safe" level of risk by setting the regulatory standard at the lowest feasible level.

The other important lower court decision in this area is Corrosion Proof Fittings v. EPA (5th Cir.1991). This case was decided under the Toxic Substances Control Act (TSCA, pages 176-182 infra). The factual finding necessary to trigger the regulatory provisions of § 6(a) of TSCA is that there is a "reasonable basis" to conclude that the chemical substance "presents or will present an unreasonable risk of injury to health or the environment." Having made such a finding, EPA may by rule apply one or more of seven types of restrictions listed in § 6(a), "to the extent necessary to protect adequately against such risk using the least burdensome requirements." The restrictions range from prohibiting the manufacture or distribution of the chemical (most burdensome) to directing the manufacturer to give notice of the risk of injury (least burdensome). Section 6(c) mandates a hybrid rulemaking procedure, including informal hearings and a limited right of cross-examination. Under § 19(c), a court of appeals must set aside a rule adopted under § 6 if the court finds that the rule is "not supported by substantial evidence in the rule-making record."

In *Corrosion Proof Fittings*, the court vacated a final EPA rule which would have prohibited the manufacture, importation, processing, and distribution of asbestos in almost all products. The rule was ten years in the making and represented the first time EPA had used its authority under section 6 to place a comprehensive ban on a dangerous substance. The court held that EPA had violated TSCA by not considering adequately the benefits and costs of less burdensome alternatives to a complete ban, by not allowing public comment and cross-examination on methodology adopted at the last minute by EPA to support its benefits calculation, and by not evaluating the toxicity of likely substitute products (some of which were also carcinogens) that would replace asbestos in its various applications.

The court emphasized that TSCA is not a "zero-risk" statute, and that the substantial evidence standard for judicial review under TSCA is less deferential than the arbitrary and capricious standard of the Administrative Procedure Act. The court said that while agency rules have a presumption of validity, "The burden remains on the EPA . . . to justify that the products it bans present an unreasonable risk, no matter how regulated," citing the plurality opinion in *Industrial Union*. The court of appeals reacted unfavorably to the fact that EPA's benefit-cost analysis resulted in figures as high as $74 million per life saved. For example, EPA said that its ban on asbestos pipe would save three lives over 13 years at a cost of $128–227 million; that its ban on asbestos shingles would cost $23–34 million to save 0.32 statistical lives; that its ban on asbestos coatings would cost $46–181 million to save 3.33 lives; and that its ban of asbestos paper products would save 0.60 lives at a cost of $4–5 million. The court said, "[U]ntil an agency 'can provide substantial evidence that the benefits to be achieved by [a regulation] bear a reasonable relationship to the costs imposed by the reduction, it cannot show that the standard is reasonably necessary.' "

While the estimated dollar costs per life saved under EPA's asbestos rule seemed very high, subsequent studies have shown that costs almost as high are expected under some other EPA regulatory programs, such as those related to pesticides and carcinogenic air pollutants. A study by Resources for the Future indicated that EPA implicitly had attached a value of $15–45 million to the prevention of one case of cancer (much more than individuals appear to be willing to spend themselves to reduce their own risk of death). On the other hand, some government programs seem to set the implicit value of life lower than do individuals.

TSCA (like FIFRA, the federal pesticide law, pages 169-174 infra) accords greater weight to industry interests, in relation to environmental and health considerations, than do the Clean Air and Clean Water Acts. Hence, *Corrosion Proof Fittings* should not imply an "unreasonable risk" threshold to toxics regulation in general. However, the vinyl chloride case, page 163 supra, decided under Clean Air Act, does seem to draw from *Industrial Union* a requirement that regulation should respond only to "significant risks," and should aim at reducing them to "acceptable" rather than zero-risk levels.

The extent to which the *Industrial Union* and vinyl chloride decisions impair the precedential value of *Reserve Mining* is unclear, though they do seem consistent with its progeny, such as *Ethyl* and *Lead Industries*, pages 153-156 supra. The approach of *Reserve Mining* does still seem to be followed in cases arising under the "imminent hazard" provisions of the general pollution statutes and of RCRA (see page 203 infra).

CHAPTER 5

CONTROL OF TOXIC SUBSTANCES

Sections A, B and C-1, 2 and 3 of this chapter examine legislation regulating the sale of toxic chemicals and the disposal of hazardous wastes. Sections C-4, D and G discuss statutory and common law civil liability for cleanups of waste disposal sites and for personal injuries and property damages caused by toxic substances. Section E outlines federal requirements that businesses publicly report toxic chemical inventories, usage, manufacture, and releases. Section F concerns criminal liability under RCRA, the Clean Water Act, and other federal environmental laws.

A. REGULATING THE SALE OF TOXIC SUBSTANCES

1. PESTICIDE REGULATION

The earliest toxic chemical problem to receive widespread public attention was that of pesticides, thanks in large part to Rachael Carson's *Silent Spring*. The principal federal statute regulating pesticides is the Federal Insecticide, Fungicide and Rodenticide Act. Congress amended FIFRA in 1972 by enacting the Federal Environmental Pesticide Control Act, 7 U.S.C.A. § 136, which then was amended substantially in 1975, 1978, 1988, 1990 and 1996. In its present form, FIFRA provides a comprehensive framework for regulating the sale and distribution of pesticides within the United States.

Under the statute, a pesticide may receive EPA approval only if it "will not generally cause unreasonable adverse effects on the environment" when used in accordance with any EPA-imposed restrictions and "with widespread and commonly recognized practice." 7 U.S.C.A. § 136a(5)(D). "Unreasonable adverse effects on the environment" are defined to include "any unreasonable risk to man or the environment, taking into account the economic, social, and environmental costs and benefits of the use of any pesticide." § 136(bb). With few exceptions, FIFRA prohibits the sale, distribution, and professional use of unregistered pesticides. §§ 136a(a) and 136j(a)(1).

Because of the explicit requirement of a cost/benefit analysis, FIFRA's "unreasonable adverse effects" standard is unusual among federal environmental statutes: most others employ risk-based standards qualified only by the availability of control technologies. (But see TSCA, pages 177-182 infra.) By disregarding the benefits of the regulated substances, the risk-based statutes provide more protection to health and the environment and less protection to industry than do FIFRA and TSCA.

As part of a registration, EPA must classify the pesticide for either "general" or "restricted" use. § 136a(d). Restrictions relate to such factors as methods of application, qualifications of applicators, amounts to be used, geographic areas of use, and species of targeted pests. EPA may "conditionally" register a pesticide if the pesticide and its proposed use are similar to any currently registered pesticide and use thereof, or differ only in ways that would not significantly increase the risk of unreasonable adverse effects. A pesticide containing an active ingredient not contained in any currently registered pesticide also may be conditionally registered for a period reasonably sufficient for the generation of required data if EPA determines that use of the pesticide during such period will not cause any unreasonable adverse effects on the environment, and that use of the pesticide is in the public interest. § 136a(c)(7).

Once registered, pesticides are still subject to continuing scrutiny by EPA. § 136d. Indeed, § 6 of FIFRA requires EPA to cancel a pesticide's registration after the first five years in which the registration has been effective (and at the conclusion of subsequent five year periods if the registration is renewed) "unless the registrant, or other interested person with the concurrence of the registrant, . . . requests . . . that the registration be continued in effect." § 136d(a). And at any time, EPA may propose cancellation of a registration and initiate elaborate cancellation proceedings if "it appears to the Administrator that a pesticide . . . does not comply with [FIFRA] or . . . generally causes unreasonable adverse effects on the environment." § 136d(b).

During the pendency of cancellation proceedings, the registration remains in effect unless EPA "suspend[s] the registration of the pesticide immediately." § 136d(c). But before suspending, EPA must determine that an "imminent hazard" exists—that continued use of the pesticide during the time required for cancellation proceedings "would be likely to result

in unreasonable adverse effects on the environment."
§ 136(*l*). Even then, FIFRA guarantees registrants the
right to an expedited administrative hearing on that
issue, and the pesticide's registration remains effective
during this latter proceeding. § 136d(c)(2). Only if
EPA determines that "an emergency exists that does
not permit [it] to hold a hearing before suspending"
may the agency ban sale of the pesticide in advance of
administrative proceedings. § 136d(c)(3).

While commerce in unregistered pesticides is
generally prohibited, EPA may permit continued sale
and use of existing stocks of pesticides whose registra-
tions have been cancelled, provided that it determines
that the sale or use is "not inconsistent with the purposes of this subchapter and will not have unreasonable
adverse effects on the environment." § 136d(a)(1).

The 1988 amendments to FIFRA dealt with three
problems that had hampered implementation of the act.
First, about 50,000 "old" pesticides had been registered
under permissive pre–1972 safety and testing requirements. Between 1972 and 1988, EPA had been able to
identify data needs for only about 25 of those pesticides
each year. The 1988 FIFRA amendments called for re-
registration or cancellation of the rest within nine years,
shifting many tasks and costs from EPA to the registrants. Second, the amendments shifted from the EPA
budget to the Federal Judgment Fund (which relies on
general appropriations to pay claims against the government) liability to *indemnify* producers, distributors and
others for economic loss when EPA suspends or cancels
a registration. Third, the amendments shifted, from
EPA to the pesticide industry, responsibility for the
costs of *disposing* of cancelled pesticides.

In a series of opinions arising out of disputes between EPA and the Environmental Defense Fund, the D.C. Circuit has created an extensive case law applying FIFRA. These opinions have established a number of rules concerning the burden of proof in suspension and cancellation proceedings. Once EPA decides to issue a notice of cancellation, a presumption arises in favor of suspension. The suspension decision is analogous to the issuance of a preliminary injunction and calls for a balancing of the equities. Issuance of a notice of cancellation shows that a substantial question of safety exists and requires suspension in the absence of countervailing benefits. (Conceivably, EPA could find that the evidence of risk was just strong enough to justify cancellation proceedings but that the danger was not quite immediate enough to justify suspension.) When EPA does suspend registration, a presumption will arise in favor of cancellation if (a) no benefit is shown, or (b) animal tests show that the chemical causes cancer. Moreover, if evidence shows that one mode of exposure is hazardous, a presumption arises that all modes are hazardous until proven otherwise. Thus, for example, if inhalation of a chemical is dangerous, there is a presumption that ingestion of the chemical would also be dangerous.

Although these presumptions were developed on a somewhat *ad hoc* basis in a series of cases, the cases do have a unifying rationale when viewed as a group. In each case, the court has held that the burden of proof is on the manufacturer once substantial evidence of a health hazard has been shown. Essentially, once EPA has found sufficient evidence of risk to justify initiation of cancellation proceedings, the burden is on the proponent of continued registration to demonstrate that the risk is minimal or that the benefits of use outweigh the risks.

Stricter state and local regulation of pesticide use is permissible, i.e., is not preempted by FIFRA. Wisconsin Public Intervenor v. Mortier (S.Ct.1991). However, lower federal courts have held that FIFRA does preempt state tort actions against pesticide manufacturers for inadequate labeling, in cases where the federal labeling requirements were met.

Despite the requirements of FIFRA, supplemented in some situations by stronger state and local regulations, suspensions and cancellations of registered pesticides have been rare. Early in 1995 it was reported that, of some 10,000 pesticides approved for use in California, fewer than 50 had been banned since 1970. The occasion for this report was the temporary lifting of a suspension by EPA to allow use of the pesticide for one more growing season to exhaust existing domestic supplies of more than 200,000 pounds of the material.

Pesticides in and on *raw* agricultural commodities are regulated under the Federal Food, Drug and Cosmetic Act, 21 U.S.C.A. § 301 et seq. EPA sets *tolerance* levels of pesticide concentrations in or on commodities consumed in the United States; the Food and Drug Administration monitors actual pesticide *content* of commodities and can confiscate foods containing either excessive concentrations of registered pesticides or unsafe residues of unregistered pesticides. 21 U.S.C.A. §§ 342, 346a. Under § 346a, EPA is to consider, when establishing tolerances, "the necessity for the production of an adequate, wholesome, and economical food supply" as well as health effects.

When a tolerance has been established for use of a pesticide on a raw agricultural commodity, the FFDCA allows for the "flow-through" of such pesticide residue to *processed* foods, even if the pesticide is a carcinogen. This flow-through is allowed only to the extent that the concentration of the pesticide in the processed food does not exceed the concentration allowed in the raw food. Section 342(a)(2)(C). Before 1996, § 409, known as the "Delaney clause," mandated a zero-risk standard for carcinogenic pesticides in processed foods if the pesticide concentrated further during processing or was applied during or after processing. In Les v. Reilly (9th Cir.1992), the court refused to imply an exception for "reasonable risks" in the language of the Delaney clause. The court said that the FFDCA unambiguously provided that pesticides which concentrated in processed foods were to be treated as food additives; and that if such pesticides induced cancer in humans or animals, they rendered the food "adulterated" and must be prohibited.

The significance of Les v. Reilly for toxics regulation in general seems to be that if Congress prescribes a clear and unambiguous risk standard, courts and regulatory agencies may not disregard it in the name of "reason" or of judicial or administrative discretion. This is reminiscent of the Supreme Court's decision in TVA v. Hill, the "snail darter case" under the Endangered Species Act, page 20, supra.

With respect to the FFDCA, however, in 1996 Congress amended the Act to exempt pesticide chemical residues from the Delaney clause. Food Quality Protection Act of 1996, amending FFDCA § 408, 21 U.S.C. § 346a. For such residues, the Delaney distinction between "carcinogen" and "noncarcinogen" was replaced with a new distinction between "threshold" and "nonthreshold" toxicants. The "general rule," for threshold toxicants, is that the EPA Administrator may establish a tolerance for a residue in or on a food if she determines that the tolerance is "safe," i.e., "that there is a reasonable certainty that no harm will result from aggregate exposure to the pesticide chemical residue, including all anticipated dietary exposures and all other exposures for which there is reliable information." 21 U.S.C. § 346a(b)(2)(A). For nonthreshold toxicants, a tolerance must meet two sets of conditions, one concerning the health risks posed by the residue and a second concerning the economic benefits from use of the pesticide chemical that produces the residue. 21 U.S.C. § 346(b)(2)(B).

The 1996 amendments also require that, in establishing a tolerance for a pesticide chemical residue, the Administrator (i) shall assess the risk of the residue based on available information about consumption patterns (exposure) among infants and children, and about their special susceptibility to the residue, and (ii) shall ensure that there is a reasonable certainty that no harm will result to infants and children from aggregate exposure to the residue. 21 U.S.C. § 346a(b)(2)(C).

2. THE TOXIC SUBSTANCES CONTROL ACT

Prior to 1976, federal regulation of toxics consisted of an assortment of specialized provisions, most of them contained in statutes whose main focus was elsewhere. The potential for regulatory gaps was obvious. In 1976, Congress moved to fill these gaps by passing the first comprehensive legislation governing toxic substances. Unfortunately, the statute is hardly a masterpiece of insightful policymaking or incisive drafting.

The aim of TSCA was to prevent "unreasonable risks of injury to health or the environment" associated with the manufacture, processing, distribution, use or disposal of chemical substances other than drugs and pesticides. TCSA's emphasis is on regulating products rather than wastes. Today's policy of *pollution prevention,* and of avoiding environmental and health problems by front-end regulation of chemical production and use, is the same policy that underlies TSCA.

The Act as a whole must be read in light of the policy section, § 2(b). Three policies are set forth. First, data should be developed on the environmental effects of chemicals; primary responsibility for the development of these data is placed on industry. Second, the government should have adequate authority to prevent unreasonable risks of injury to health or the environment, particularly imminent hazards. Finally, this authority should be exercised so as "not to impede unduly or create unnecessary economic barriers to technological innovation while fulfilling the primary purpose of this Act to assure that . . . such chemical substances . . . do not present an unreasonable risk of injury." (Note the similarity to FIFRA's mandate to balance adverse effects on human health or the environment against economic and social benefits of the use of a pesticide.) Obviously, much depends on the relative weights given to these potentially conflicting goals of protecting technological development and assuring human and environmental safety.

The most important substantive provisions of the Act are found in §§ 4, 5, and 6. These sections concern testing, premanufacturing clearance, and regulation of manufacturing and distribution. We will consider only the main outlines of these provisions, without too much attention to the innumerable exemptions, exceptions, qualifications and procedural details.

Section 4 relates to testing. It empowers the EPA to adopt rules requiring testing by manufacturers of substances. Such rules must be based on a finding that insufficient data are currently available concerning the substance, and that the substance may "present an unreasonable risk," "enter the environment in substantial quantities," or present a likelihood of "substantial human exposure." There are a variety of complicated procedural devices set out in exhaustive detail in the section. In addition to § 4, the statute contains several other provisions aimed at collection of information.

Section 5 requires a manufacturer to give notice to the EPA before manufacturing a new chemical substance, or manufacturing or processing any chemical substance for a "significant new use." If the substance is covered by a § 4 rule, the § 4 test results must be submitted along with the § 5 notice. For substances not covered by § 4, but listed by EPA as possibly hazardous, the manufacturer is to submit data it believes show the absence of any unreasonable risk of injury. Normally, the next step would be a § 6 proceeding. But if EPA finds that an unreasonable risk may be presented before a § 6 rule can be promulgated, it can issue a "proposed section 6 rule" which will be immediately effective, issue an administrative order prohibiting manufacture, or seek an injunction, § 5(f). Often, of course, EPA will not have sufficient information to make a definite finding about safety. EPA can then make findings similar to those triggering the § 4 testing rules and issue an administrative order prohibiting manufacture or use. (If a timely objection to the order is filed, however, EPA must seek injunctive relief, § 5(e).)

Section 6, unlike § 5, applies to all chemicals, not just to new chemicals or new uses. The finding necessary to trigger § 6 is that "there is a reasonable basis to conclude" that the substance "presents or will present an unreasonable risk of injury to health or the environment." Having made such a finding, EPA may by rule apply any of a number of restrictions "to the extent necessary to protect adequately against such risk using the least burdensome requirements" (§ 6(a)). Obviously, much depends on whether more weight is given to the "protect adequately" standard or to the "least burdensome" standard. In general, § 6(c) directs EPA to use its powers under other statutes in preference to § 6. The effective date of a proposed rule may be accelerated if the EPA finds a likelihood of "an unreasonable risk of serious or widespread injury to health or the environment" before the effective date of the final rule. The requirements for acceleration under § 6(d), it should be noted, are somewhat different from those applicable to new chemicals under § 5(f). Finally, § 6 contains a special provision for the phasing out of polychlorinated biphenyls (PCBs).

One other provision which deserves mention is § 7, which allows EPA to obtain emergency judicial relief in cases of "imminent hazards". The Act also contains the usual panoply of provisions on civil and criminal penalties, judicial enforcement, judicial review, and preemption.

By 1983, EPA had only begun to put the statutory scheme into operation. It had compiled an inventory of 62,000 "old" chemicals. Using the inventory, an expert Interagency Testing Committee (ITC) had started to identify the riskiest existing chemicals and to designate them as high priority. Under § 4, EPA then was either to propose a testing rule for each such chemical or to decide that testing was not necessary. Of the first 33 priority chemicals recommended by the ITC, EPA concluded that no testing was necessary for about half. Although the agency had *proposed* testing rules for the others, it had not actually adopted any rules. Instead, it had adopted a policy of negotiating voluntary testing agreements with industry, though the agreements were not legally enforceable. NRDC v. EPA (S.D.N.Y.1984) held that this practice violated § 4, which directs that test rules "shall" be promulgated and shall identify the specific effects for which testing must be done, the test standards, and the deadlines for test completion and submission of data. This decision resulted in a complete revamping of EPA's procedures for negotiating test rules under § 4 of TSCA. The agency now seeks to make consent agreements enforceable on the same basis as test rules. 40 CFR 790. Manufacturers sometimes challenge EPA test rules judicially, and the courts review in detail the agency's findings and reasons for demanding tests. See Chemical Manufacturers Ass'n v.

EPA (5th Cir.1990), in which a rule requiring manufacturers and processors of chemical cumene to perform toxicological testing was remanded for EPA to articulate the standards on the basis of which it found both the quantities of cumene entering the environment from the facilities in question and the potential human exposure to be "substantial."

The requirement that EPA issue a rule before requiring testing distinguishes TSCA from food, drug, and pesticide statutes, which mandate production of safety data prior to marketing. It seems that TSCA essentially establishes a presumption of safety, which EPA must overcome before it may even require further testing of a chemical.

Many of the problems concerning "new" chemicals have related to compliance with § 5's requirement that a "premanufacture notice" (PMN) be submitted to EPA before a chemical is manufactured or imported into the United States. The statute calls for submission of information on chemical identity, proposed use, anticipated production volume, expected by-products, estimates of the number of people likely to be exposed during manufacture, and methods of disposal. Test results—and therefore tests—are not required unless the company has them on hand. (Other data on environmental and health effects must be submitted "insofar as known . . . or reasonably ascertainable.")

If EPA decides that a PMN does not provide sufficient information on which to base the necessary determination of risk, the agency may request more data. If such data are not provided, EPA can take no action (thus allowing manufacture), issue an order for additional information, or take steps to limit production or use of the chemical.

The most important judicial interpretation of TSCA to date occurred in Corrosion Proof Fittings v. EPA (5th Cir.1991), discussed at length in Chapter 4 supra at pages 164-167. EPA had adopted a rule, under § 6, which would have prohibited most uses of asbestos. The court held that EPA had violated TSCA by not considering adequately the benefits and costs of *less burdensome* alternatives to a complete ban, by not allowing public comment and cross-examination on methodology adopted at the last minute to support its benefits calculation, and by not evaluating the toxicity of likely *substitutes* for asbestos. Substantively, the court found that EPA had not provided substantial evidence of an "unreasonable risk of injury" to human health or the environment. *Corrosion Proof Fittings* raises serious doubts about the usefulness of § 6 of TSCA to regulate individual toxic chemicals.

3. REGULATION OF RELEASES OF GENETICALLY MODIFIED ORGANISMS

Biotechnology is likely to revolutionize much of our economy. Its effects already are evident, and controversial, in agriculture and medicine. To develop or use products such as corn and soybean plants which are resistant to, or contain, pesticides, genetically modified organisms (GMOs) must be released into the environment.

There are legitimate concerns about possible adverse effects of such releases. Among ecologists the greatest source of apprehension is the potential hazards of introducing non-native organisms into a new environment. Experience has shown that putting a non-native or "exotic" species into a new environment sometimes results in that species displacing native varieties and dominating the environment. GMOs introduced into new environments might have ecological impacts similar to those of exotic species. Theoretically, the GMOs may multiply and exchange genetic material, or hybridize, with other organisms. For example, corn that has been genetically modified to resist pesticides may pass the pesticide-resistant gene on to weeds, creating new ecological and farming problems.

Individual nations have taken different approaches to protecting the environment from possible adverse effects of GMO releases. Denmark and Germany follow a process-oriented approach, which views the technique of genetic engineering itself as a risk. Hence those countries regulate the use of DNA techniques, even if the end-product is not a GMO. On the other hand, the United States has adopted a product-specific approach. Its regulations are concerned not with the use of biotechnology techniques, but with the use of GMO end-products, such as foods or seeds. The GMO end-products are regulated like similar products created by more traditional techniques, under the statutory authority of FIFRA, FFDCA, TSCA, and the Federal Plant Pest Act.

The 1986 Coordinated Framework for Regulation of Biotechnology, issued by the U.S. Office of Science Technology Policy, divided jurisdiction over the environmental regulation of biotechnology among several federal agencies. EPA has primary responsibility. It treats biopesticides as chemical pesticides under FIFRA, page 169 supra, and other biotech products as new chemicals under TSCA, page 178 supra.

The Food and Drug Administration reviews genetically engineered food products for food safety, under the Federal Food, Drug and Cosmetic Act (FFDCA), page 174 supra. The U.S. Department of Agriculture regulates the release of genetically modified plants, animals, and microorganisms, under the Federal Plant Pest Act, which applies to environmental releases of insects or worms considered to be plant pests, or of organisms containing genetic material from plant pests. 7 U.S.C.A. § 150aa – 150jj; 7 C.F.R. § 340.

B. TOXIC SUBSTANCES UNDER THE GENERAL POLLUTION STATUTES

1. WATER POLLUTION

As originally enacted in 1972, the Clean Water Act required EPA to publish a list of toxic pollutants and to implement standards for these pollutants providing an "ample margin of safety." For various reasons, implementation of this requirement proved impractical. The agency lacked sufficient information about toxic pollutants and was given too little time to develop such information under the statutory timetable. Furthermore, because of the "ample margin of safety" requirement, the agency believed it had no leeway to consider feasibility. As a result, implementation of the statutory scheme threatened extensive plant closures and severe economic injury to some major industries.

The 1977 amendments to the Clean Water Act were an outgrowth of these problems. Because of the difficulty of implementing the original requirement, EPA had entered into a consent decree with the NRDC governing toxic pollutants. The decree required EPA to issue effluent limitations and new source performance standards for 21 major industries requiring the use of BAT. The 1977 amendments essentially codified this consent decree. Under the present statute, a list of toxic pollutants is specified in § 307(a)(1). Each pollutant on the list is subject to effluent limitations based on the BAT standard. This requirement is contained in § 307(a)(2) and is also incorporated in § 301(b)(2)(A). EPA in its discretion may impose more stringent limitations based on the "ample margin of safety" standard. Section 307 also provides for pretreatment standards for wastes — especially industrial wastes — that are to be introduced into municipal treatment systems rather than being discharged directly into the nation's waterways. These pretreatment standards are intended to prevent introduction of substances that cannot be adequately treated by public facilities or that might damage those facilities.

The Clean Water Act was amended again by the Water Quality Act of 1987. Congress had become concerned that certain waters could not meet applicable water quality standards despite the imposition of BAT requirements. In particular, numerous "toxic hotspots" needed more stringent controls. Section 304(*l*), added in 1987, established a comprehensive system for toxics control. States were directed to identify, within two years, such "hotspots" — waters where technology-based controls and existing water quality-based controls were not adequate to meet water quality standards because of toxic pollutants, even after implementation of BAT, new source performance standards, and standards requiring pretreatment of industrial wastes discharged into publicly owned treatment plants. The states then were to identify the specific point sources preventing the attainment of standards, and the amount of each toxic pollutant discharged by each such source. After these identifications, every state was required to devise an individual control strategy to achieve standards at each "hotspot" within three years after the date of the establishment of the strategy. By 1989 all states except Arizona had submitted the required lists and control strategies, and by 1997 more than 675 permits prescribing "individual control strategies" for specific point sources had been issued.

Another statute related to water pollution is the Safe Drinking Water Act, 42 U.S.C.A. §§ 300f to 300j–26. The Act, as amended extensively in 1986 and 1996, requires EPA to set maximum levels for contaminants in water delivered to users of public water systems. Of special concern are toxic contaminants in water from underground sources. A 1984 report by the Congressional Office of Technology Assessment (OTA) identified more than 200 contaminants in groundwater used for drinking, many of them associated with cancer and damage to the central nervous system, liver, and kidneys. The report documented serious incidents of such contamination by toxic chemicals, including pesticides and wastes leaked from landfills or disposed of in underground injection wells, in at least 34 states.

The Safe Drinking Water Act directs EPA to set health-based standards for contaminants in drinking water and to require water supply system operators to come as close as possible to meeting the standards by using the best available technology that is economically and technologically "feasible." Primary enforcement responsibility may be delegated to states which request it, if they adopt drinking water regulations no less stringent than the national standards and implement adequate monitoring and enforcement procedures.

EPA has developed a special regulatory program to deal specifically with pesticide contamination of groundwater. The program rests on a combination of state pesticide management plans and federal groundwater quality standards. Most prominent among the federal statutes invoked are FIFRA and the Safe Drinking Water Act.

2. AIR POLLUTION

Prior to 1990, § 112 of the Clean Air Act required EPA to regulate hazardous air pollutants at a level which provided an "ample margin of safety" to protect the public health. This was similar to the standard in the 1972 Clean Water Act governing regulation of toxic water pollutants. As discussed in the preceding section, implementation of that provision proved impractical, and the Clean Water Act was amended in 1977. The amendment prescribed a list of toxic water pollutants and provided that they were to be subject to effluent limitations based on a BAT standard, with EPA having discretion to impose more stringent limitations based on an "ample margin of safety" standard.

Until 1987, EPA's regulatory approach under old § 112 of the Clean Air Act was similar to that authorized in the 1977 Clean Water Act amendments, even though

§ 112 did not mention BAT or technological feasibility. However, as to hazardous air pollutants, that approach was found to be unlawful in NRDC v. EPA (D.C.Cir.1987) (en banc), the "vinyl chloride case" discussed at pages 163-164 supra. There the court held that "safe" need not mean "risk-free," and that the EPA Administrator should use his "expert judgment" regarding the level of emissions that would result in an "acceptable" risk to health. Only after this degree of "safety" was assured could the Administrator consider what was an "ample margin," and then he might "diminish" the statistically determined "safe" level of risk by setting the regulatory level at the lowest feasible level.

In 1989, EPA published some final and proposed regulations governing industrial benzene emissions. These were the first toxic air pollutant standards developed under the two-step procedure ordered by the court of appeals. Concerning "acceptable risk" to health, EPA said it would generally presume that a maximum individual risk ("MIR") no higher than 1 in 10,000 was acceptable, i.e., a person living very near to the pollution source and exposed to the maximum, modeled long-term concentration of the pollutant, 24 hours per day for 70 years, should not face an estimated incremental risk greater than 1 in 10,000 of contracting cancer. Concerning "ample margin of safety," EPA sought to provide protection to the greatest number of persons possible — estimated at 99 percent of all persons within 50 kilometers of all the emission sources — to an individual lifetime incremental risk level no higher than approximately 1 in 1 million.

The Clean Air Act Amendments of 1990 included a totally new § 112, somewhat similar in approach to § 307 of the Clean Water Act. However, the risk management methodology prescribed in the 1987 vinyl chloride case and employed in EPA's 1989 regulations governing industrial benzene emissions was endorsed by Congress and continues to be important under new § 112.

Section 112(b) now contains an initial list of 189 chemicals to be regulated. For each of two categories of sources, "major" and "area" (non-major), EPA is to promulgate emission standards which require installation of maximum achievable control technology (MACT). Standards for 40 of the highest priority source categories were to be issued by 1992. Other standards were to be issued in stages, with the final deadline being in the year 2000. Existing sources must comply with MACT standards within three years after issuance, unless EPA or a state agency grants a one-year extension.

Beyond MACT standards, § 112(f)(2) contemplates subsequent adoption, within 8 years after promulgation of MACT standards for each category of sources, of more stringent emission standards where necessary "to provide an ample margin of safety to protect public health in accordance with this section (as in effect before the date of enactment of the Clean Air Act Amendments of 1990) or to prevent, taking into consideration costs, energy, safety, and other relevant factors, an adverse environmental effect." If MACT standards applicable to a "known, probable or possible human carcinogen do not reduce lifetime excess cancer risks to the individual most exposed to emissions from a source . . . to less than one in one million, the Administrator shall promulgate standards under this subsection for such source category." Section 112(f)(2)(B) provides that nothing in § 112 "shall be construed as affecting, or applying to the Administrator's interpretation of this section, as in effect before the date of enactment of [the 1990 amendments] and set forth in [the 1989 industrial benzene emissions regulations]."

C. THE RESOURCE CONSERVATION AND RECOVERY ACT (RCRA)

Enacted in 1976, RCRA was a response to growing public awareness of serious problems related to disposal of hazardous wastes. According to EPA estimates, 290 million tons of hazardous wastes were produced in the United States in 1981. The principal industries generating the wastes were chemicals and petroleum (71%) and metals (22%). The wastes included organic materials from industrial processes (e.g., benzene and PCBs), heavy metals, biological wastes with bacterial and viral contaminants, sludge (the solid or semisolid byproduct of most air and water pollution control methods), and various chemicals.

Before RCRA, many such wastes were stored or disposed of at sites where water contamination could occur, for example, sites located in floodplains, over aquifers unprotected by impervious rock or soil, and in filled wetlands. Water filtering through such sites can leach chemicals into groundwater, and surface runoff from rain and snowmelt can carry chemicals to nearby streams. In either case, the result may be impairment or destruction of public water supplies.

Congress was confronted with the dual problems of dealing with serious threats posed by many existing waste disposal sites, and regulating future disposal activities so as not to multiply those threats. The lawmakers responded by enacting RCRA in 1976 and, thereafter, the Comprehensive Environmental Response, Compensation, and Liability Act of 1980 (CERCLA).

RCRA was primarily a forward-looking statute. Most of its provisions were aimed at creating a regulatory program to control future waste treatment, storage and disposal (TSD) activities. However, it also was retrospective, imposing civil liability upon past contributors to TSD facilities which currently present an "imminent and substantial endangerment" to health or the environment.

CERCLA was primarily backward-looking. Its main thrust was to create broad civil liability for cleanup of leaking TSD sites, most of which presumably were expected to antedate the implementation of RCRA's regulatory program. However, CERCLA also was forward-looking. It contained some regulatory provisions, including one requiring that persons in charge of TSD facilities notify EPA of any hazardous substance releases. More importantly, however, strict liability for cleanup of leaking sites provided a strong economic incentive for proper TSD activities by future generators and handlers of hazardous wastes.

1. OVERVIEW OF THE ACT

The hazardous waste provisions of RCRA are contained in subtitle C, as amended in 1984 and 1986. § 3001 requires EPA to promulgate criteria for "identifying the characteristics" of hazardous waste, and for "listing" hazardous wastes, which should be subject to

RCRA regulation, "taking into account toxicity, persistence, and degradability in nature, potential for accumulation in tissue," and other hazardous traits such as corrosiveness and flammability. The remaining provisions of subtitle C relate to standards and enforcement.

Three sets of standards are required, covering generators, transporters, and disposal sites. EPA has broad authority to prescribe such standards "as may be required to protect human health and the environment." Certain types of standards are required. § 3002 requires standards for generators of hazardous wastes covering record-keeping, reporting, labeling, and use of appropriate containers. Section 3002(5) requires use of a "manifest" system to ensure that the hazardous waste generated by the source is ultimately processed on site or at a facility with a § 3005 permit. (A manifest is a list or invoice of cargo for a transporter, identifying the cargo and its intended destination.) The manifest system is incorporated into § 3003, which requires standards for transporters. (Transporters are also subject to recordkeeping and labeling requirements.) As the last phase of this "cradle to grave" system for hazardous wastes, § 3004 requires standards covering treatment, storage and disposal (TSD) facilities. These standards cover compliance with the manifest system and other recordkeeping requirements. More importantly, they also cover TSD methods, as well as location, construction, and operation of disposal sites.

Under § 3004 (as amended in 1984), new landfills and surface impoundments, as well as expansions of existing units, must have double plastic liners, leachate collection systems, and groundwater monitoring facilities unless EPA specifically finds for a particular site that an alternative design or operating practice will be equally effective in preventing migration of hazardous substances into ground or surface water. The 1984 amendments also direct EPA to require the owner or operator of a disposal site to provide assurances of financial responsibility to comply with applicable regulatory standards. Assurances may consist of one or a combination of insurance, guarantee, surety bond, letter of credit, or qualification as a self-insurer.

An important feature of the 1984 amendments is that they shifted the focus of hazardous waste management away from land disposal to *treatment* alternatives. Section 1002(b)(7) now states that "land disposal . . . should be the least favored method for managing hazardous wastes." Consistent with this, § 3004 prohibits hazardous wastes from being disposed of on land unless one of two conditions is satisfied: (1) EPA determines, "to a reasonable degree of certainty, that there will be no migration of hazardous constituents from the disposal unit . . . for as long as the wastes remain hazardous," or (2) the waste is pretreated to meet standards established by EPA under § 3004(m). Pursuant to this subsection, EPA in 1986 issued regulations requiring that hazardous wastes be treated to levels achievable by application of "best demonstrated available technology" (BDAT).

A permit system established under § 3005 is the key enforcement provision for TSD facilities. EPA is given broad inspection powers, § 3007, and the power to issue compliance orders (with violators subject to a civil penalty) or bring a civil action against violators of any requirement, § 3008. Criminal penalties are also available for violation of the permit requirements or falsification of documents, § 3008(d). Finally, RCRA makes careful provision for state regulation. Under a provision modeled on the Clean Water Act, states may assume responsibility for hazardous waste control, § 3006. State laws less stringent than federal requirements are preempted, § 3009.

The 1984 amendments also provided for regulation of underground storage tanks containing petroleum products and other hazardous liquids such as solvents and pesticides, §§ 9001–9010. EPA regulations provide for detection and correction of leaks in existing tanks and establish performance standards for new tanks. The aim is to avoid groundwater pollution. 1986 amendments established a $500 million Leaking Underground Storage Tank Trust Fund, derived from federal taxes on motor fuels and to be used for correction of releases of petroleum when EPA cannot identify a financially responsible owner or operator of the tank who will undertake action properly.

2. "SOLID" AND "HAZARDOUS" WASTE DEFINED

RCRA's coverage extends to all "solid waste." However, the waste need not be in solid form. Section 1003(27) defines "solid waste" to include any garbage, refuse, sludge, "and other *discarded* material, including solid, liquid, semisolid, or contained gaseous material" (emphasis added), excluding, however, solid or dissolved materials in domestic sewage, irrigation return flows, or industrial discharges from point sources. The statutory exclusions leave large quantities of hazardous materials unregulated by RCRA.

An important issue is the extent to which RCRA covers materials that are *recycled* or held for future recycling. Can such materials be considered "discarded"? In American Mining Congress v. EPA (*AMC I*) (D.C.Cir.1987), a divided court held that Congress did not intend RCRA to regulate "spent" materials that are recycled and reused "in an *ongoing* manufacturing or industrial process." The majority said that such materials have not yet become "part of the waste disposal problem," but are "*destined for beneficial reuse or recycling in a continuous process by the generating industry itself.*" In a dissent, Judge Mikva said that RCRA's definition of "disposal" encompasses more than just "discarding or throwing away." Rather, he said, the definition was "functional": waste is disposed of if it is put into contact with land or water in such a way as to pose the risk to health and the environment that moved Congress to adopt RCRA. "Simply because a waste is likely to be recycled will not ensure that it will not be spilled or leaked before recycling occurs."

Two subsequent decisions of the D.C. Circuit limited the effect of *AMC I*. In American Mining Congress v. EPA (*AMC II*)(D.C.Cir.1990), the court sided with EPA, saying: "*AMC*'s holding concerned only materials that are 'destined for *immediate reuse* in another phase of the industry's ongoing production process' (emphasis added), and that 'have not yet become part of the waste disposal problem.' Nothing in *AMC* prevents the agency from treating as 'discarded' the wastes at issue in this case, which are managed in land disposal units that *are* part of wastewater treatment systems, which *have* therefore become 'part of the waste disposal problem,' and which are *not* part of ongoing industrial processes."

In American Petroleum Institute v. EPA (D.C.Cir.1990), the court held that even if materials are in fact recycled, they may be considered wastes at the time of recycling and therefore subject to RCRA regulation. The court overturned an EPA determination that materials utilized in a metals reclamation process ceased to be solid waste when they arrived at a reclamation facility because they no longer were "discarded material." The court said that the materials were discarded before being subject to reclamation, and that they had become "part of the waste disposal problem."

Section 1004(5) of RCRA defines "hazardous waste" to mean a "solid waste, or combination of solid wastes, which because of its quantity, concentration, or physical, chemical, or infectious characteristics may (A) cause, or significantly contribute to an increase in mortality or an increase in serious irreversible, or incapacitating reversible, illness; or (B) pose a substantial present or potential hazard to human health or the environment when improperly treated, stored, transported, or disposed of, or otherwise managed." Under § 3001, EPA is to promulgate regulations identifying the *characteristics* of hazardous waste and *listing* particular hazardous wastes to be regulated under subtitle C, "taking into account toxicity, persistence and degradability in nature, potential for accumulation in tissue, and other related factors such as flammability, corrosiveness, and other hazardous characteristics."

EPA regulations provide two principal ways in which solid waste may be deemed to be "hazardous": by exhibiting one of four hazardous characteristics ("*characteristic* wastes"), or by being identified specifically as hazardous waste by EPA ("*listed* wastes"). 40 CFR 261.3. EPA has established four general categories of listed wastes (the "F," "K," "P," and "U" lists). On the "P" list are acutely hazardous chemical products. The "U" list includes non-acutely hazardous chemical products. The "F" and "K" lists of waste mixtures and combinations include wastes that meet the criteria for the "P" and "U" lists or one of the four "characteristics" (toxicity, ignitability, corrosivity, and reactivity). Within these lists, EPA has identified hundreds of specific types of wastes as "hazardous."

To prevent generators from evading hazardous waste regulations by diluting or otherwise changing the composition of listed wastes, EPA has adopted two important rules, the "*mixture*" rule and the "*derived-from*" rule. The former provides that a mixture of "listed" hazardous waste with other solid waste is also a hazardous waste. The derived-from rule provides that any solid waste "generated from the treatment, storage, or disposal of a hazardous waste . . . (but not including precipitation run-off)" is hazardous waste.

Chemical Waste Management, Inc. v. EPA (D.C.Cir.1989) concerned EPA's treatment standards for *leachate*, which is produced when liquid such as rainwater percolates through wastes stored in a landfill. The derived-from rule provided that leachate derived from hazardous waste was also a hazardous waste. The court held that EPA did not act arbitrarily and capriciously by mandating that environmental media (such as soils) contaminated by hazardous wastes must themselves be treated as hazardous wastes. The court said that the rule on contaminated soil was part of a coherent regulatory framework, "one application of a general principle, consistently adhered to, that a hazardous waste does not lose its hazardous character simply because it changes form or is combined with other substances."

The mixture and derived-from rules do not require that materials which are not really hazardous nevertheless be managed as hazardous waste. The derived-from rule merely establishes a presumption, which can be overcome, for example, by showing that a leachate is nonhazardous. EPA's regulations explicitly exempt a mixture which "no longer exhibits any characteristic of hazardous waste."

Edison Electric Institute v. EPA (D.C. Cir.1993) demonstrates the complexity of formulating and applying rules pertaining to *characteristic* wastes, solid wastes which are not specifically "listed" by EPA as hazardous but which manifest one or more of the four characteristics (toxicity, ignitability, corrosivity, and reactivity) set out in EPA regulations for the purpose of identifying other (non-listed) hazardous wastes. EPA regulations prescribed a testing procedure, the Toxicity Characteristic Leaching Procedure (TCLP), for determining the "toxicity" characteristic of solid waste. The TCLP was based on a scenario involving disposal of toxic waste in an actively decomposing municipal landfill overlying a groundwater aquifer. The test required a waste generator to mix a sample of its waste with an acidic leaching medium and then to test the resulting liquid waste to see if it contained unsafe levels of toxic contaminants identified in the National Primary Drinking Water Standards. In *Edison*, generators of mineral processing wastes and manufactured gas plant wastes challenged EPA's application of the TCLP to their wastes. The court held that the TCLP did not bear a rational relationship to the wastes in question because EPA had not shown that such wastes had ever been disposed of in municipal landfills or in any other manner which would cause them to come into contact with an acidic leaching medium. The court remanded to allow EPA to provide a fuller and more reasoned explanation for its decision to apply the TCLP to the wastes in question.

3. THE LAND DISPOSAL BAN

When it amended RCRA in 1984, Congress sought to discourage land disposal of hazardous waste. Section 3004(d)(1) provided a staged prohibition on land disposal of *untreated* hazardous waste unless EPA "determines the prohibition of one or more methods of land disposal of such waste is not required in order to protect human health and the environment for as long as the waste remains hazardous." In making these determinations, EPA was directed to take into account the characteristics of the waste, "the long-term uncertainties associated with land disposal," and the importance of encouraging proper management of hazardous waste initially. Section 3004(d)(1), (e)(1), and (g)(5) limited EPA's discretion by specifying that a method of land disposal may not be determined to be protective of human health and the environment "unless, upon application by an interested person, it has been demonstrated to the Administrator to a reasonable degree of certainty, that there will be *no migration* of hazardous constituents from the disposal unit or injection zone for as long as the wastes remain hazardous." (Emphasis added).

Congress did not entirely ban the land disposal of wastes unable to meet this standard. It provided an exception for wastes treated to "substantially diminish the toxicity of the waste or substantially reduce the likelihood of migration of hazardous constituents from the waste so that short-term and long-term threats to human health and the environment are minimized." Section 3004(m). The statute directed EPA to promulgate treatment standards specifying how waste otherwise subject to the "land ban" could satisfy the standard. Thus, the land disposal ban, in effect, applies to *untreated* hazardous wastes and authorizes EPA to require pre-treatment of wastes that can not be shown to be capable of safe disposal on land in untreated form.

To prevent generators of hazardous waste from frustrating the land ban by simply storing waste indefinitely, § 3004(j) prohibits the *storage* of waste subject to the land disposal ban "unless such storage is solely for the purpose of the accumulation of such quantities of hazardous wastes as are necessary to facilitate proper recovery, treatment or disposal." In Edison Electric Institute v. EPA (D.C.Cir.1993), electric power companies challenged EPA's interpretation of this section, making it unlawful to store "mixed" wastes for an indefinite period pending the development of adequate treatment techniques or disposal capacity. The companies contended that the interpretation was inconsistent with the statute, and unreasonable as applied to generators of wastes containing both hazardous and radioactive components, for which there were then few lawful treatment or disposal options. EPA's regulations established a burden-shifting scheme for determining when storage would be viewed as "solely for the purpose of the accumulation of such quantities of hazardous waste as are necessary to facilitate proper recovery, treatment, or disposal." Basically, if waste was stored for longer than one year, the owner or operator had the burden of proving that the storage was solely for the purpose of accumulating sufficient quantities for proper recovery, treatment, or disposal. The court concluded that EPA's interpretation of § 3004(j) was consistent with RCRA's status as a "highly prescriptive, technology-forcing statute." The court said that RCRA's "draconian incentives" for the rapid development of adequate treatment and disposal capacity would be significantly diminished if generators could rely on the possibility of indefinite storage. The fact that technology may not be able to keep up with statutory timetables did not mean that the courts were at liberty to ignore them. Any relief would have to come from Congress.

Chemical Waste Management, Inc. v. EPA (D.C.Cir.1992), concerned the *extent* to which "characteristic" wastes must be *treated* prior to land disposal. The "NRDC petitioners" (environmental organizations and companies in the business of treating hazardous wastes) challenged EPA's decision not to require the use of "best demonstrated available technologies" (BDAT) in *all* situations. "Industry petitioners" (waste generators) objected to regulations mandating levels of treatment which in some situations went *beyond* removal of the characteristic (ignitability, corrosivity, reactivity or toxicity) which had led to the waste's classification as hazardous. The court rejected the

NRDC claim that some form of technology must be used to treat waste in *all* instances, and that dilution is never sufficient. The court found that RCRA does not bar *dilution* of ignitable, corrosive, or reactive (ICR) wastes, but merely defines the purposes that a method of treatment must achieve. The court rejected the generators' argument that the moment a waste ceases to meet the regulatory definition of a hazardous waste, EPA loses its authority to regulate that waste any further. The court concluded that, in combination, subsections 3004(g)(5) and (m) provide EPA with authority to bar land disposal of certain wastes unless they have been treated to reduce risks *beyond* those needed to trigger the characteristics themselves. The rationale was that the environmental concerns related to wastes displaying the *toxic* characteristic are different from the concerns for ICR wastes. Toxic constituents can pose a *cumulative* impact on land disposal, even where waste is below the characteristic level. On the other hand, treatment that removes the ICR characteristics "fully addresses the environmental concern from the properties themselves."

4. CIVIL LIABILITY: IMMINENT HAZARDS

In addition to EPA's regulatory powers, RCRA also gives EPA authority to seek injunctive relief under certain circumstances. Section 7003 provides:

> Notwithstanding any other provision of this chapter, upon receipt of evidence that the past or present handling, storage, treatment, transportation or disposal of any solid waste or hazardous waste may present an imminent and substantial endangerment to health or the environment, the Administra-

tor may bring suit on behalf of the United States in the appropriate district court against any person (including any past or present generator, past or present transporter, or past or present owner or operator of a treatment, storage, or disposal facility) who has contributed or who is contributing to such handling, storage, treatment, transportation, or disposal to restrain such person from such handling, storage, treatment, transportation, or disposal, to order such person to take such other action as may be necessary, or both.

Section 7002, the citizen suit provision, empowers "any person" to commence a civil action against parties whose past or present hazardous waste activities contribute to an imminent hazard, under a standard similar to that of § 7003. The two sections make RCRA important not only for dealing with present hazardous waste disposal activities but also as a complement to CERCLA in securing judicially mandated cleanups of abandoned disposal sites.

In applying the "imminent and substantial endangerment" standard, the courts have required only a relatively low level of danger as a trigger. Further, proof of actual harm is not necessary. Plaintiff need only prove that an existing dangerous condition creates a *risk* of harm to the environment or human health. Compare the decision in Reserve Mining Co. v. EPA, under the Clean Water Act, page 151 supra.

United States v. Waste Industries, Inc. (4th Cir.1984) is one of several important cases giving an expansive reading to the liability provisions of § 7003. The court noted that this section stands apart from other portions of RCRA defining EPA's regulatory authority, since § 7003 is designed to deal with situations in which the regulatory schemes break down or have been circumvented. Thus, § 7003 has a retrospective dimension—authorizing action against "inactive" sites to which wastes no longer are being added—whereas §§ 3001–3020 are prospective. Section 7003 (like 7002) authorizes actions against persons who have "contributed" to the "handling, storage, treatment, transportation or disposal" of hazardous waste which may pose an imminent hazard. The court emphasized that inclusion, in § 1004(3), of the word "leaking" as one of the definitional components of "disposal" demonstrated that Congress intended the latter term to have "a range of meanings, including conduct, a physical state, and an occurrence." A person who in the past contributed to a present occurrence ("leaking") can be ordered not only to stop this "conduct" but also to "take such other action as may be necessary," e.g., to reimburse the government for cleanup costs, to monitor for and prevent further contamination, and to restore groundwater.

United States v. Northeastern Pharmaceutical & Chemical Co., Inc. (8th Cir.1986) held that § 7003 does not require a finding of fault or negligence in order to hold past offsite generators and transporters liable for response costs. Such parties are strictly liable even for acts of disposal which occurred before RCRA became effective in 1976. Persons liable as "contributors" can include *officers and employees* of corporate generators and transporters. Because the remedies available to the government under § 7003 are essentially equitable, defendants are not entitled to jury trials. Presumably the result would be the same in citizen suits under § 7002.

Among the citizen-suit provisions found in various federal environmental laws, § 7002 of RCRA is unique in authorizing suits by private and other non-EPA plaintiffs to abate potential imminent hazards. An important question is whether § 7002 authorizes the courts in citizen suits to exercise their full equitable powers, including the power to order restitution, not merely to issue injunctions. In Meghrig v. KFC Western, Inc. (S.Ct. 1996), the owner of contaminated land cleaned it up and then sued the prior owner responsible for the contamination. The Supreme Court held that § 7002(a)(1)(B) does not authorize a private plaintiff to seek restitution for past cleanup costs where the "imminent and substantial endangerment" does not still exist when the suit is filed. Plaintiff should have sued *before* spending $200,000 to comply with a county order to remove the oil-tainted soil.

D. THE COMPREHENSIVE ENVIRON-MENTAL RESPONSE, COMPENSATION, AND LIABILITY ACT

CERCLA, also known as the "superfund" law, was enacted in 1980 and revised by the Superfund Amendments and Reauthorization Act of 1986 (SARA). Its principal purpose is the cleanup of leaking hazardous waste disposal sites.

1. OVERVIEW OF THE ACT

The Act has four basic elements. First, it establishes an information-gathering and analysis system to enable federal and state governments to characterize chemical dump sites and develop priorities for response actions. Section 102 directs the EPA Administrator to issue regulations designating as "hazardous" those substances which, when released into the environment, may present "substantial danger" to the public health or welfare or the environment. (Section 101(14) also incorporates by reference any substance designated by EPA as hazardous or toxic pursuant to § 311(b)(2)(A) or 307(a) of the Clean Water Act, § 3001 of RCRA, § 112 of the Clean Air Act, or § 7 of TSCA. Petroleum and natural gas are expressly excluded.) Section 103 requires owners and operators of hazardous waste storage, treatment or disposal sites to notify EPA of the amount and types of hazardous substances to be found there, and of any known, suspected, or likely releases of such substances from the sites. This information is important for EPA's development of a National Priorities List (NPL) of uncontrolled sites, used in planning appropriate responses.

Second, the Act establishes federal authority to respond to hazardous substance emergencies and to clean up leaking sites. Section 104 authorizes the President to provide for "removal" and "remedial" actions consistent with the National Contingency Plan (NCP) referred to in § 105. Removal actions are short-term, emergency responses, while remedial actions are intended to provide long-term solutions. Response actions may be carried out by the federal government directly, through contractors, or through cooperative agreements with states. The NCP was originally developed under § 311(c) of the Clean Water Act. Under § 105(a) of CERCLA, a section of the NCP known as the national hazardous substance response plan establishes procedures and standards for responding to releases of hazardous substances. The President is required to employ a Hazard Ranking System in determining the sites or facilities to be added to the NPL. Federal response actions at listed sites are limited to cases in which the responsible parties either cannot be found or do not take the necessary actions.

Third, the Act creates a Hazardous Substances Trust Fund (the "superfund") to pay for removal and remedial actions. However, the special corporate and excise taxes (particularly on petroleum and chemical feedstocks) expired in 1995. Without further action by Congress, which has been unwilling to provide more money except as part of a long-stalled comprehensive "reform" of CERCLA, the superfund may run dry. It has been operating recently on interest from unexpended funds and on recoveries from private parties required to reimburse EPA for cleanup costs.

Fourth, the Act makes persons who are responsible for hazardous substance releases liable for cleanup and restitution costs. Section 106 authorizes the Attorney General to seek injunctive relief where an actual or threatened release poses an "imminent and substantial endangerment" to the public health or welfare or the environment. Alternatively, the President may issue administrative orders directing responsible parties to take protective action. Section 107 provides that generators and transporters of hazardous substances, as well as owners and operators of treatment, storage or disposal (TSD) facilities, shall be liable for: (a) all costs of removal or remedial action incurred by the federal or state government "not inconsistent with" the NCP; (b) any other "necessary" response costs incurred by any other person "consistent with" the NCP; and (c) damages to "natural resources" resulting from release of hazardous substances. The courts have held that § 107 imposes strict liability, not dependent on fault. Section 107(b) contains narrow exceptions for releases caused solely by acts of God or war or acts or omissions of certain "third parties." As discussed below, liability is usually joint and several among responsible generators, transporters, owners and operators, although § 107 does not expressly say so.

2. IMPLEMENTING CLEANUPS

In implementation of CERCLA, the guiding policy is to achieve private-party cleanup, either voluntary or through enforcement action, if possible. Response actions financed from the superfund are undertaken only when federal and state governments determine them to be appropriate. An important part of implementation is federal negotiation of cooperative agreements with states, under which they take lead responsibility for cleanup, with later recovery of costs from responsible parties.

Sections 116 and 121, added in 1986, established schedules for response actions, and preferences among types of responses. Section 121 establishes a preference (in remedial actions under § 104 or 106) for treatment which permanently and significantly reduces the volume, toxicity or mobility of the hazardous substances. Offsite transport and disposal of the hazardous substances or contaminated materials are least favored where "practical [onsite] treatment technologies" are available. Remedial actions are to be "cost-effective," considering total short-term and long-term costs. The actions taken are to attain a degree of cleanup and control of further releases which, at a minimum, "assures protection" of human health and the environment.

Before SARA, both potentially responsible parties (PRPs) and environmental groups often sought judicial review of EPA's proposed remedial actions at particular sites before the cleanups were implemented. Rather than waiting to raise defenses in subsequent cost recovery actions under § 107, PRPs directed early challenges to the selection of remedial actions, claiming, for example, that EPA had chosen unreasonably elaborate or expensive remedies. Environmental groups, on the other hand, had different reasons for seeking pre-enforcement review of proposed remedial actions. They wanted early access to the courts to halt implementation of remedies that, in their view, failed to go far enough in protecting public health and the environment. Before 1986, CERCLA provided little guidance on the propriety of pre-enforcement judicial review. A leading case, Lone Pine Steering Committee v. EPA (3d Cir.1985), held that the courts lacked jurisdiction to conduct pre-enforcement review of EPA's method of cleanup. The court was concerned that such suits would frustrate Congress' intention that EPA act quickly to remedy problems posed by hazardous waste sites.

In SARA, Congress codified in § 113(h) the general denial of access to the courts to obtain pre-enforcement review of remedial action. Congress remained troubled, however, by the effect that the rule might have on citizen groups wishing to challenge the adequacy of remedial action before cleanups were completed.

Therefore, Congress created an exception authorizing the filing of citizens suits after a removal or remedial action has been taken under § 104 or secured under § 106. Congress then defined this exception liberally by explaining that such suits can be filed after the completion of "distinct and separate phases" of a remedial action, indicating in the conference report that it is not necessary to wait until the entire action has been completed. The intent was to permit judicial review early enough so that the direction of a multi-stage cleanup could be modified, if necessary, prior to completion.

3. LIABILITY OF RESPONSIBLE PARTIES

United States v. Monsanto Co. (4th Cir.1988) was typical of early enforcement suits by the federal government to recover its costs of removing hazardous substances from disposal sites. The four-acre site contained more than 7,000 fifty-five gallon drums of chemical waste, many of them leaking toxic, carcinogenic, mutagenic, explosive and highly flammable substances. Defendants, who had refused to enter into settlement agreements with the government, included three generators and the two owners of the site (who had leased it to the firm which then accepted wastes for disposal, perhaps without the site owners' knowledge). The government moved for partial summary judgment on the issue of defendants' joint and several liability. The court found that each defendant fell within one of the four classes of persons identified in § 107(a) as liable for response costs. Once the requisite nexus with the waste site was established, each class was *strictly* liable unless they could prove under § 107(b) that the release or threat of release of hazardous substances was caused solely by unrelated persons or events.

A *generator* was liable under § 107(a)(3) if the government could prove that:

> a. The generator's hazardous substances were, at some point in the past, shipped to the facility;

> b. The generator's hazardous substances, or hazardous substances *like* those of the generator, were present at the site;

> c. There was a release or threatened release of *any* hazardous substance at the site; and

> d. The release or threatened release caused the incurrence of response costs.

The court rejected defendants' contention that plaintiff must prove that hazardous substances traceable to each generator were released at the site. The court said that to require specific proof of causation would be at odds with the express language of the statute and would frustrate the intent of Congress because of the technological infeasibility of tracing a given generator's substances at the site.

The court also held that *joint and several* liability was appropriate under CERCLA in circumstances of "indivisible" injury. The court expressly approved the rationale and discussion in United States v. Chem–Dyne Corp. (S.D.Ohio 1983), in which the district court said:

> If the harm is divisible *and* there is a reasonable basis for apportionment of damages, each defendant is liable only for the portion of the harm he

himself caused * * *. In this situation, the burden of proof as to apportionment is upon each defendant * * *. On the other hand, if the defendants caused an entire indivisible harm, each is subject to liability for the entire harm.

The *Monsanto* court found that defendants had failed to meet their burden of establishing a reasonable basis for apportioning liability among the responsible parties:

> To meet this burden, the generator defendants had to establish that the environmental harm at [the site] was divisible among responsible parties. They presented no evidence, however, showing a relationship between waste volume, the release of hazardous substances, and the harm at the site. Further, in light of the commingling of hazardous substances, the district court could not have reasonably apportioned liability without some evidence disclosing the individual and interactive qualities of the substances deposited there. . . . [T]he defendants still have the right to sue responsible parties for contribution, and in that action they may assert both legal and equitable theories of cost allocation.

The defendants in *Monsanto* also argued that "retroactive" application of CERCLA, to create liability for conduct which occurred prior to the Act's passage, would violate due process. The court rejected the argument, saying that a presumption of constitutionality attaches to "legislative Acts adjusting the burdens and benefits of economic life," and that the burden is on one complaining of a due process violation to establish that the legislature has acted in an arbitrary and irrational way. "CERCLA operates remedially to spread the costs of responding to improper waste disposal among all parties that played a role in creating hazardous conditions."

Two other leading decisions on CERCLA are in agreement with *Monsanto* on the foregoing issues. See United States v. Northeastern Pharmaceutical & Chemical Co., Inc. (8th Cir.1986)(also holding that the federal government could recover retroactively response costs which it *incurred* before enactment of CERCLA); State of New York v. Shore Realty Corp. (2d Cir.1985).

Northeastern Pharmaceutical dealt with several other significant issues. It held that liability under § 107(a)(3) attached not only to a corporate generator but also to an individual corporate officer or employee who personally participated in making arrangements for the disposal of wastes. The statute provides that any person who "arranged" for disposal shall be liable for the government's response costs; there is no requirement that the person own or possess the waste or the facility from which it is transported for disposal.

It should be noted that § 107(a)(2), prescribing liability for any person who at the time of disposal of a hazardous substance owned or "operated" the disposal facility, has been applied to senior corporate officers and lower-ranking employees who personally participated in the disposal. See *Shore Realty*, supra, and United States v. Gurley (8th Cir.1994). On the other hand, a "consultant" who also was the corporate secretary and chairman of the board and owned 85% of the company's stock, was held not to be an "operator" because there was no evidence that he personally participated in any conduct that violated CERCLA. Riverside Market Development Corp. v. International Building Products, Inc. (5th Cir.1991). "Operator" liability also has been imposed on *parent corporations* whose subsidiaries owned disposal facilities. The parent itself, e.g., acting through an agent who is not an officer of the subsidiary, must have "actively participated in, and exercised control over, the operations of the *facility itself*." United States v. Bestfoods (S.Ct. 1998).

The *Northeastern Pharmaceutical* court also held that under § 107(a)(4)(A)—which imposes liability for governmental response costs "not inconsistent with the national contingency plan"—the burden of proof of inconsistency with the NCP is upon the defendants; and that all costs incurred by the government that are not inconsistent with the NCP are conclusively presumed to be reasonable and recoverable. On the other hand, under § 107(a)(4)(B)—which imposes liability for response costs incurred by "any other person consistent with" the NCP—*non*governmental plaintiffs have the burden of proving that their expenditures were consistent with the NCP. Finally, the court held that defendants do not have a right to a jury trial where the government seeks response costs under § 107, since CERCLA affords essentially equitable relief in the form of restitution.

Shore Realty, supra, held that a state could recover its emergency, or short-term, costs from a corporate site owner (which neither owned the site when hazardous wastes were placed there nor caused the presence or release of the wastes) and from its principal officer and stockholder (as an "operator"), even though the site was not on EPA's National Priorities List. The court held that while NPL listing may be a requirement for the use of superfund money under §§ 104 and 111, it is not requisite to liability under § 107. NPL listing, said the court, is not a general requirement under the National Contingency Plan, since the NPL is a "limitation on remedial, or long-term, actions—as opposed to removal, or short-term, actions—particularly federally funded remedial actions." Nor was the state's recovery barred by its failure to obtain EPA's prior approval of the response action, since the NCP's requirements concerning collaboration in joint federal-state cleanup efforts are inapplicable where a state acts on its own without seeking reimbursement from the superfund.

Section 107(a)(2)(B) also creates a *private* cause of action for recovery of response costs if they are "necessary" and "consistent with" the NCP. Potential plaintiffs include owners of land adjacent to a leaking disposal site, and even the owner of the site itself on which defendant deposited hazardous waste. Although reimbursement of private response costs from the *superfund* requires that they be approved under the NCP and federally certified, § 111(a)(2), private recovery from a generator, transporter, owner or operator under § 107(a)(2)(B) does not require that plaintiff's response actions have been taken pursuant to a governmentally authorized cleanup program. It is sufficient, for example, if the actions were required by a state or local agency and were consistent with provisions of the NCP in effect at the time of the response. NL Industries, Inc. v. Kaplan (9th Cir.1986); Wickland Oil Terminals v. Asarco, Inc. (9th Cir.1986).

Prior to 1986, there was a division among the courts regarding whether the possible joint and several liability of CERCLA defendants was a matter of federal or state common law. Although SARA was silent on this point, legislative history indicates that Congress intended federal law to control. As Representative John Dingell explained on the floor of the House, "[t]he courts have established, as a matter of federal common law, that the liability of potentially responsible parties at superfund sites is strict, joint and several, unless the responsible parties can demonstrate that the harm is divisible." He said that the reasoning of the court in United States v. Chem–Dyne Corp., page 211 supra, correctly expressed congressional intent.

Because § 107(a) extends liability for cleanup costs to all "owners" of contaminated properties, regardless of the circumstances of their ownership, parties who involuntarily or innocently acquired former disposal sites have been required to pay for cleanup, even when the cost exceeded the value of the land. Several well publicized cases helped to focus Congress' attention on this aspect of CERCLA's liability scheme. In United States v. Maryland Bank & Trust Co. (D.Md.1986), for example, a bank made a mortgage loan of $335,000 on a piece of land. The borrower defaulted, and the bank instituted a foreclosure suit. After the bank took title to the property, state and federal authorities determined that it was a contaminated waste site requiring cleanup under CERCLA. The bank was held liable for response costs of more than $550,000.

Prompted by the perceived unfairness of such results, Congress included a new defense in SARA to protect "innocent landowners." While § 107(a)'s general liability standard for "owners and operators" was maintained, Congress expanded § 107(b)(3)'s third-party exception by redefining the term "contractual relationship" in § 101(35). Now, "innocent landowners" who acquire property without "reason to know" that hazardous substances have been disposed of there are not liable as owners or operators under § 107. However, § 101(35) provides, "To establish that the defendant had no reason to know . . ., the defendant must have undertaken, at the time of acquisition, all appropriate inquiry into the previous ownership and uses of the property consistent with good commercial or customary practice in an effort to minimize liability." Section 101(35) also states that innocent owners who learn of contamination at the site and then transfer ownership without disclosing such information to subsequent purchasers are fully liable under § 107(a).

What about landowners who *know* the condition of the site when they acquire ownership, and who then transfer it to another person after *disclosing* the condition? Are such "passive intervening landowners" liable under § 107(a)? The answer depends on the definition of "disposal" in § 107(a)(2). Section 101(29) states that "disposal" shall have the meaning provided in § 1004(3) of the Solid Waste Disposal Act, which defines it to include "discharge, deposit, injection, dumping, spilling, *leaking,* or placing of . . . hazardous waste into or on any land or water . . ." (emphasis added). The courts have split on the question of CERCLA liability of passive intervening landowners. Nurad, Inc. v. William E. Hooper & Sons Co. (4th Cir. 1992), held that § 107(a)(2) imposes liability not only for active involvement in the "dumping" or "placing" of hazardous waste at a facility, but for ownership of the facility at a time when such waste was "spilling" or "leaking." However, United States v. 150 Acres of Land (6th Cir. 2000) held that "disposal" requires "human intervention;" and United States v. CDMG Realty Co. (3d Cir. 1996) held that "while 'leaking' and 'spilling' may not require affirmative human conduct, neither word denotes the gradual spreading of contamination." Note the importance of the issue to lending institutions which foreclose, take title, and resell the property.

With respect to *lender* liability, § 101(20)(A) excludes from the definition of "owner or operator" any "person, who, without participating in the management of a . . . facility, holds indicia of ownership primarily to protect his security interest in the . . . facility." Financial institutions and other secured creditors were shocked by the decision in United States v. Fleet Factors Corp. (11th Cir.1990), which denied Fleet's motion for summary judgment because Fleet's activities as a secured creditor might make it liable if it participated in the "financial management of a facility to a degree indicating a *capacity* to influence the [bankrupt debtor] corporation's treatment of hazardous wastes" (emphasis added). The court said that it was not necessary, for liability, that the creditor actually involve itself in day-to-day operations of the facility; it was enough if the involvement with management was "sufficiently broad to support the inference that it could affect hazardous waste decisions if it so chose." Congress then amended § 101(20) by adding a new subsection (E), "Exclusion of lenders not participants in management." The phrase "participate in management" is defined to mean "actually participating in the management or operational affairs" of a facility, and "does not include merely having the capacity to influence, or the unexercised right to control" facility operations. Note the similarity between this treatment of lenders and the treatment of parent corporations under United States v. Bestfoods, page 214 supra.

4. RIGHT OF CONTRIBUTION

Although apportionment of response costs among responsible parties is appropriate under § 107(a) when there is a reasonable basis for division of the harm, joint and several liability is the general rule. The government thus is relieved of the obligation to join all potentially responsible parties (PRPs) and to prove their individual contributions to the hazardous waste site. The burden of proving divisibility of harm is on the defendant seeking to limit its liability. In this situation, the subject of contribution among PRPs is of great importance, especially to those against whom the government initially chooses to proceed for recovery of response costs.

In an action for contribution, one joint tortfeasor which has discharged more than its fair share of the common liability seeks to recover the excess costs from another tortfeasor. Before the 1986 amendments to CERCLA, a few district courts had recognized an implicit right to contribution under CERCLA. They conceived of the area of contribution as one for development of a federal common law. On the other hand, at least one court looked to state law. SARA amended § 113 to provide explicitly for a right to contribution. Any person may seek contribution from any other person who is liable or potentially liable under § 107(a), during or following any civil action under § 106 or 107(a). Such claims are governed by federal law. In resolving them, the court may allocate response costs "using such equitable factors as the court determines are appropriate." Factors frequently considered include the relative amounts of waste disposed of by the various generators and transporters, the relative toxicity of the wastes, the degree of involvement by each party in the generation, transportation or disposal, the degree of care exercised by the various parties, and the degree of their cooperation with public officials to prevent harm to public health or the environment. Section 113(f) also says that nothing therein shall diminish the right of any person to bring an action for contribution in the absence of a civil action under § 106 or 107(a), e.g., after a voluntary settlement.

Allocation of liability in a contribution action can be complicated by the insolvency or unavailability of some PRPs. For example, suppose that each of five generators sent 20 percent of "the problem" to a disposal site. One of them, E, went out of business many years ago, and the owner and operator of the site is now insolvent. Firm A has paid for the entire $500,000 cleanup, pursuant to an administrative order from EPA, and now brings a contribution action against B, C and D, the other PRPs. However, D has only $20,000 of assets. Each of B and C argues that its liability is limited to $100,000, which would leave A out of pocket in the amount of $280,000. Two interrelated issues are presented: (1) May the court find B and C jointly liable, as they would be under § 107(a), or only severally liable for their 20-percent shares of the total response costs? (2) May the court allocate some of E's

$100,000 "orphan share" (and perhaps some of D's unpaid $80,000) of the response costs to B and C, or, again, is their liability limited to $100,000 each?

While contribution liability usually has been held to be only several, a few courts have said that joint liability may be imposed in appropriate circumstances because §113(f) expressly provides for allocation based on "equitable factors." Browning-Ferris Industries of Illinois, Inc. v. Ter Maat (7th Cir. 1999). With respect to the second issue, one court has said, "Under § 113(f)(1), the cost of orphan shares is distributed equitably among all PRPs just as cleanup costs are." Pinal Creek Group v. Newmont Mining Corp. (9th Cir. 1997). In the hypothetical case above, by finding joint liability, or apportioning the orphan shares of E and perhaps D, a court could allocate to each of B and C one-fourth or one-third of E's $100,000 share of the response costs, and perhaps also one-third of the $80,000 of D's share which D will not be able to pay. Otherwise, A would be left in a much less favorable position than B and C, simply because EPA moved against A alone rather than against all three of them.

5. MEASURE OF DAMAGES

Another important matter is the kinds of costs for which PRPs may be held liable. Section 107(a) defines in general terms the costs and damages recoverable under CERCLA. It mentions "costs of removal or remedial action" incurred by the federal or state government, "other necessary costs of response" incurred by any other person, and "damages for injury to, destruction of, or loss of natural resources, including the reasonable costs of assessing such injury, destruction, or loss." Before SARA, there were numerous disputes about recoverability of contractor costs, enforcement costs, and even interest. SARA attempted to remedy this problem by expanding the list of recoverable costs and damages to include virtually every conceivable expense associated with superfund cleanup activity. The costs of health assessments and health effects studies now are recoverable, as are enforcement costs and costs related to indemnification agreements with response action contractors. However, private plaintiffs may not recover compensation for lost property value or individual medical monitoring. Price v. U.S. Navy (9th Cir.1994). Nor may they recover reimbursement for their attorneys' fees. Key Tronic Corp. v. United States (S.Ct.1994).

Under § 107(f), CERCLA liability for injury to *natural resources* is owed to the United States government, to any state for resources "within the State or belonging to, managed by, controlled by, or appertaining to such State," and to any Indian tribe in specified situations. The statute creates no private cause of action for natural resource damage. Authority to recover is in the President, for the United States, or the "authorized representative of any State," who "shall act on behalf of the public as trustee of such natural resources." Sums recovered shall be used by the trustee only to "restore, replace, or acquire the equivalent of" the natural resources injured, destroyed or lost. "Natural resources" are defined by § 101(16) to mean land, fish, wildlife, biota, air, water, ground water, and other such resources belonging to, or managed or held in trust by, the United States, a state or local government, a foreign government, or an Indian tribe.

How are the recoverable damages to be measured? Section 301(c) directs the President to promulgate regulations for "the assessment of damages for injury to, destruction of, or loss of" natural resources:

> (2) Such regulations shall specify (A) standard procedures for simplified assessments requiring minimal field observation, including establishing measures of damages based on units of discharge or release or units of affected area, and (B) alternative protocols for conducting assessments in individual cases to determine the type and extent of short- and long-term injury, destruction, or loss. Such regulations shall identify the best available procedures to determine such damages, including both direct and indirect injury, destruction, or loss and shall take into consideration factors including, but not limited to, replacement value, use value, and ability of the ecosystem or resource to recover.

The "standard procedures" are referred to as "Type A" rules, and the "alternative protocols" as "Type B" rules.

The President assigned responsibility for promulgating the regulations to the Department of Interior. In 1986, the Department belatedly published final regulations containing both Type A and Type B assessment rules. Both were challenged in court by state governments, environmental organizations, and industry groups. The Type A rules were upheld in State of Colorado v. United States Dept. of Interior (D.C.Cir.1989). However, major portions of the Type B rules were found to violate CERCLA in Ohio v. United States Dept. of Interior (D.C.Cir.1989).

The most significant issue in the *Ohio* case concerned the validity of a provision that damages for despoilment of natural resources should be "the *lesser* of: restoration or replacement costs; or diminution of use values" (emphasis added). The court held that, under CERCLA, the Department of the Interior was not entitled to treat use value and restoration cost as having "equal presumptive legitimacy" as measures of damages to natural resources. Primary among the statutory provisions cited by the court was § 107(f)(1), which states that natural resource damages recovered by a government trustee are "for use only to restore, replace, or acquire the equivalent of such natural resources," and that the measure of damages "shall not be limited by the sums which can be used to restore or replace such resources." The court concluded that Congress intended a "distinct preference" for restoration cost as the measure of damages.

6. SETTLEMENTS

CERCLA § 122(a) directs that "[w]henever practicable and in the public interest," settlement agreements should be sought in order to expedite effective remedial actions at superfund sites and to minimize litigation. Among the tools authorized by § 122 to facilitate cost allocations, reduce transaction costs, and otherwise promote settlements, are (1) de minimis settlements—expedited settlements for small-volume waste contributors; (2) nonbinding preliminary allocations of responsibility ("NBARs") for cleanup costs—developed by EPA for PRPs; (3) mixed-funding agreements to share cleanup costs—permitting use of a combination of federal, state and PRP funds; (4) covenants not to sue—protecting PRPs who settle from future liability to the United States related to the hazardous substance release addressed by a remedial action; and (5) alternative dispute resolution—the use of neutral third parties to help resolve liability and cost-allocation problems.

Section 122(d)(1)(A) provides that whenever the President enters into a settlement agreement with a PRP with respect to remedial action under § 106, except as otherwise provided in § 122(g) concerning de minimis settlements, "the agreement shall be entered in the appropriate United States district court as a consent decree."

In addition to § 122, another CERCLA provision of great significance to settlements is § 113(f)(2) concerning *contribution*:

> A person who has resolved its liability to the United States or a State in an administrative or judicially approved settlement shall not be liable for claims for contribution regarding matters addressed in the settlement. Such settlement does not discharge any of the other potentially liable persons unless its terms so provide, but it reduces the potential liability of the others by the amount of the settlement.

7. REFORM OF CERCLA

Throughout the 1990s there were several unsuccessful efforts in Congress to "reform" CERCLA. The perceived need for change stemmed from the slow pace and enormous cost of CERCLA cleanups, and from the inordinate amounts of money consumed by transaction costs, primarily legal fees. The basic problems were disagreements over how clean sites should be made, and disagreements among PRPs and their insurers over who should pay what portions of the costs. As a result of the disagreements, the entire program was bogged down in litigation.

A 1994 bill supported by the Clinton administration and by environmentalists, industrial interests, and insurers would have (1) set uniform national standards governing how clean sites should be made, based on formulas that, while still complex, would have been more workable than existing standards; (2) related the extent of cleanup to how the particular site was to be used in the future, saving time and expense in some cases; (3) increased the influence of local citizen groups in cleanup decisions; (4) encouraged arbitration rather than litigation by those who would have to pay for cleanups; and (5) increased federal financing of some cleanups by collecting $8 billion over ten years from insurance companies which, in exchange, would have been protected against some liability.

Republican opponents blocked the bill in the House of Representatives by demanding amendments that would have relaxed cleanup standards for groundwater contaminated by carcinogenic chemicals, and changed how the costs and benefits of cleanups would be weighed and balanced. If the House had approved the bill, Senate Republicans would have sought to abolish CERCLA's retroactive liability for pre–1980 disposal activities.

In 1997, congressional Republicans unsuccessfully sought a "comprehensive reform" which would have included an appropriation of $650 million for the superfund; financial assistance to state and local governments and prospective purchasers for cleanup and development of contaminated urban sites, known as "brownfields"; elimination of "retroactive" liability for generators and transporters who disposed of waste before 1980; elimination of liability for "small" waste generators and transporters that contributed only small amounts of waste, employed less than 50 people, or had less than $3 million in gross annual revenues; "caps" on the allocation of liability for response costs to a municipal solid waste generator (10%) or a municipal landfill owner or operator (20%); replacement of the broad preference for costly "treatment" remedies at all contaminated sites, with a narrower preference applicable only to "hot spots" posing a "substantial threat to human health and the environment"; limitations on the recovery of damages for injury to "non-use" values of natural resources; restrictions on federal payment of "orphan shares" of response costs; and provision for the "reopening" of consent decrees allocating response costs among private PRPs.

E. MANDATORY REPORTING OF CHEMICAL HAZARDS

The Emergency Planning and Community Right-to-Know Act (EPCRA) was enacted by Congress with the 1986 amendments to CERCLA. The two general objectives of EPCRA are to support emergency planning by local governments with regard to chemical hazards, and to provide citizens and local governments with information about potential community-based chemical hazards. Congress included three provisions to implement these objectives. The first concerns governmental emergency response planning. The second addresses emergency release notification by private industry. The third requires compilation and reporting of information concerning chemical properties, manufacturing, usage, and releases.

The first provision requires each state to establish a state emergency response commission and local emergency planning committees. The latter must have emergency response plans which include, among other things, identification of local facilities at which any statutorily designated "extremely hazardous substances" are present; methods and procedures for reporting any release of such a substance; public notification procedures; and evacuation plans.

The second component requires the owner or operator of a "facility" to give notice of a hazardous substance release to the state emergency response commission and the local emergency planning committee. The notification must contain specific information, including data about the chemical released, the estimated quantity, the time and duration of the release, any known or anticipated acute or chronic health risks, and advice regarding appropriate medical attention or precautions for exposed individuals.

The final provision requires owners and operators of certain facilities to inform citizens about chemicals located in their communities, by submitting to state and local authorities information about toxic chemical inventories, usage, manufacture, and releases.

All information collected under EPCRA is available to the public. A citizen-suit provision authorizes self-help enforcement of EPCRA against facility owners and operators, state and local governments, and EPA. Facilities' annual Toxic Release Inventory (TRI) reports give the public unprecedented pictures of the industries that put it at risk, and give the industries a strong incentive to protect or repair their reputations by reducing their releases.

F. CRIMINAL LIABILITY

Almost every federal environmental statute imposes criminal liability. Congress has made virtually all "knowing" and some "negligent" violations of pollution control standards, limitations, permits, and licenses subject to criminal as well as civil sanctions. These statutes rarely define thresholds indicating when violators' conduct justifies adding criminal to civil penalties. Congress also has criminalized both the failure to report releases of hazardous substances and the filing of false reports, e.g., CERCLA § 103(b) and EPCRA §325(b).

1. KNOWING VIOLATIONS

The legal issue which arises most frequently in environmental criminal cases is the extent of the "knowledge" which defendants must be shown to have had in order to justify convictions. For example, § 3008(d) of RCRA — one of the environmental criminal provisions most often used by federal prosecutors — prescribes fines and imprisonment for any person who:

(1) *knowingly* transports or causes to be transported any hazardous waste identified or listed under this subchapter to a facility which does not have a permit under this subchapter . . . ;

(2) *knowingly* treats, stores, or disposes of any hazardous waste identified or listed under this subchapter —

> (A) without a permit under this subchapter . . .;
>
> (B) in *knowing* violation of any material condition or requirement of such permit . . . [emphasis added].

In United States v. Laughlin (2d Cir. 1993), defendant appealed from a judgment convicting him of knowingly disposing of hazardous waste without a permit, in violation of § 3008(d)(2)(A). The trial court had instructed the jury that the government was required to prove that defendant knowingly disposed of creosote sludge and knew that it "had the potential to be harmful to others or the environment or, in other words, it was not a harmless substance like uncontaminated water." On appeal, defendant contended that the word "knowingly" in subsection (2) applied not only to the prohibited act—treatment, storage, or disposal of a hazardous waste—but also to the fact that the waste had been identified or listed as hazardous under RCRA and the fact that his corporate employer lacked a permit. He urged that the jury should have been instructed that the government was required to prove, as essential elements of the violation, that he was aware of RCRA regulations applicable to creosote sludge and knew that the employer had not obtained a permit to dispose of the sludge. In rejecting defendant's contention, the court invoked what is known as the "public welfare offense" doctrine:

When knowledge is an element of a statute intended to regulate hazardous or dangerous substances, the Supreme Court has determined that the knowledge element is satisfied upon a showing that a defendant was aware that he was performing the proscribed acts; knowledge of regulatory requirements is not necessary. See *United States v. International Minerals & Chem. Corp.* [S.Ct. 1971] (in prosecution for knowingly violating a hazardous materials regulation, Government was not required to prove that defendant was aware of regulation, but only that he was aware of shipment of the hazardous materials).

Similarly, in United States v. Sinskey (8th Cir. 1997), the court affirmed defendant's conviction under the Clean Water Act. Defendant challenged jury instructions given with respect to CWA § 309(c)(2)(A), which among other things punishes anyone who "knowingly violates" § 301 or a condition or limitation contained in a permit that implements § 301. The trial court had instructed that in order for the jury to find defendant guilty of acting "knowingly," the proof had to show that he was "aware of the nature of his acts, perform[ed] them intentionally, and [did] not act or fail to act through ignorance, mistake, or accident." The court of appeals held that the government was not required to prove that defendant knew that his acts violated either the CWA or the corporate employer's NPDES effluent-discharge permit, "but merely that he was aware of the conduct that resulted in the permit's violation."

This interpretation comports not only with our legal system's general recognition that ignorance of the law is no excuse . . . , but also with Supreme Court interpretations of statutes containing similar language and structure. In *United States v. International Minerals & Chemical Corp.*, . . .[t]he Court [noted] that where "dangerous or . . . obnoxious waste materials" are involved, anyone dealing with such materials "must be presumed" to be aware of the existence of the regulations.

The court in *Sinskey* distinguished United States v. Ahmad (5th Cir. 1996), in which a convenience store owner had pumped out an underground gasoline storage tank into which some water had leaked, discharging gasoline into city sewer systems and nearby creeks. At trial, defendant asserted that he thought he was discharging water, and that CWA § 309(c)(2)(A) required proof not only that he knew he was discharging something, but also that he knew he was discharging gasoline. The Fifth Circuit reversed his conviction. The *Sinskey* court said that *Ahmad* "involved a classic mistake-of-fact defense, and is not applicable to a mistake-of-law defense such as that asserted by Sinskey."

2. NEGLIGENT VIOLATIONS

In United States v. Hanousek (9th Cir. 1999), defendant appealed his conviction for "negligently" discharging a harmful quantity of oil into a navigable water of the United States, in violation of CWA §§ 309(c)(1)(A) and 311(b)(3). Defendant contended that the trial court had erred by failing to instruct the jury that the government had to prove that he acted with *criminal* negligence, as opposed to ordinary negligence. In his proposed instruction, defendant defined criminal negligence as "a gross deviation from the standard of care that a reasonable person would observe in the situation." However, the district court had instructed the jury that the government was required to prove only that defendant acted negligently, which that court defined as "the failure to use reasonable care." In affirming the conviction, the court of appeals said:

> If Congress intended to prescribe a heightened negligence standard, it could have done so explicitly, as it did in [§ 311(b)(7)(D), which] provides for increased civil penalties "[i]n any case in which a violation . . . was the result of gross negligence or willful misconduct." . . .
>
> In light of our holding in [United States v.] *Weitzenhoff* [9th Cir. 1993] that the criminal provisions of the CWA constitute public welfare legislation, and the fact that a public welfare statute may impose criminal penalties for ordinary negligent conduct without offending due process, we conclude that section [309(c)(1)(A)] does not violate due process by permitting criminal penalties for ordinary negligent conduct.

3. RESPONSIBLE CORPORATE OFFICERS

Congress has explicitly incorporated the category of "responsible corporate officer" into the definition of a liable "person" in the criminal provisions of the Clean Air Act and Clean Water Act. In United States v. Brittain (10th Cir. 1991), a prosecution under the Clean Water Act for unlawful discharges of raw sewage into a stream, the individual defendant contended that he was not a "person" subject to criminal prosecution under the statute. The court suggested that a responsible corporate officer (RCO) would not have to personally direct, or commit, a violation of the statute to be criminally liable. The court said:

> Under this interpretation, a "responsible corporate officer," to be held criminally liable, would not have to "willfully or negligently" cause a permit violation. Instead, the willfulness or negligence of the actor would be imputed to him by virtue of his position of responsibility

However, since the individual defendant in *Brittain* did, in fact, have actual knowledge of the illegal conduct, and directed that it occur and be concealed from the authorities, the court's analysis of the extent to which knowledge may be imputed to a corporate officer, by virtue of his position alone, was dicta. Federal prosecutors have not followed this dicta in subsequent prosecutions.

In United States v. McDonald and Watson Waste Oil Co. (1st Cir. 1991), the president of the company was convicted under RCRA § 3008(d)(1) of knowingly transporting and causing the transportation of hazardous waste to a facility which did not have a permit. In reversing the criminal conviction, the court said:

> We agree . . . that knowledge may be inferred from circumstantial evidence, including position and responsibility of defendants such as corporate officers, as well as information provided to those defendants on prior occasions. Further, willful blindness to the facts constituting the offense may be sufficient to establish knowledge. However, . . . a mere showing of official responsibility . . . is not

an adequate substitute for direct or circumstantial proof of knowledge.

The United States Department of Justice has followed this decision in its subsequent environmental prosecutions.

A recent case applying the RCO doctrine is United States v. Iverson (9th Cir. 1998). Defendant was the founder, president, and chairman of the board of a chemical blending company. The company shipped its chemical in drums, which were returned for cleaning and reused. The cleaning process generated a wastewater regulated by the CWA, but the company failed to obtain a discharge permit and resorted to various illegal disposal methods. Although defendant "officially" retired prior to the events which led to criminal charges against him, he continued to receive money from the company, to be listed as president in documents which it filed with the state, and to give orders to employees, including the employee responsible for the drum-cleaning operation. Defendant sometimes was present when drums were cleaned, and he told employees involved that if they got caught, the company would receive only a slap on the wrist.

In affirming Iverson's conviction, the court of appeals approved the trial court's instruction that the jury could find him liable as a "responsible corporate officer" if it found, beyond a reasonable doubt: (1) that he knew that pollutants were being discharged to the sewer system by company employees, (2) that he had the "authority and capacity to prevent the discharge," and (3) that he failed to prevent the ongoing discharge. The court rejected defendant's argument that a corporate officer is "responsible" only when he "in fact exercises control over the activity causing the discharge or has an express corporate duty to oversee the activity."

4. PROSECUTORIAL DISCRETION

As noted at the beginning of this section on criminal liability, Congress generally has not defined thresholds indicating at what points violations of environmental laws or regulations are serious enough to justify adding criminal to civil penalties. Those judgments are left to enforcement officials in the executive branch.

Most cases come to federal prosecutors by referral from EPA. In 1994, EPA issued a guidance on the exercise of investigative discretion by its criminal investigators. The guidance established specific criteria which EPA investigators are to consider before initiating a criminal investigation. Case selection is based on two general measures, "significant environmental harm" and "culpable conduct." These measures, in turn, are divided into several factors which serve as indicators that a case is suitable for criminal investigation. The factors identified as possible indicators of environmental harm are (1) actual harm, (2) threat of significant harm, (3) failure to report environmental releases, and (4) a trend or common attitude toward noncompliance within the regulated community. Culpable conduct is based on (1) a history of repeated violations, (2) deliberate misconduct, (3) concealment of misconduct or falsification of records, (4) tampering with pollution monitoring or control equipment, or (5) conducting pollution-related activities without necessary permits or approvals.

In a policy statement issued in 1995, EPA said that it generally will not recommend criminal prosecution against those who find violations of environmental laws "through an environmental audit" or through "an objective, documented, systematic procedure or practice reflecting the regulated entity's due diligence in preventing, detecting, and correcting violations." However, a decision not to recommend prosecution also is dependent on prompt disclosure of the violations; correction and remediation; prevention of recurrence; and an absence of prior violations.

5. STATE PRIVILEGES FOR ENVIRONMENTAL AUDITS

Approximately twenty states have enacted laws making information gathered through voluntary environmental audits *privileged*, or protected from disclosure, in various types of enforcement proceedings. Thus, the information is not accessible to third parties, including the government, absent a waiver or court order. About half of the laws also provide *immunity* from criminal, civil, or administrative prosecution and penalties with respect to violations that are disclosed voluntarily.

The laws typically define an environmental audit as a systematic review of a facility's practices to determine noncompliance with certain environmental laws. Most specify a variety of documents which may be considered parts of such reports and to which the privilege extends. These include field notes, records of observations, findings, opinions, suggestions, conclusions, drafts, memoranda, photographs, maps, charts, graphs, and surveys. Most of the laws prohibit persons who participated in audits from disclosing, testifying, or being compelled to testify about the audit reports or underlying facts. Included among participants are those who were made privy to audits, those who did any of the work, and those who provided estimates for corrective work resulting from the audit.

The federal EPA and Department of Justice strongly oppose state privilege and immunity laws, fearing that federal officials may have to step in and expend federal resources to pursue enforcement actions in cases that would be a state responsibility absent restrictions preventing the states from acting. EPA has threatened to withdraw or refuse delegations of authority to implement federal environmental laws and programs, for states whose environmental audit laws interfere unduly with the states' enforcement capabilities. EPA and the Department of Justice also take the position that they are not bound by state privilege or immunity laws in federal enforcement proceedings.

G. COMMON LAW REMEDIES

While Congress and state legislatures have been enacting regulatory statutes aimed at preventing future problems and cleaning up current hazards, state and federal courts have been faced with increasing numbers of tort actions seeking compensatory and punitive damages, and occasionally injunctions, for injuries allegedly caused or threatened by toxic substances. These cases have presented the legal system with a wide range of novel issues, and sometimes strained the system to its limits.

A variety of causes of action may be available to private plaintiffs, frequently adjoining landowners, injured or threatened by hazardous waste sites. Such causes of action include nuisance, negligence, trespass, strict liability, mental distress, and medical monitoring. Branch v. Western Petroleum, Inc. (Utah 1982)(all except medical monitoring); Potter v. Firestone Tire & Rubber Co. (Cal.1993)(mental distress); In re Paoli R.R. Yard PCB Litigation (3d Cir.1990)(medical monitoring).

Governmental plaintiffs may seek abatement of hazardous conditions by challenging them as public nuisances. In Village of Wilsonville v. SCA Services, Inc. (Ill.1981), the court compelled defendant, the owner and operator of a state-licensed hazardous-waste landfill located above an abandoned coal mine, which created a possibility of subsidence, to remove (at an eventual cost of $50 million) all wastes deposited there because they constituted a "prospective nuisance."

In toxic waste damage actions, the plaintiff's first problem is to establish that defendant's conduct met the requisite liability standard. Although many toxic tort plaintiffs have brought actions under products liability theories holding manufacturers strictly liable for defective products, the liability standard is less clear in cases not involving manufacturers. The generally accepted liability test for hazardous waste releases is stated in the Second Restatement of Torts. Under this test, liability exists despite the exercise of due care if an activity was "abnormally dangerous." To determine whether an activity is abnormally dangerous, a court must weigh the probability and severity of foreseeable harm, whether the activity is unusual or is in an inappropriate location, and other factors. Restatement (Second) of Torts § 520 (1977). Thus, fault plays a role in the Restatement assessment. A few courts have rejected this fault element, however, and have begun to move beyond the abnormally dangerous test. In State Dept. of Environmental Protection v. Ventron Corp. (N.J.1983), the court imposed strict liability for harm caused by toxic substances escaping from a landowner's property.

Even if the defendant's conduct meets the requisite legal standard for liability, several possible barriers may prevent recovery. Statutes of limitations used to create major difficulties in some states. For example, a New York trial judge in 1983 dismissed 54 of 91 personal injury actions by residents of Love Canal. The judge held that the actions were barred by New York's statute of limitations because they were filed more than three years after *exposure* to the toxic chemicals. The statute of limitations problem has also received great attention in the asbestos cases.

Approximately forty states have rejected the "exposure" rule in favor of the "discovery" rule, taking the position that the period of limitation does not begin to run until plaintiff discovers her illness. For the remaining states, § 309 of CERCLA was adopted in 1986. It provides that in any action brought under state law for personal injury or property damages "which are caused or contributed to by exposure to any hazardous substance . . . released into the environment from a facility," the limitation period for the action shall commence on "the date plaintiff knew (or reasonably should have known)" that the injury or damages were caused or contributed to by the hazardous substance.

Another problem is establishing a link between the defendant and the release of the substance. For example, many hazardous waste generators may have shipped similar materials to the site in question. It may be quite difficult to establish whose containers leaked or in what quantities. A similar issue has arisen in products liability cases. In Sindell v. Abbott Laboratories (Cal.1980), the plaintiff's mother was administered the drug diethylstilbesterol (DES) during pregnancy. Although DES was routinely given to prevent miscarriage, it now is known to cause a rare form of cancer in some daughters of women who took the drug. After developing such cancer, the plaintiff sued eleven of the more than two hundred manufacturers of DES. Although plaintiff was unable to identify the manufacturer of the particular DES which her mother took, the court held that she had stated a cause of action against all manufacturers of the drug using an identical formula. Resting this holding on a broad social policy, the court noted that the defendants were "better able to bear the costs of injury resulting from the manufacture of a defective product." The Sindell court then adopted a novel theory of liability by making each defendant liable for a share of plaintiff's damages, based on its share of the DES market. A similar approach could be applied where a plaintiff's illness can be traced to releases from a waste disposal site but not to any specific contributor to the site.

Sindell and related theories address the problem of linking the defendant to the chemical exposure. An even more difficult problem is that of linking the exposure to plaintiff's injury. As we have seen, toxic chemical regulation involves matters at the boundaries of scientific knowledge. This scientific uncertainty causes severe problems for government regulators, but even more serious problems result for private plaintiffs who must establish a defendant's liability by a preponderance of the evidence.

In considering compensation, it is important to keep in mind that there are really two causation problems. One is the problem of establishing that the chemical involved is *capable* of causing the type of harm from which the plaintiff suffers. This is often difficult because the causation of diseases like cancer is so poorly understood. For this reason, medical theory is relatively unhelpful in filling in gaps in the factual picture. Facts themselves are hard to come by. Many toxic substances are relatively novel, and, given the long latency periods associated with cancer, sufficient evidence concerning health effects is not likely to be available for the foreseeable future. Animal studies, although useful, generally involve much higher doses that are difficult to extrapolate to low doses over prolonged periods; there is also the question of whether extrapolation of results between species is valid. Epidemiological studies are helpful, but often inconclusive regarding the level of risk created by a toxic substance.

The other problem relating to proof of causation is that of establishing, given that the toxic substance in question *can* cause harm of the type suffered by plaintiff, that the plaintiff's harm *did* in fact result from such exposure. A chemical may increase the prevalence of a disease enough to leave no doubt that *some* members of the exposed population were injured by that chemical. Others, however, may have suffered injuries from independent sources, and the two groups may be impossible to distinguish. The statistical association between exposure and illness may be too weak to justify a finding that a particular plaintiff's disease is causally linked to an exposure to a hazardous substance.

Despite the novelty of tort litigation over toxic causation, clear patterns have evolved in some areas. Litigation about Agent Orange, a defoliant and herbicide used by American forces in the Vietnam war, has provided the most extensive judicial discussion of toxic causation. See In re Agent Orange Product Liability Litigation (E.D.N.Y.1984). Numerous lawsuits were filed against the manufacturers by veterans, their families, and others who contended that Agent Orange had caused various illnesses. Ultimately the litigation was consolidated in the Eastern District of New York. The weakness of the plaintiffs' causation evidence persuaded Judge Weinstein to approve a $180 million settlement, which was considered highly favorable to the defendants.

As Judge Weinstein explained, the evidence concerning the possible dangers from Agent Orange would have been enough for a court to uphold an administrative order limiting its use. Emphasizing the distinction between preventive regulatory measures and compensatory legal actions, however, the judge noted that "[in] the latter [case], a far higher probability (greater than 50%) is required since the law believes it unfair to require an individual to pay for another's tragedy unless it is shown that it is more likely than not that he caused it." The key flaw in the plaintiffs' case was that government epidemiological studies showed no statistical link between Agent Orange exposure and significant health effects. Hence, Judge Weinstein agreed that a settlement was in the best interests of the class.

In companion cases, involving opt-outs or individuals never included in the class, Judge Weinstein was forced to rule on the merits of the plaintiffs' claims. In these cases, he granted summary judgment for the defendants despite plaintiffs' tender of expert testimony linking Agent Orange with health effects. The epidemiological studies played a key role in these decisions. "The numerous epidemiological studies . . . are sufficient to shift the burden to plaintiffs of showing that a material fact exists as to causation." Judge Weinstein ruled the plaintiffs' expert testimony inadmissible, and then granted summary judgment because the plaintiffs had no admissible evidence to counter the defendants' epidemiological studies.

The D.C. Circuit has permitted recovery solely on the basis of expert clinical assessments despite a lack of statistical evidence. In Ferebee v. Chevron Chemical Co. (D.C.Cir.1984), the court stated that a cause-effect relationship need not be clearly established by animal or epidemiological studies before a doctor can testify that, in his opinion, such a relationship exists. "As long as the basic methodology employed to reach a conclusion is sound, such as use of tissue samples, standard tests, and patient examination, products liability law does not preclude recovery until a 'statistically significant' number of people have been injured or until science has had the time and resources to complete sophisticated laboratory studies of the chemical." A few courts have followed Ferebee's broader view of admissibility.

However, cases like Ferebee must be viewed with caution. In Daubert v. Merrell Dow Pharmaceuticals, Inc. (S.Ct.1993), the lower courts had ruled that expert testimony which plaintiffs wanted to present to the jury could not be admitted because it did not rely on epidemiological studies and was not "generally accepted" in the scientific community. The Supreme Court remanded, ruling that the "general acceptance" test applied by the lower courts, see Frye v. United States (D.C.App.1923), has been supplanted by a broader and more flexible inquiry under the legislatively enacted Federal Rules of Evidence. "[I]n order to qualify [under Rule 702] as 'scientific knowledge,' an inference or assertion must be derived by the scientific method" and must have been tested, said Justice Blackmun. While publication in a journal subject to peer review is not essential, it is a "relevant" factor for a judge to consider in assessing whether a method or technique is valid. The Court "recognize[d] that in practice, a gatekeeping role for the judge, no matter how flexible, inevitably on occasion will prevent the jury from learning of authentic insights and innovations. That, nevertheless, is the balance that is struck by Rules of Evidence designed not for the exhaustive search for cosmic understanding but for the particularized resolution of legal disputes." The Court rejected plaintiffs' argument that Congress intended to permit juries to resolve scientific disputes through the adversarial process in the same manner as they resolve disputes about economic theories or other complex subjects.

On remand in *Daubert*, the court of appeals again held that plaintiffs' proffered expert testimony was inadmissible. The court emphasized plaintiffs' failure to show either that the testimony grew out of research conducted by the expert prior to and independently of the litigation, or that the research had been subjected to peer review. Daubert v. Merrell Dow Pharmaceuticals, Inc. (9th Cir.1995).

CHAPTER 6

PRESERVATION OF NATURAL AREAS

Cleaning up the air and water is clearly an important goal of environmental law, as is protecting the public from toxic chemicals. There is, however, another strand of federal environmental law which seeks different, though related, goals. Indeed, this strand pre-dates the federal anti-pollution effort. The reference, of course, is to the goal of preserving wilderness and other natural areas.

Several statutes that we have already considered incorporate this goal. For example, NEPA requires the government to "fulfill the responsibilities of each generation as trustee of the environment for succeeding generations," to "assure for all Americans safe, healthful, productive, and esthetically and culturally pleasing surroundings," and to "preserve important . . . natural aspects of our national heritage. . . ." Section 101(b). Much litigation under NEPA relates to whether factors such as these have been adequately discussed in environmental impact statements. As we will see, the Clean Water Act also contains protections for wetlands, and the Clean Air Act contains specific provisions relating to the protection of parks and wilderness areas.

In this chapter, we will be concerned primarily with direct restrictions on land development in natural areas.

The effect of these restrictions is to prevent individuals who wish to do so from using certain areas for economically profitable purposes. This chapter explores the statutory and constitutional implications of these restrictions. We begin by considering government restrictions on the development of privately owned land. We next consider efforts to protect coastal waters, and turn then to restrictions on resource development on publicly owned lands. We close with a brief discussion of protection for endangered species, a policy that applies in each of these geographic areas.

A. PRESERVATION AS A GOAL

Before considering these legal restrictions on development, an understanding of their rationale is helpful. A century ago the idea of preventing the development of "useless" wilderness areas might have been widely regarded as completely irrational. Obviously, individuals who share this judgment will regard the legal mechanisms under discussion here as incomprehensible at best and perhaps perverse at worst. What are the arguments in favor of protecting natural areas?

Because the alternative land uses typically are economically profitable, it is useful to begin by examining this question from an economic perspective. As we saw in Chapter 3, economists typically regard the free market as the ideal means of determining resource allocation. It has been argued that this model should be extended to wilderness areas, so that, for example, the Grand Canyon would be sold to the highest bidder. If the highest bidder was the Sierra Club, the Canyon would be saved; if the highest bidder was a strip mining company, the Canyon would be mined. Any attempt to defend wilderness preservation must confront and attempt to refute this position.

Several economic arguments can be made in favor of wilderness preservation. As we saw earlier, the market mechanism breaks down when public goods or externalities are present. Arguably, both are involved in wilderness preservation. Individuals may consider preservation of wilderness worthwhile even though they have no present plans to use the wilderness. They may be considered as having a so-called "option demand" for wilderness. That is, these individuals would be willing to pay to preserve the option of using the wilderness in the future for themselves and their descendants. More broadly, some individuals who have no desire to use wilderness at any time may nevertheless have a preference for the preservation of wilderness as an ethical value. These individuals' preferences arguably make wilderness preservation a public good. The reason is that if the wilderness is preserved, these individuals cannot be excluded from enjoying the resulting satisfaction of their preferences. Furthermore, externalities are also present. Many biologists would suggest, on the basis of studies of prior ecological changes, that widespread changes in undeveloped areas are likely to have unforeseen negative consequences there and elsewhere. For example, development of estuaries or marsh areas may indirectly affect wildlife and marine life, thereby impinging on the interests of hunters and fishermen. The existence of these externalities provides a basis for preserving wilderness areas that is not unlike the basis for preventing pollution.

Moreover, temporal externalities also exist, for many of the affected individuals belong to future generations. Some economists have argued that these intertemporal effects may be quite large. The amount of wilderness is limited by present supplies; indeed, the future amount of available wilderness probably will be even less than that existing today. As the supply decreases, the price individuals would be willing to pay to use any one piece of wilderness will tend to increase. Moreover, preservation of wilderness seems to be a "normal" good—that is, a good which is in greater demand as income rises. If we assume that economic growth will continue, the result will be higher individual incomes and therefore a higher demand for wilderness. Hence, future generations may have a stronger demand for wilderness areas than current generations. Ignoring the preferences of future generations thus could result in greatly distorted resource allocation over time. Thus, from the perspective of neoclassical economics, a strong argument can be made against leaving decisions about wilderness to the market.

As a descriptive science, economics can tell us only the consequences of a decision but not its desirability. Society must make a value judgment about those consequences. Today's society clearly has made a judgment in favor of preserving wilderness. This can be seen in the various environmental statutes considered in this chapter. It can also be seen in more direct measurements of public opinion in various opinion polls, which show consistent support for wilderness preservation.

With this background in mind, we will turn to the problems raised by attempting to prevent individuals from developing privately owned lands.

B. RESTRICTIONS ON DEVELOPMENT OF PRIVATE LAND

Much environmentally significant land, particularly in wetlands and coastal areas, is in the hands of private individuals. We will not attempt to survey the various state laws restricting the development of this land. Instead, we will focus on the constitutional issues. We will first consider the extent to which attempts to regulate development of private land may violate the taking clause of the Constitution. We will then turn to the public trust doctrine and some related doctrines which legitimize restrictions that might otherwise be constitutionally dubious.

1. THE TAKING PROBLEM

The Fifth Amendment provides that private property shall not "be taken for public use, without just compensation." This provision applies only to the federal government. The Fourteenth Amendment, which imposes constitutional restrictions on the States, does not contain similar language. The Supreme Court, however, has construed the Fourteenth Amendment as imposing a similar requirement by implication from its due process clause. Consequently, courts have not distinguished between the federal and state governments for purposes of taking clause analysis.

The earliest relevant taking case is Hadacheck v. Sebastian (S.Ct.1915). *Hadacheck* involved a Los Angeles city ordinance making it unlawful to operate a brickyard within certain portions of the city. Hadacheck owned a brickyard in one of those areas. He had purchased the land when it was well outside the city limits and not near any residential district. He alleged that he had had no reason to anticipate that the area would ever be annexed to the city, that much of the property had been excavated for clay, that the land was worth $800,000 if used for brick-making purposes but no more than $60,000 for any other purpose, and that the ordinance would force him out of business. He also made two additional allegations that were rejected by the state courts: (1) that the operation of his business did not have detrimental effects on adjoining property, and (2) that the real purpose of the ordinance was to give brickyards located elsewhere in the city a monopoly. The Supreme Court decisively rejected the attack on the ordinance:

> It is to be remembered that we are dealing with one of the most essential powers of government, one that is the least limitable. It may, indeed, seem harsh in its exercise, usually is on some individual, but the imperative necessity for its existence precludes any limitation upon it when not exerted arbitrarily. A vested interest cannot be asserted against it because of conditions once obtaining. To so hold would preclude development and fix a city forever in its primitive conditions. There must be progress, and if in its march private interests are in the way they must yield to the good of the community.

Hadacheck was decided at a time when the Supreme Court was much more willing than it is today to strike down state statutes regulating economic activities. Yet, even in that pro-business period, the Court firmly upheld the *Hadacheck* ordinance.

Hadacheck might seem to suggest that the impact of a regulation on private individuals is irrelevant to determining constitutionality. The theory of the case seems to be that if a statute is otherwise legitimately within the police power—that is, if it is reasonably related to the public health, welfare, or morals—then individuals who suffer severe losses because of the regulation have no remedy. Less than a decade after *Hadacheck,* the Supreme Court drew back from this conclusion in Pennsylvania Coal Co. v. Mahon (S.Ct.1922). This case involved a Pennsylvania statute making it unlawful for coal companies to cause the subsidence of any public building, street, or private residence. The Mahons were bound by a covenant to permit a coal company, which had conveyed only the surface rights to their lot, to remove all the coal without liability. The effect of the statute was to annul this covenant. Pennsylvania law recognized three separate property rights: the right to use the surface, ownership of the subsurface minerals, and the right to have the surface supported by the subsurface earth. The coal company claimed that the statute operated as a taking of the second and third rights, both of which belonged to them under their deed with the Mahons. In perhaps the most important single decision under the taking clause, Justice Holmes held that the statute was indeed a taking. The heart of the opinion is to be found in the following famous passage:

> Government hardly could go on if to some extent values incident to property could not be diminished without paying for every such change in the general law. As long recognized, some values are enjoyed under an implied limitation and must

yield to the police power. But obviously the implied limitation must have its limits, or the contract and due process clauses are gone. One fact for consideration in determining such limits is the extent of the diminution. When it reaches a certain magnitude, in most if not in all cases there must be an exercise of eminent domain and compensation to sustain the act. So the question depends upon the particular facts. The greatest weight is given to the judgment of the legislature, but it always is open to interested parties to contend that the legislature has gone beyond its constitutional power.

In applying this test, the Court stressed that the statute made coal mining in certain areas commercially impracticable and thus had "very nearly the same effect for constitutional purposes as appropriating or destroying it." The Court concluded that so long as "private persons or communities have seen fit to take the risk of acquiring only surface rights, we cannot see that the fact that the risk has become a danger warrants the giving to them greater rights than they bought." Justice Brandeis filed a strong dissent.

At the very least, *Pennsylvania Coal* makes it clear that *Hadacheck* cannot be taken to its logical extreme. That is, cases exist in which there is a legitimate public purpose for regulation but the regulation falls too heavily on a single individual, who must be compensated under the taking clause. As the Court says in *Pennsylvania Coal,* this is a matter of degree and therefore difficult to predict in advance.

The next case made it clear, however, that even the physical destruction of property may sometimes be permissible without compensation. In Miller v. Schoene (S.Ct.1928), the Court upheld a Virginia statute authorizing the state entomologist to order the destruction of ornamental red cedar trees. The purpose of the statute was to prevent the transmission of a plant disease to neighboring apple orchards. The Court held that the existence of cedars was incompatible with the existence of the apple trees, so that the state was forced to choose which form of property to preserve. As the Court said, "[W]hen forced to such a choice the state does not exceed its constitutional powers by deciding upon the destruction of one class of property in order to save another which, in the judgment of the legislature, is of greater value to the public."

For several decades, the Supreme Court paid little attention to takings issues. In the late 1970s, the Court's interest returned to this area. Penn Central Transportation Co. v. New York (S.Ct.1978) involved a New York historic preservation ordinance. Briefly, under the ordinance a special commission was empowered to designate buildings as landmarks, subject to administrative and judicial review. After designation, the exterior of a building had to be kept in good repair and exterior alterations had to be approved by the Commission. Development rights lost because of the landmark designation could be transferred to nearby plots of land, thereby allowing additional development on that land beyond the normal restrictions of the applicable zoning and building codes. Penn Central owned Grand Central Terminal, a designated landmark. A plan by Penn Central to build a multistory office building perched above the terminal was rejected by the Commission. Penn Central then brought suit claiming that its property had been taken without compensation. It conceded, however, that the transferable development rights had some value and that the company could still earn a reasonable return on its initial investment.

The opinion of the Court by Justice Brennan begins by reviewing the factors that had shaped prior decisions. The Court conceded that it had been unable to develop any "set formula" for determining when compensation was required. Instead, it referred to the prior cases as involving "essentially ad hoc, factual inquiries." The Court did, however, point to several relevant factors. The most important were (1) whether the regulation had "interfered with distinct investment backed expectations," and (2) whether the government had physically invaded the property or had simply enacted "some public program adjusting the benefits and burdens of economic life to promote the common good." In reviewing the specific regulation before it, the Court concluded that the purposes of the ordinance were permissible because the ordinance was "expected to produce a widespread public benefit applicable to all similarly situated property." The Court then held that the regulation passed the *Pennsylvania Coal* test because it did not deprive the company of all use of the property, but instead allowed continuation of a past use and more importantly, permitted the company to obtain a "reasonable return" on its investment.

Since *Penn Central*, taking cases have been a regular part of the Court's docket. A year after *Penn Central*, the Supreme Court decided two additional significant taking cases. The first case, Andrus v. Allard (S.Ct.1979), involved a statute prohibiting commercial transactions in certain "artifacts" such as eagle feathers.

The plaintiffs owned bird feathers when the statute was passed and were subject to prosecution for selling them. In rejecting a taking claim, the Court stressed that the plaintiffs retained the rights to possess, donate and devise the feathers. The Court noted that the feathers could conceivably be exhibited for profit, but then went on to add that a loss of future profits, unaccompanied by any physical property restriction, "provides a slender reed upon which to rest a takings claim." The second case, Kaiser Aetna v. United States (S.Ct.1979), involved a private fishpond which the owners connected to the ocean and converted into a "marina-style subdivision community." Although the government did not initially object to this project, it later contended that the marina was subject to a right of public access. The Court held that imposing this right of access would constitute a taking. The opinion does not purport to establish a general test, but instead stresses that the pond was not commercially navigable in its original state, that the government acquiesced in the marina conversion, and that the right to exclude others is a fundamental element of property ownership. We will consider this case again in the next subsection when we discuss the federal navigational servitude.

In 1987, the Supreme Court decided three important takings cases. One related to remedies. In First English Evangelical Lutheran Church of Glendale v. County of Los Angeles (S.Ct.1987), the Court significantly strengthened the remedy available to a property owner whose land has been "over-regulated." Under *First English,* the land owner is entitled not only to an injunction against enforcement of the ordinance, but also to damages for the temporary restriction on development between the ordinance's passage and the injunction invalidating it. Thus, governments may become liable for substantial damage awards if they misjudge the location of the blurred and wavering line between valid regulations and invalid takings. This may deter stringent environmental regulations.

The other two 1987 cases increased the uncertainty about the difference between regulation and taking. In one case, Keystone Bituminous Coal Ass'n v. DeBenedictis (S.Ct.1987), the Court upheld a statute strikingly similar to that struck down in the old *Pennsylvania Coal* case. This time, the Court found that protection of surface land from subsidence was a valid public purpose, and that the mining companies could still earn a fair return on their holdings, since only a small percentage of the coal had to be left in the ground to support the surface. The Court was sharply divided, however, with four dissenters insisting that *Pennsylvania Coal* was controlling.

In the final case in this trilogy, the Court found a taking based on quite a different analysis. Nollan v. California Coastal Commission (S.Ct.1987) involved an owner's effort to construct a bungalow on his beachfront property. As a condition of approval, the California Coastal Commission required him to record an easement giving the public lateral access to the beach from adjacent beach property. In an opinion by Justice Scalia, the Court held that this requirement was a taking. Justice Scalia assumed that the Commission could have simply forbidden construction of the bungalow, but held that any conditions on approval had to be "reasonably related" to problems created by the new construction. The four dissenters accused the majority of substantially raising the level of scrutiny applied to land use regulations. The dissent also pointed out that the permit condition was not alleged to diminish the value of the owner's investment in the land.

In a follow-up to *Nollan*, the Court fleshed out the "nexus" requirement in Dolan v. City of Tigard (S.Ct.1994). Like *Nollan*, *Dolan* involved conditions on a building permit: a requirement that in order to expand a hardware store, the owner dedicate a flood-plain area and the adjacent 15 feet to a public "green-space" and bicycle path. The court upheld the conditions to the extent that they limited development in this part of the land, but found it difficult to see why the owner was also required to give up her "right to ex-clude" others from use of the greenway. Applying a test of "rough proportionality," the Court concluded that the city had failed to provide any quantitative evidence that the bikeway would offset the increased traffic demand from the store expansion. As a practical matter, it is unclear whether *Dolan* actually places substantive restrictions on government action, or merely imposes the expense of paying a consultant to deliver the appropriate estimates in support of the government. In any event, later precedent indicates that the nexus and proportionality tests apply only when the govern-ment conditions a permit on the grant of a property interest such as an easement. These requirements do not apply when the government merely restricts the use of property.

None of these cases involved the core question raised by Justice Holmes in *Pennsylvania Coal*: When does a diminution in value become so great as to become a taking? In Lucas v. South Carolina Coastal

Council (S.Ct.1992), the Court made it clear at least that a *complete* destruction of land value is normally a taking. *Lucas* involved a takings claim by the owner of two beachfront residential lots, who could not build on the property at all because of a state law protecting fragile breaches. Although dicta in a number of previous cases had suggested that a 100% loss of property value would be a taking, regardless of the government's regulatory justification, *Lucas* is the first square holding to that effect. Justice Scalia's opinion for the Court sets some limits on this rule: it does not apply when the land use would be a common law nuisance or otherwise in excess of the owner's common law rights; it does not apply to personal property; it may not apply to regulations that are not specifically directed to land use. Justice Scalia also found it somewhat difficult to explain the basis for the rule, perhaps because his usual philosophy of reliance on constitutional text and original intent provides little support. In a concurring opinion, Justice Kennedy argued for a more fluid balancing approach, while Justices Blackmun and Stevens sharply dissented.

Obviously, the Court has not steered a steady course in construing the takings clause, and the theoretical foundations for the endeavor remain mysterious. At this point, however, it is possible to discern a fairly clear pattern in the results of the cases. The Court seems to divide land-use regulations into three categories.

First are the access mandates. Such a regulation mandates that a landowner open up his land to the public or allow it to be physically occupied by a third-party. Such regulations are much like condemnation of an easement and not surprisingly are considered virtually per se takings. *Kaiser Aetna* is an illustrative case.

Second are use limitations. The regulation may restrict the landowner's use of the property so greatly as to impose a severe economic loss. Assuming that the land use would otherwise have been lawful, the regulation is a taking if it renders the land completely valueless. The Court has never precluded the possibility that a partial use restriction might be severe enough to constitute a taking even if the government is pursuing a bona fide public policy. Notably, however, in the 80 years since *Hadacheck*, the Court has never found such a taking in a specific case if the government was pursuing a bona fide public policy. So, perhaps Holmes's reference to a sufficiently great diminution in value actually means the complete destruction of value. If so, *Lucas* represents the rare case of a taking due to diminution of value.

The third category involves tie-ins between use restrictions and access mandates. The government may require the landowner to allow public access (normally a taking) in order to escape from land use restrictions (normally not a taking). Here, the Court requires that the access requirement relate to the proposed use of the land and be "roughly proportionate" to the problems created by the new use.

This three-part scheme provides a tidy account of the cases. Takings law has been so doctrinally unruly, however, that it would be unwise to count on future consistency. Perhaps the Court will find that some public access requirements are not takings, after all, or that some partial use restrictions are takings. In the meantime, however, this scheme does at least put the cases into some coherent order.

One response to the taking problem has been to attempt to limit the kinds of interests that can claim the status of property rights. By preventing certain kinds of economic interests from rising to the status of property rights, a court can avoid any taking problem. The court can simply say that whatever was taken was not property and thus not subject to the taking clause. In the next section, we will consider several of the doctrines which have served this function.

2. THE PUBLIC TRUST DOCTRINE

Both the federal and state governments possess certain quasi-property rights stemming from their regulatory powers over waterways. These rights have become important in the environmental context because they serve to justify government regulations in coastal and wetland areas that might otherwise be challenged under the taking clause.

At the state level, these quasi-property rights are defined by the public trust doctrine. The leading case concerning this doctrine is Illinois Central Railroad Co. v. Illinois (S.Ct.1892). This case involved the validity of a land grant to the Illinois Central Railroad. In 1869, the Illinois legislature had granted fee title to certain submerged lands under Lake Michigan to the railroad. (When the bill was introduced, it had conveyed these lands to the City of Chicago, but somehow before final passage the grantee had been changed to the railroad.) Four years later, the State repealed the prior statute. Illinois then filed a quiet title suit to establish its ownership of the submerged lands. It should be noted that if the 1869 statute was valid, the statute reclaiming ownership of the lands could hardly avoid attack as a taking

since it seized title to private property. The Supreme
Court, however, avoided any such constitutional problem by holding that the original grant of land to the
railroad was invalid, so that the railroad never had
anything except at most a voidable title to the property.
The 1869 Act was invalid because it violated the public
trust in which the property was originally held by the
State, as the following passage explains:

> That the State holds the title to the lands under
> the navigable waters of Lake Michigan . . . we have
> already shown, and that title necessarily carries with
> it control over the waters above them whenever the
> lands are subjected to use. . . . It is a title held in
> trust for the people of the State that they may enjoy
> the navigation of the waters, carry on commerce
> over them, and have liberty of fishing therein freed
> from the obstruction or interference of private
> parties. . . . The trust devolving upon the state for
> the public, and which can only be discharged by the
> management and control of property in which the
> public has an interest, cannot be relinquished by a
> transfer of property. The control of the state for
> the purposes of the trust can never be lost, except
> as to such parcels as are used in promoting the
> interests of the public therein, or can be disposed of
> without any substantial impairment of the public
> interest in the lands and waters remaining.

Thus, private property interests in land subject to the
public trust are severely limited. To the extent private
individuals can hold title to this land at all, that title is
necessarily subject to the requirements of the trust. As
the Supreme Court later made clear, the public trust
extends not only to navigable waters but also to all

waters affected by the tides. Phillips Petroleum Co. v. Mississippi (S.Ct.1988).

The evolution of the public trust doctrine is well illustrated by three cases from California. In a 1928 case, Boone v. Kingsbury (Cal. 1928), the California Supreme Court upheld a statute authorizing oil drilling in offshore tidal areas. The court held that this form of development was a justifiable exercise of the public trust. The court stressed the public interest in encouraging "citizens to devote waste and unused lands to some useful purpose." As an example of such useless lands, the court referred to a prior case involving a salt marsh. By 1971, the court's attitude had changed completely. In Marks v. Whitney (Cal.1971), the court gave a much more expansive reading to the public trust doctrine. The court stressed that in administering the trust, the state is not bound by traditional classifications of land uses. Instead, the state can give recognition to the need to preserve lands in their natural state, so they can serve as "ecological units for scientific study, as open space, and as environments which provide food and habitat for birds and marine life, and which favorably affect the scenery and climate of the area." As a result, the court held that a neighboring landowner could sue to prevent tidelands from being filled and developed. Such a suit could be brought even if lands had already been reclaimed with or without prior authorization from the state, since neither reclamation nor prior authorization "*ipso facto* terminate the public trust nor render the issue moot." Later, in National Audubon Society v. Superior Court of Alpine County (Cal.1983), the same court held that the public trust doctrine limited "prior appropriation" rights over use of water, so that Los Angeles was not automatically entitled to the full use of its water rights where the result would be to completely dry up a lake. Given the almost sacrosanct place of prior appropriation rights in western water law, this was a notable expansion of the public trust doctrine.

The public trust doctrine is not the only property law concept that has been used to uphold restrictions on private land development. In an innovative decision, the Oregon Supreme Court held that fencing beach land violated a property interest on the part of the public deriving from longstanding custom. State ex rel. Thornton v. Hay (Or.1969). Opinions such as this, or such as those applying the public trust doctrine, should not be seen simply as a means of finding a loophole in taking law. Rather, they are best seen as attempts to adjust the technicalities of taking and property law to the realities of modern life. As a realistic matter, certain activities involve longstanding public interests and therefore must reasonably be expected to be subject to broad government regulation. Given the long history of public control over waterways, no individual claiming to own legal title to a public waterway can really have a reasonable expectation of uninhibited use of his "property." Thus, the kinds of firm expectations that taking law was intended to protect simply cannot arise in some contexts.

3. THE NAVIGATIONAL SERVITUDE

Like the states, the federal government has a quasi-property interest in navigable waters. The federal interest is called the navigational servitude. The operation of the servitude is illustrated in United States v.

Rands (S.Ct.1967). The issue in *Rands* was whether a condemnation award for land along the Columbia River should include that portion of its market value attributable to potential use as a port site. The court held that no individual can own a property interest in the use of navigable waters, for such use is always completely subject to government control. "Thus, without being constitutionally obligated to pay compensation, the United States may change the course of a navigable stream, or otherwise impair or destroy a riparian owner's access to navigable waters, even though the market value of the riparian owner's land is substantially diminished." Indeed, later in the opinion, the Court referred to the "constitutional power of Congress *completely* to regulate navigable streams to the *total* exclusion of private power companies or port owners" [emphasis added].

The *Rands* case may have been somewhat limited by Kaiser Aetna v. United States (S.Ct.1979). That case, discussed in the previous subsection, involved the private improvement of a pond which originally was incapable of being used for navigational purposes. As a result of the improvements, the pond was to be used as a private marina. The Court acknowledged that the strict logic of *Rands* and similar cases might allow the government to require public access to the marina, converting it into a public aquatic park. But, the Court concluded, the facts in the *Kaiser Aetna* case were too far removed from previous cases involving navigable waterways. For one thing, the pond was unlike the sort of "great navigable stream" that had previously been held "incapable of private ownership." The Court also stressed the government's consent to the marina project:

> We have not the slightest doubt that the Government *could have refused to allow such dredging* on the ground that it could have impaired navigation in the bay, or could have conditioned its approval of the dredging on petitioners' agreement to comply with various measures that it deemed appropriate for the promotion of navigation. But what petitioners *now* have is a body of water that was private property under Hawaiian law, linked to navigable water by a channel dredged by them with the consent of the respondent.... In this case, we hold that the "right to exclude," so universally held to be a fundamental element of the property right, falls within this category of interests that the Government cannot take without compensation.... Thus, if the Government wishes to make what was formerly Kuaapa Pond into a public aquatic park *after petitioners have proceeded as far as they have here,* it may not, without invoking eminent domain power and paying just compensation, require them to allow free access to the dredged pond while petitioners' agreement with their customers calls for an annual $72 regular fee. [Emphasis added]

This was obviously a guarded holding. Two decades later, *Kaiser Aetna* seems to have found its place as a narrow exception to the *Rands* rule.

It is important to note that the navigational servitude applies only to waters meeting the traditional test of navigability. While statements of the traditional test vary, the central concern behind these tests relates to potential use for navigational purposes. On the other hand, federal regulation has not been limited to this class of waterways. The courts have held, with strong support in the legislative history, that the Clean Water Act extends beyond traditional navigable waters to all bodies of water within the United States. The reason, obviously, is that the purity of navigable waterways cannot be maintained unless other bodies of water which directly or indirectly connect to those navigable waters are also cleaned up. To the extent that Congress has extended its jurisdictional net beyond the traditional navigable waterways, however, it can no longer claim the protection of the navigational servitude as a defense to taking claims. Thus, at least some applications of the Clean Water Act possibly might be found to limit the use of certain parcels of land so drastically as to constitute takings.

Perhaps the most significant exercise of congressional authority is § 404 of the Clean Water Act. Section 404 requires permits for the discharge of dredged or fill material. In an important early district court opinion, the permit requirement was applied to manmade canals and mangrove wetlands which are periodically covered by tides. The discharges, which ultimately would have resulted in converting these areas into dry land, were held to violate the Act. United States v. Holland (M.D.Fla.1974).

The Supreme Court ratified this expansive construction of the statute by the lower courts in United States v. Riverside Bayview Homes, Inc. (S.Ct.1985), which upheld a regulation defining the Corps' permit authority broadly. The regulation at issue gave the Corps jurisdiction over any area flooded or saturated often enough to support "vegetation typically adapted for life in saturated soil conditions." Thus, a broad range of wetlands are subject to the permit requirement. Courts have aggressively enforced the permit requirement, sometimes going so far as to require that land illegally filled be returned to its natural condition.

This tremendous expansion of federal jurisdiction has given rise to some administrative problems. It would obviously be impractical to require a federal permit every time a farmer digs a ditch that connects to an existing drainage system. EPA adopted regulations exempting discharges from agricultural activities, with certain exceptions for relatively major pollution sources. These regulations, however, were held invalid in NRDC v. Costle (D.C.Cir.1977). The D.C. Circuit rejected EPA's argument that issuing permits would be impractical in view of the number of sources involved (around 500,000) and the difficulty of setting quantitative effluent limits. Instead, the court held, EPA could issue general permits for whole classes of discharges, setting various restrictions on the discharger's actions. The 1977 amendments to the Act exempt a number of "normal farming, silvaculture, and ranching activities" from permit requirements insofar as these activities involve discharges of dredged or fill material. The exemption does not apply to any "activity having as its purpose bringing an area of the navigable waters into a use to which it was not previously subject, where the flow or circulation of navigable waters may be impaired or the reach of such waters be reduced" (§ 404(f)(2)).

Because both the federal and state governments, as we have seen, have legitimate interests in regulating the use of water bodies and adjacent lands, a cooperative effort is clearly indicated. A beginning has been made toward such cooperation. The Clean Water Act provides for delegation of the permit system to state governments, subject to certain safeguards. In addition, another statute, the Coastal Zone Management Act, 16 U.S.C.A. §§ 1451–1464, attempts to encourage state governments to implement land use plans for coastal areas. The incentive is financial; the requirements are essentially procedural. Congress was less concerned about controlling the eventual form of state regulation than in encouraging the states to engage in some structured form of regulation of coastal areas. The CZMA is discussed in more detail below.

C. PROTECTING COASTAL WATERS

Disputes over the exploration and development of offshore oil and gas deposits have multiplied ever since the disastrous 1969 blowout and spill in California's Santa Barbara channel, which killed birds and marine organisms, damaged beaches and seafront properties, and impaired fishing and recreational activities over a large area. The disputes most frequently have arisen in connection with federal leasing of tracts in the outer continental shelf (OCS). The United States government, rather than the states, exercises sovereign rights over the seabed and subsoil of the continental shelf beyond three miles from the coastline. United States v. Maine (S.Ct.1975); Outer Continental Shelf Lands Act (OCSLA), 43 U.S.C.A. § 1331. Acting primarily through the Department of the Interior, the government leases OCS areas to private firms through a competitive bidding process prescribed by OCSLA. Leasing and the resultant exploration, development, production and transportation of OCS oil and gas also are subject to the mandates of NEPA, the Coastal Zone Management Act (CZMA), and the Clean Water Act.

The process leading to production and transportation of oil and gas from OCS lands involves several stages at which environmental considerations are to be taken into account. As amended in 1978, OCSLA charts a path which begins with promulgation of a five-year leasing program and continues through lease sales and exploration to development, production, and sale of the recovered minerals. 43 U.S.C.A. §§ 1344, 1337, 1340, 1351 and 1353. To ensure that the Secretary of the Interior takes into account all relevant policy considerations and the views of all interested persons, the Act provides for participation by Congress, affected state and local governments, other federal agencies, and the public.

Section 18 of the Act, 43 U.S.C.A. § 1344, requires the Secretary to establish a five-year OCS leasing program, consisting of a schedule of proposed lease sales indicating as precisely as possible the size, timing and location of leasing activity. The Secretary must prepare and maintain the program consistent with four basic principles:

(1) Management of the OCS shall be conducted in a manner which considers economic, social, and environmental values. . . .

(2) Timing and location of exploration, development, and production among the oil and gas-bearing physiographic regions of the OCS shall be based on consideration of an equitable sharing of developmental benefits and environmental risks among the various regions. . . .

(3) The Secretary shall select the timing and location of leasing, to the maximum extent practicable, so as to obtain a proper balance between the potential for environmental damage, the potential for discovery of oil and gas, and the potential for adverse impact on the coastal zone.

(4) Leasing activities shall be conducted to assure receipt of fair market value for the lands leased and the rights conveyed by the federal government.

Section 18 also establishes a mechanism for state governments to offer suggestions and comments. The Secretary must submit the proposed program and any comments received to Congress and the President at least sixty days before he approves it, indicating why any specific recommendation of a state government was not accepted.

Following approval by the Secretary, a leasing program is subject for sixty days to judicial review exclusively in the D.C. Circuit, upon suit by any person who participated in the administrative proceedings related to the program and is adversely affected or aggrieved by it. 43 U.S.C.A. § 1349. The court of appeals must consider the matter solely on the record before the Secretary, and his findings are conclusive if supported by substantial evidence.

In State of California v. Watt (D.C.Cir.1981), the states of California and Alaska and several environmental groups obtained judicial review of the five-year OCS leasing program approved in 1980 during the Carter administration. The court noted that § 18 of OCSLA seeks to assure that the size, timing, and location of proposed lease sales within the program achieve a proper balance among economic, environmental, and coastal state concerns. The court found that Secretary Andrus had erred in failing (a) to specify the location of certain proposed lease sales more precisely than simply "California", (b) to consider the need to share developmental benefits and environmental risks among the various OCS regions, (c) to consider the relative environmental sensitivity and marine productivity of different areas of the OCS, (d) to base timing and location of leasing on some of the standards of subsection 18(2), (e) to strike a proper balance incorporating environmental and coastal zone factors, and not simply administrative and economic factors, and (f) to quantify environmental costs to the extent they are quantifiable. The court remanded the leasing program to Secretary Andrus' successor, James Watt, for reconsideration in connection with a revised leasing program then being prepared.

In 1982 Secretary Watt approved a new 1982–1987 program to lease virtually the nation's entire OCS, almost one billion acres in 41 oil and gas lease sales. The program excluded almost no areas for environmental reasons, and clearly evidenced the belief of Watt and others in the Reagan administration that natural resources are best used by the private sector. On the following day, eight environmental groups and several state and local governments challenged the program in a consolidated lawsuit in the D.C. Circuit. They complained that the program did not reflect a proper balance among the potentials for environmental damage, hydrocarbon discovery, and adverse coastal effects, and that it violated the court's 1981 order in *California*

v. Watt. However, the court rejected each of the petitioners' arguments and upheld the program in its
entirety. State of California v. Watt (D.C.Cir.1983).
The program later ran into political roadblocks, however.

After a five-year OCS leasing program has been
approved by the Secretary of Interior and survived
judicial review, later steps toward production of oil and
gas include the proposal and conduct of lease sales by
the Secretary, and proposal by lessees of exploration
plans and then development and production plans. As
stated previously, OCSLA requires at all these stages
that the Secretary consider environmental factors and
the views of other federal officials, state and local
governments, and the public.

Related to federal action under OCSLA, there has
been extended controversy over the requirements of the
Coastal Zone Management Act. CZMA seeks to
achieve sound use of coastal land and water resources
by providing monetary assistance to states to develop
and administer management programs consistent with
standards prescribed in §§ 305 and 306. Approval of a
state management program by the Secretary of Commerce triggers "federal consistency" provisions in §
307(c). As originally enacted, this provision required
federal agencies, permittees and licensees to show that
their proposed developments in or "directly affecting"
coastal zones, including the OCS, would be consistent
with the state program. In certain instances the consistency requirement is qualified by the phrase "to the
maximum extent practicable" or "unless [found by the
Secretary of Commerce to be] consistent with the
objectives of this title or otherwise necessary in the

interest of national security." (A 1990 revision of § 307(c) is discussed below.)

California was one of the first states to receive federal assistance to develop a management program under CZMA. In 1976 the legislature enacted the California Coastal Act, and the National Oceanic and Atmospheric Administration (NOAA), the approving agency under the Secretary of Commerce, began working with state officials to ensure that the new legislation complied with the requirements of CZMA. In 1977, oil industry trade associations sued to enjoin NOAA's approval of the California management program. They contended, among other things, that it failed to satisfy the requirement of § 306(c)(8) that such a program provide for "adequate consideration of the national interest involved in planning for, and in the siting of, facilities (including energy facilities in, or which significantly affect, such state's coastal zone) which are necessary to meet requirements which are other than local in nature." In American Petroleum Institute v. Knecht (9th Cir.1979), the court upheld NOAA's approval of the California management program, rejecting plaintiffs' argument that § 306(c)(8) required "explicit commitments" by the state to accommodate new energy facilities.

In 1981, over the protests of state and local officials in California, Secretary of the Interior Watt announced an OCS lease sale of the entire Santa Maria Basin, offshore from an extraordinarily scenic stretch of coastline extending between Big Sur and Santa Barbara. The court of appeals held that Secretary Watt had violated § 307(c)(1) by selling tracts without making a determination of consistency with the state's program, because the sale would "directly affect" the state's coastal zone by establishing "the first link in a chain of events which could lead to production and development of oil and gas on the individual tracts leased." The Supreme Court reversed in Secretary of the Interior v. California (S.Ct.1984), holding that the CZMA consistency provisions apply only to the later stages of the oil production process, namely exploration and development. The Court also held that the CZMA does not extend to activities on the OCS.

As a rider to the 1990 Omnibus Budget Reconciliation Act, Congress overruled Secretary of the Interior v. California by amending § 307(c)(1) of the CZMA to read as follows:

Each Federal agency activity within or outside the coastal zone that affects any land or water use or natural resource of the coastal zone shall be carried out in a manner which is consistent to the maximum extent practicable with the enforceable policies of approved State management programs.

Subsection (B) provides for federal exemption if the federal activity is found by the President to be "in the paramount interest of the United States."

So far, we have considered the process leading up to issuance of leases. Suppose environmental problems arise later. Leases issued by the Secretary of Interior contain provisions intended to protect against damages from oil spills. The Act confirms that Congress intended to exercise both the proprietary powers of a landowner and the police powers of the legislature in regulating leases of publicly owned resources. Safeguards are not limited to those provided by lease covenants; the Secretary may prescribe at any time rules and regulations which he finds "necessary and proper" for the "conservation of natural resources." 43 U.S.C.A. § 1334(a)(1). Rules in effect at the time a lease is executed are incorporated statutorily into the terms of the lease, and the Secretary may obtain cancellation of the lease if the lessee breaches any such rule. However, violations of rules issued after the lease has been executed do not enable the Secretary to cancel the lease; the property rights of the lessee are determined only by those rules in effect when the lease is executed.

In Union Oil Co. of California v. Morton (9th Cir.1975), four oil companies brought suit to set aside an order of the Secretary denying them permission to construct a drilling platform in the Santa Barbara Channel which they alleged was necessary for full exercise of their lease rights. The lease gave plaintiffs the right to erect floating drilling platforms, subject to the provisions of OCSLA and to "reasonable regulations" not inconsistent with the lease. After the blowout which caused the disastrous 1969 Santa Barbara oil spill, the Secretary had ordered all activities on this and other leases suspended pending further environmental studies. A few months later he had issued a regulation authorizing emergency "suspension" of any operation which threatened immediate, serious or irreparable harm or damage to the environment, and providing that the suspension should continue until in the Secretary's judgment the threat had terminated. Plaintiffs claimed a distinction between suspension and revocation, asserting that the Secretary had not merely suspended their operations, because a suspension by definition was of a "temporary nature."

The court held that Congress had intended vested rights under the lease to be invulnerable to defeasance by subsequently issued regulations. Although the regulation in question provided that a "suspension" should be limited in time only by the Secretary's judgment that the environmental threat had ended, and although § 1334(a)(1) authorized regulations providing not only for suspensions but for any other conservation action the Secretary determined to be necessary and proper, the court said that Congress had not intended leases to be so tenuous that the Secretary could terminate them at will. Therefore, while Congress itself could order the leases forfeited, subject to payment of just compensation, without congressional authorization the Secretary had no power to revoke.

The *Union Oil* decision is open to question. The Second Circuit strongly suggested two years later that, after leasing, the Secretary was empowered to take any measures necessary to protect the environment. County of Suffolk v. Secretary of the Interior (2d Cir.1977). When the *Union Oil* lease was executed, § 1334(a)(1) expressly authorized the Secretary to subject the lease to later regulations necessary for protection of the environment. Presumably, the Secretary could not contract away his statutory authority. If an indefinite suspension for environmental protection constitutes a "taking" in violation of the Fifth Amendment, it seems that the Secretary's regulatory power vanishes whenever a pollution problem is so serious that no solution is foreseeable within a reasonable period of time.

When a spill does occur, the issue is no longer regulation but liability. Several federal laws impose liability for oil spills. OCSLA amendments of 1978 established liability for cleanup costs and damages resulting from OCS activities and created the Offshore Oil Spill Pollution Fund. The amendments apply to offshore facilities and to vessels carrying oil from such facilities. Strict liability for cleanup costs and damages is imposed jointly and severally on the owner and operator, subject to monetary caps. These caps, however, are not applicable if an incident is caused by willful misconduct or gross negligence, or by knowing violation of federal safety regulations. The Fund, which is derived from a fee of 3 cents per barrel imposed on the owner of oil obtained from the OCS, is liable for all losses not otherwise compensated.

Until 1990, the broadest liability for spills was imposed by § 311 of the Clean Water Act. It made vessels strictly liable for cleanup costs incurred by the government unless the owner proved that the spill was solely a result of an Act of God, an act of war, an act or omission of a third party, or negligence by the federal government. These exceptions from liability were narrowly construed. Section 311 placed limits on liability. For the Exxon Valdez, the limit would have come to $32 million. However, the limits were not applicable if the government could show that the discharge was due to "willful negligence or willful misconduct within the privity and knowledge of the owner." A jury returned a $5 billion verdict against Exxon.

The Oil Pollution Act of 1990 replaced the liability provisions of § 311. Section 1002 imposes liability on "each responsible party" for removal costs, damage to natural resources, damages "for injury to, or economic losses, resulting from destruction of, real or personal

property," and lost profits "due to the injury, destruction, or loss of any real property, personal property, or
natural resources, which shall be recoverable by any
claimant." "Responsible parties" are defined in §
1001(32) to include the owners and operators of vessels,
on-shore facilities, or pipelines. Defenses to liability are
modeled on CERCLA § 107, which is discussed in
Chapter 5. Liability limits for tankers are now at least
$10 million for ships weighing 3000 or more gross tons,
or $1200 per ton. Owners of offshore facilities are liable
for up to $75 million. Like § 311, the new statute
provides for unlimited liability if the spill is caused by
gross negligence, willful misconduct, or a safety violation. The statute also tracks CERCLA in establishing
an oil spill trust fund ($1 billion), granting the President
federal response authority, and requiring the President
to issue regulations governing the measurement of
damages for injury to natural resources.

Measuring damages for injuries to natural areas
poses interesting issues. This issue was raised in Commonwealth of Puerto Rico v. SS Zoe Colocotroni (1st
Cir.1980). The government of Puerto Rico was seeking
to recover for injuries to an area of coastal mangrove
wetlands. The court rejected a commercial or market-
value test as the basis for recovery. The proper measure
of damages, it said, was the reasonable cost to restore or
rehabilitate the environment to its pre-existing condition. Applying this standard, the court rejected a plan
to remove all the oil-impregnated mangrove plants and
replace them with containerized plants as too costly and
destructive to the remaining natural environment. The
court also rejected an abstract calculation of six cents
per marine animal killed. The case was remanded for

the taking of testimony on a plan that "would have a beneficial effect on the ... ecosystem without excessive destruction of existing natural resources or disproportionate cost."

Section 1006(d)(1) of the 1990 Oil Pollution Act, 33 U.S.C.A. § 1706, now provides that the measure of natural resource damages is:

> (A) the cost of restoring, rehabilitating, replacing, or acquiring the equivalent of, the damaged natural resources;
>
> (B) the diminution in value of those natural resources pending restoration; plus
>
> (C) the reasonable cost of assessing those damages.

These costs are to be assessed with respect to the restoration plans promulgated by federal or state trustees. Double recoveries are precluded by subsection (d)(3). Section 1006(e) requires the President to issue damage assessment regulations; damage determinations pursuant to those regulations enjoy a rebuttable presumption of correctness.

D. PROTECTION OF PUBLIC LANDS

1. PUBLIC LANDS POLICY

Although few individuals in the eastern half of the United States are aware of this fact, the federal government owns vast amounts of land. In 1989, the public lands were estimated at over 690 million acres, an area nearly the size of India or roughly one-third of the land area in the United States. About half of this land was located in Alaska. The percentage of federally owned lands, excluding Indian reservations, in the western states ranges from about 30% in Washington to almost 90% in Nevada. The average is close to 50%. Thus federal land policy is of critical importance to the western states.

Land policy is also of great importance to a number of important economic interests. The public lands contain much of the nation's commercial forest land, as well as large amounts of minerals such as copper, mercury, and nickel. In addition, federal lands account for a significant share of the nation's production of oil. Thus, the federal lands also have tremendous economic importance.

Of course, the public lands also have tremendous importance to conservationists. In perhaps the single most important conservation action of the past century, Congress in 1980 set aside vast tracts of land in Alaska as national monuments, parks, and wilderness areas. Roughly 30 million acres were added to the national parks system alone. Even before this legislation, more than 180 million acres had been reserved for national forests and parks. It takes little imagination to foresee the possibility of considerable conflict between environmentalists and resource developers.

In order to understand the environmental aspects of public land law, a basic understanding of the non-environmental aspects is necessary as background. Unfortunately, there is no comprehensive statutory scheme governing federal lands. The numerous existing statutes are complicated and poorly coordinated. We will not attempt here to cover them in detail since to do so would require an undue amount of space. Nevertheless, we will attempt to give a basic outline of public land law.

Until the Twentieth Century, the federal government's main purpose with respect to public lands was to dispose of them as quickly as possible. This policy was evidenced by several homestead acts which conveyed large portions of land to farmers and ranchers. The most important survivor from this period is the Mining Law of 1872, 30 U.S.C.A. § 22 et seq. The Act allows private purchase of "all valuable mineral deposits in lands belonging to the United States." (This statute does not apply to certain important minerals such as oil, gas, coal and oil shale.) Any individual who discovers a valuable mineral deposit on public lands can obtain a mining claim for that deposit. The locater of the minerals acquires a possessory interest in the claim, which is a form of transferable property. Beginning at the time of location, this property interest gives the holder the right to extract, process and market the minerals. The holder of the claim also has the right to obtain outright title to the land on which the claim is located. The locater is not required to apply for a government patent to the land, but if it chooses to do so, the Secretary of the Interior has no discretion about issuing the patent. The sole purpose of this statute is to promote mining. Thus, this statute gives the federal government little power to control mining.

In 1976, mining activities were finally subjected to some degree of government control. As part of the Federal Land Policy and Management Act, Congress provided that in "managing the public lands" the Secretary "shall, by regulation or otherwise, take any action necessary to prevent unnecessary or undue degradation of the lands." 43 U.S.C.A. § 1732(b). The preceding sentence in the statute makes it clear that this provision is applicable to mining. Until this statute was passed, the federal government was essentially powerless to deal with environmental problems relating to mining, and even today its power is limited.

State governments may also require permits for mining on federal lands. These permit requirements are not preempted if the state is regulating mining methods to limit environmental damage, as opposed to prohibiting mining altogether in certain locations. See California Coastal Commission v. Granite Rock Co. (S.Ct.1987). Distinguishing between "environmental" and "land use" regulations, as the Court attempted to do in *Granite Rock*, may prove difficult in practice.

As mentioned earlier, some important natural resources such as oil have been exempted from the 1872 statute. Under the Mineral Leasing Act of 1920, the Secretary of the Interior was empowered to issue prospecting permits and leases for certain minerals such as oil and gas. Unlike the limited government role under the Mining Act, the government's powers to control mineral leasing are quite broad because of its discretion over the issuance of permits and leases.

The other major resource use with which we will be concerned is logging. Since 1891, the President has been authorized to set aside land as national forests. See 16 U.S.C.A. § 471. Under an 1897 statute, the purposes of establishing national forests were declared to be water control and "a continuous supply of timber." 16 U.S.C.A. § 475. The motivation for the statute was the fear that forest lands might soon disappear, leaving the United States with a shortage of timber and of watersheds needed to control stream flows. In 1960, Congress broadened the purposes of the national forest system by passing the Multiple–Use Sustained Yield Act, 16 U.S.C.A. §§ 528–531. This statute provides that national forests shall be administered for various purposes, including outdoor recreation, timber, and wildlife purposes. Because the Act gave the administrator no guidance as to what weight to give these various purposes, the Act was held to leave the administrator almost complete discretion. In 1974 and 1978, Congress called upon the Secretary of Agriculture to establish land management plans for national forests. This legislation also addresses matters such as clearcutting, a logging practice which had previously given rise to considerable controversy. See 16 U.S.C.A. §§ 1601 et seq. In 1976, the Federal Land Policy and Management Act was passed, which calls for similar planning on the 450 million acres administered by the Bureau of Land Management. See 43 U.S.C.A. §§ 1701–1784.

2. WITHDRAWALS

Historically, resource development on public lands has been the rule rather than the exception. Most public land law was geared toward encouraging resource development, while preservation was an exception. Thus, historically, preservation of public lands has taken place when either the executive or the legislature took action to withdraw lands from the "normal" development process.

Presidential authority to withdraw land from development was upheld by the Supreme Court in United States v. Midwest Oil Co. (S.Ct.1915). Because of the encouragement offered by the public land laws of the time, a race among oil companies arose in California to remove as much oil as possible, with each company attempting to pump out the oil before owners of nearby wells could do so. In 1909, the Geological Survey reported that all the oil lands might be in private hands within a few months. This, in turn, might have jeopardized the Navy's fuel supply. In response, the President issued an order "in aid of proposed legislation" withdrawing certain public lands from disposal to the public. The oil companies argued strenuously that the President lacked statutory authority to take this action. The Court held, however, that Congress had been aware of numerous prior instances of similar Presidential actions. Because Congress did not repudiate these previous withdrawals and indeed acquiesced in the practice, Congress was held to have impliedly consented to the Executive practice. The Court stressed the need for Presidential flexibility in administering the public lands.

The Presidential power at issue in *Midwest Oil* was confirmed by the Pickett Act. The Act authorized the President "in his discretion" to "temporarily withdraw from settlement . . . any of the public lands of the United States . . . and reserve the same for water-power sites, irrigation, classification of lands, or other public purposes to be specified in the orders of withdrawal, and such withdrawals shall remain in force until revoked by him or by an Act of Congress." Such withdrawals did not affect the application of the mining laws to metallic minerals on withdrawn land. Despite the use of the word "temporary", a temporary withdrawal remained in effect until expressly revoked. Consequently, such a "temporary" withdrawal could in fact last 50 years or more, long after its original purpose has ceased. In part, the rationale for this rule was the need for certainty in the determination of property claims with respect to public lands.

In 1976, the Pickett Act was repealed. The power of the Secretary of the Interior to withdraw public lands is now governed by 43 U.S.C.A. § 1714. The goal of this legislation was to give Congress greater control over Executive withdrawals. Withdrawals of large tracts of land (over 5,000 acres) can be made only for 20–year periods, subject to a legislative veto by concurrent resolution of both houses. (The constitutionality of this legislative veto provision is dubious.) The Secretary is authorized to make smaller withdrawals for various periods of time, ranging from 5 years to infinity depending on the reason for the withdrawal. The statute does provide for emergency 3–year withdrawals, which must be made when either the Secretary or the Interior Affairs Committee of either house of Congress determines that "an emergency situation exists and that extraordinary measures must be taken to preserve values that would otherwise be lost." (The grant of power to congressional committees here is also constitutionally dubious.) This provision was used in 1978 to make an emergency withdrawal of 105 million acres in Alaska. The legislative history shows that the 1976 legislation was intended to eliminate the President's implied withdrawal power under the *Midwest Oil* doctrine. The President does retain withdrawal power under certain other statutes, such as the Antiquities Act, 16 U.S.C.A. § 431, which was also used by President Carter with respect to large tracts of land in Alaska.

Congress can also withdraw land from development through legislation. The most important legislative land withdrawal, apart from the 1980 Alaskan Lands Act, was the Wilderness Act of 1964, 16 U.S.C.A. §§ 1131–1136. This statute created the National Wilderness Preservation System. Section 1132 of the Act designates certain lands as wilderness areas and provides for review of other national forest lands to determine the desirability of further legislation adding them to the wilderness system.

The most important effect of wilderness designation is found in § 1133 of the Wilderness Act, which sharply restricts the use of wilderness land. Section 1133 makes the agency administering any wilderness area "responsible for preserving the wilderness character of the area" and for insuring that these areas are devoted to "the public purposes of recreational, scenic, scientific, educational, conservational, and historical use." Except where the Act expressly provides otherwise, no commercial enterprise and no permanent roads are allowed within any wilderness area. Mineral use remained a major exception, with the mining laws having remained applicable to wilderness areas until 1983. One area of uncertainty is the relationship between the Wilderness Act and other previous legislation, since the Act sharply changes the status of these lands but purports not to repeal such previous legislation.

The 1976 Federal Land Policy and Management Act required an inventory by 1991 of all roadless areas of 5,000 acres or more outside of the national forest system. Subject to existing rights, FLPMA required that areas under study be managed "in a manner so as not to impair the suitability of such areas for preservation as wilderness." This provision was held to apply to mineral leasing, except for activities actually underway when the 1976 Act was passed. Rocky Mountain Oil & Gas Association v. Watt (10th Cir.1982).

3. PREVENTION OF CONFLICTING PRIVATE USES

In addition to limiting development of public lands themselves, preservation of these lands often requires restrictions on activities on private lands. For example, preserving a water supply for public lands may be critical if they are to fulfill their purposes. Other public lands cannot be effectively used for their intended purposes without clean air and good visibility. In the remaining part of this chapter, we will briefly consider the statutory and common law doctrines protecting public lands from conflicting uses of adjacent private lands. As we saw in Chapter 2, congressional power under the property clause to regulate the use of private lands is not altogether clear. This has not proved a major problem with respect to the restrictions we are about to discuss. Restrictions on water use have been considered to be federal property rights reserved when lands were originally granted to private individuals. The restrictions relating to air pollution are part of a general statute clearly authorized under the commerce clause.

To understand the federal government's special prerogatives in water law, it is necessary to recall some basic facts about western water law. In much of the western half of the country, water is a scarce commodity. To allocate this commodity, the western states generally use a priority system based on order of use together with some kind of filing system. Generally speaking, individuals who first appropriate part of a water supply have priority over those whose appropriation is later in time. Of course there are numerous complications and local variations, but this is the general scheme. The federal government has often failed to comply with the state priority systems. The question that arises is whether the federal government can claim a greater right to the use of water than it is given by state law.

As Cappaert v. United States (S.Ct.1976) illustrates, the federal government does indeed have some special prerogatives in water law. *Cappaert* involved an underground pool in the Devil's Hole Cavern in Nevada. The land surrounding Devil's Hole is part of the Death Valley National Monument. In a pool within the cave, the Devil's Hole pupfish live and breed. If the water level falls below a certain level in the pool, uncovering a rock shelf, the fish cannot breed. Nearby landowners began pumping operations which resulted in declining water levels in the pool. The Court held that the Presidential proclamation establishing the cave as part of the national monument had the effect of reserving the necessary underground water to fulfill the purposes of the reservation. One of the purposes of the reservation was preservation of the pool and the fish that live within it. Thus, although it had not obtained any property interest in the groundwater under state law, as a matter of federal law the government was entitled to insist that sufficient underground water be left to maintain the pool level.

Some of the limits of the implied reservation doctrine became clear in United States v. New Mexico

(S.Ct.1978). The question in that case was whether the creation of a national forest reserves water for recreation and wildlife-preservation purposes. In an opinion by then–Justice Rehnquist, the Supreme Court held that the sole purposes of creating national forests were to preserve timber supply and watersheds. Although a secondary purpose of preserving wildlife may later have developed, according to the Court such a secondary purpose does not suffice to trigger the implied-reservation doctrine. The Court's opinion shows great sensitivity to state's rights in the water law area. Four Justices dissented, arguing that the congressional desire to "improve and protect" the forests included a desire to preserve the wildlife that inhabit those forests. Even after *New Mexico,* apparently it is open to the federal government to prove that preservation of wildlife is necessary to preserve the vegetation in the forest and is therefore part of the primary congressional purpose. Such a showing presumably would be sufficient to justify use of the implied-reservation doctrine.

The implied-reservation doctrine has deep historical roots. A more recent protection for federal lands is to be found in the Clean Air Act. Section 162 designates major national wilderness areas and parks as Class I areas. These Class I areas are subject to special protection under the PSD (prevention of significant deterioration) provisions of the Act. As we saw in Chapter 3, air in Class I areas must be kept cleaner than would otherwise be required by the national air quality standards. To implement this clean air requirement, the Act contains special permit provisions and requires changes in state implementation plans.

Under § 165, a facility can receive a permit even if its emissions would violate the Class I limits, if the manager of the affected federal lands certifies that there will be no adverse impact on the federal lands. If the federal land manager refuses to issue the permit, the state governor may request a limited Presidential exemption. On the other hand, even if a facility does meet the Class I requirements, it may be denied a permit if it will have an adverse impact on visibility or other "air quality-related values" in a Class I area. Another significant provision of the Clean Air Act is found in § 169A. This section is designed to maintain high visibility in mandatory Class I areas. To some degree, retrofitting is required in the interests of improved visibility, although major weight is given to the cost factor.

E. PRESERVING ENDANGERED SPECIES

We close this book with the subject of biodiversity. Protection of endangered species raises the full panoply of issues we have discussed in this book: the division of labor between courts, agencies, and legislatures; the meaning and validity of environmental values; and the necessity or avoidability of trade-offs between environment and economic factors. As we will see, it also raises questions about the rights of governmental and private property owners.

Endangered species receive particularly strong protection under U.S. law. The Endangered Species Act (ESA) stems from the formative period of U.S. environmental law in the 1970s. Section 4 requires the Secretaries of Commerce and Interior to determine whether any species is endangered and to designate critical habitat, based on the best scientific data available. Section 7, entitled "Interagency Cooperation," requires consultation to ensure that agency actions do not jeopardize any endangered species—the "consultation" has turned out to be less important than the "do not jeopardize." Section 9 goes on to forbid "taking" any endangered species.

As we saw in Chapter 1, the Supreme Court's decision in *TVA v. Hill* strongly supported a broad interpretation of the ESA by requiring an injunction against an almost-completed multimillion dollar project. The Court's opinion stressed the nearly absolute priority Congress had placed on preserving endangered species. In response to *TVA v. Hill*, Congress amended the ESA to provide an escape hatch in the form of a special committee (commonly called the "God committee"), which can override § 7 if there are no reasonable alternatives to the agency action, the benefits clearly outweigh those of compliance with the statute, and the action is in the public interest and has at least regional significance. 16 U.S.C. 1536(e), (h). This committee has hardly ever intervened, so the net effect of the amendment was to leave § 7 about as strong as it had been previously.

Section 7, which prohibits the government from jeopardizing any endangered species, has also received strong support from the courts. For example, in National Wildlife Federation v. Coleman (5th Cir.1976), the court enjoined construction of an interstate highway that would cross a critical habitat of the Mississippi Sandhill Crane. The court was also concerned about the effect of the highway in encouraging development in the area, placing the crane in further risk. The court emphasized that § 7 "imposes on federal agencies the mandatory duty to insure that their actions will not either (i) jeopardize the existence of an endangered species, or (ii) destroy or modify critical habitat of an endangered species."

Section 7 has not lacked for controversies, most notably in the Northwest where efforts to protect the spotted owl have led to substantial logging restrictions, and where salmon protection may become equally controversial. But under § 7, at least the government is only restricting its own activities or the use of its own lands or funds. Section 9 has been even more hotly resented by private landowners, who may be deprived of the right not only to destroy animals causing them economic losses, but also to modify areas of critical habitat needed by the endangered species. Not surprisingly, the concept of "property rights" has been fervently invoked in support of these claims.

In Babbitt v. Sweet Home Chapter of Communities for a Great Oregon (S.Ct.1995), the Court held that habitat destruction may violate § 9 of the ESA. Section 9 is a ban on "taking" endangered species; "taking" in turn is defined to encompass any effort to "harass, harm, pursue, hunt, shoot, wound, kill, trap, capture, or collect." 16 U.S.C. 1532(19). The Secretary of the Interior had defined "harm" by regulation to encompass "significant habitat modification or degradation where it actually kills or injures wildlife by significantly impairing essential behavioral patterns, including breeding, feeding, or sheltering." As construed by the government, the regulation required a clear showing of proximate cause. The question before the Court was whether this was a permissible reading of the statute. In a careful opinion by Justice Stevens, the Court concluded that the agency's interpretation of the statute was valid, relying on the broad statutory reference to "harm" and the legislative purpose of reversing the trend toward extinction.

Justice Scalia wrote a scathing dissent. The centerpiece of the dissent was his assertion that the word "take", as applied to wildlife, is "as old as the law itself," and means "to reduce those animals, by killing or capturing , to human control." "It should take the strongest evidence," he said, "to make us believe that Congress has defined a term in a manner repugnant to its ordinary and traditional sense." Scalia's reading of the statute may not be impermissible, but under the *Chevron* doctrine (discussed in Chapter 2), he had the burden of showing that the agency's contrary interpretation was not merely wrong but unreasonable. His dissent fell short of overcoming the strong textual argument in the other direction.

It would be peculiar to say that Mrs. O'Leary's cow didn't "harm" the people of Chicago when it kicked over the lantern that started the Chicago fire. Similarly, as a matter of ordinary English usage, someone who destroys the breeding grounds used by an endangered species or eliminates its food supply surely harms them. Thus, rather than being based on the plain language of the text, the dissent seems to be more motivated by concern over the rights of property owners. Congress is now considering legislation to provide compensation to these property owners. Substantial revisions of the ESA are also under consideration.

As always in environmental law, the only thing that can be confidently predicted about the future is that it will remain interesting, as our society continues to struggle with implementing the goal of environmental protection while respecting other important social values.

As we have seen, environmental regulation involves difficult tradeoffs. Partly as a result of the need to accommodate these tradeoffs, environmental law has evolved into a complex and highly technical body of rules. In the midst of this complexity, it is easy to lose sight of the law's fundamental underlying goal for the past several decades. At least since the late 1960s, our society has had a firm commitment to the protection of environmental quality. It is the questions of "at what cost?" and "how fast?" that continue to divide us and to cause analytical difficulties. But the basic commitment has now passed the test of time. Despite its imperfections and frustrations, environmental law is seemingly here to stay.

INDEX

References are to Pages

ENVIRONMENTAL AUDITS
Defined, 237
Factor in mitigating penalties for violators, 236–237
State privileges against disclosure, 237–238

ENVIRONMENTAL IMPACT STATEMENTS
Alternatives, 42–45
CEQ regulations, 29, 42, 46
Conflict with other statutes, 30
Contemplated actions, 38
Generally, 25
Judicial review, 30–31
   On merits, 47–49
Mitigation, 48
Nuclear weapons, 41
Procedures, 33
Ratemaking proceedings, 35–36
Research and development programs, 34
Rule of reason, 42–45
Scope,
   CEQ regulations, 41
   Dictated by proposal, 35–37
   Judicial review, 38
   Multiple pending proposals, 38, 42
   National programs, 37
   Segmentation, 33
   Synergistic effects, 38
Significant impact, 27–29
Speculative impacts, 45–46
Statutory language, 25
Supplemental EIS, 30
Threshold requirements,
   Generally, 26

Cancer, 146-149, 151-152
Defined, 145–146
Latency, 150–151
"Safe" distinguished from "risk-free," 149, 163–166, 188
Significant risk, 153, 158–159, 161–163

RISK MANAGEMENT
"Acceptable" risk, 149, 158–159, 163–164, 188
Asbestos, 151–153, 165–166
Carcinogens, 146–149, 151–152, 157–159, 163, 165–167, 173, 175, 188, 241–242
Defined, 145
"Endangerment" standard, 152–154, 202–204
Feasibility, 155, 157–158
Judicial deference, 153–155, 161, 166
Policy judgments, 154–155
"Safe" distinguished from "risk-free," 149, 163–166, 188
"Unreasonable" risk, 165–167, 170–172, 177–179
Zero-infinity dilemma, 150

RULEMAKING
See also, Administrative Procedure Act
Hybrid procedures, 19
Scope of review, 17–19
Statutory requirements, 17

SAFE DRINKING WATER ACT
Statutory scheme, 186–187

SOLID WASTE
Automobile hulks, 72
Interstate commerce, 69–71
Landfills, 202–206